FRAGMENTS
OF THE
MEXICAN REVOLUTION

FRAGMENTS
OF THE
MEXICAN REVOLUTION

Personal Accounts from the Border

Oscar J. Martínez

UNIVERSITY OF NEW MEXICO PRESS
Albuquerque

The illustrations that accompany this book are reproduced from Edwin Lieuwen, MEXICAN MILITARISM: THE POLITICAL RISE AND FALL OF THE REVOLUTIONARY ARMY (Albuquerque: University of New Mexico Press, 1968).

Design by Milenda Nan Ok Lee

Library of Congress Cataloging in Publication Data

Martínez, Oscar J. (Oscar Jáquez), 1943–
  Fragments of the Mexican Revolution.

  Bibliography: p.
  1. Mexico—History—Revolution, 1910–1920—Personal narratives.
  2. Mexico—Social life and customs.   3. Southwest, New—Social life and customs.   I. Title.
F1234.M378   1983   972.08'1   83–12370
ISBN 0-8263-0694-2
ISBN 0-8263-0709-4 (pbk.)

First edition

To Jeri

Contents

Illustrations

Preface

The accounts that appear in this volume deal with various aspects of life in Mexico and along the U.S.-Mexican border during an era of social and political upheaval. My intent is to broaden our understanding of and appreciation for the Mexican Revolution by examining selected experiences of people from the border region and the conditions that affected their everyday lives. I have sought to give a voice particularly to ordinary people, whose history in the Revolution remains too little known. Much as been written by and about military and political leaders on both sides of the border who had important roles in Mexico's affairs during the turbulent 1910s, and works have appeared that describe the course of the Revolution at the regional and local levels with some attention given to conditions among the population at large, yet common folks have lacked a forum to relate in their own words how that momentous event touched their lives. The tape recorder has made it possible in recent years to gather such reminiscences, and these accounts together with excerpts from sources written by contemporary observers permit the modern reader to glimpse daily life and the general state of affairs in the border area.

In the selections that follow, I seek to convey the personal side of certain episodes in the Revolution by drawing on interviews, letters, official testimony, newspaper articles, documents, written memoirs, and reports. Since personal reminiscences constitute most of the selections presented here, a word is in order concerning their reliability. Many of the oral history interviews were conducted in the 1970s, half a century after many of the events described. With the passage of this much time, some details have no doubt been distorted, exaggerated, or forgotten by the narrators, either consciously or unconsciously. Against these undeniable pitfalls of oral history one must set the comparable shortcomings of traditional documentary sources. In any case, factual precision is not at issue in the memoirs presented here because our concern is not with an accurate chronology of the Revolution, but with the impact of the tumultuous revolutionary decade upon individuals. The Revolution has continuing meaning for the narrators as they reflect on the events they have witnessed. Because most of our narrators consider these experiences among the most poignant of their lives, they recall them vividly and, through the years of retelling, have learned to present them in concise fashion.[1]

What a loss that historians did not begin interviewing people of that generation sooner. Fortunately some personal testimony was collected in the 1910s and 1920s, and it has proved useful for this study. Although selective and biased, the data gathered by the Albert B. Fall Committee in 1919–1920 include lively statements about conditions in the border region. Fall, who at the time wished to portray Mexico as a chaotic and lawless country, interviewed many American and some Mexican victims of the disturbances.[2] Another useful collection of personal testimony regarding border troubles resulted from the 1919 investigation of the Texas Rangers, led by State Representative J. T. Canales.[3] Also helpful are Manuel Gamio's interviews with Mexicans in the United States who had fled Mexico during the Revolution.[4]

The oral accounts presented below vary in length because extracts are taken from interviews that focused mainly on the Mexican Revolution and from others that dealt with the subject only in passing. A number of the selections have been translated from Spanish to English for this volume; many have been edited to eliminate repetition and improve clarity. Written materials such as letters and newspaper articles have been minimally edited.

The involvement and support of the many persons and institutions that have been a part of this project are gratefully acknowledged. Special thanks go to the individuals who consented to share their experiences during the Revolution through tape-recorded interviews. I am also grateful to past and contemporary oral history interviewers whose work provided material selected for this study. These interviewers include former and current staff members of the University of Texas at El Paso Institute of Oral History (IOH), which I served as Director from 1975 to 1982, students in my borderlands history classes, and volunteers from the El Paso community. Sarah E. John, IOH Acting Director, and IOH transcribers Rhonda Hartman, Nellie Barron, and Irene Ramirez, contributed significantly to the research, transcription, translation, and typing of many of the selections. César Caballero and Elvira Chavarría, of the University of Texas at El Paso and the University of Texas at Austin libraries, respectively, made my library work easier and more pleasant. Richard Estrada read the manuscript in early draft form and made helpful suggestions. Muriel Bell and David V. Holtby provided valuable editorial assistance. John U. Chávez helped me with photography work. Support for research, processing of interviews, and writing came from the University of Texas at El Paso (through the IOH), the National Fellowships Fund in Atlanta, the National Endowment for the Humanities, the Andrew W. Mellon Foundation, the National Research Council, and the Center for Advanced Study in the Behavioral Sciences, where I completed the final draft.

NOTES

1. Historians have made scant use of oral history to gather data about the Revolution from a regional perspective. A notable exception is Jessie Peterson and Thelma Cox Knowles, eds., *Pancho Villa: Intimate Recollections by People Who Knew Him* (New York: Hastings House, 1977), a biography based on 31 interviews, supplemented by reprinted newspaper articles and letters, plus descriptive narrative by the authors. An excellent example of the use of oral history to view the Revolution at the national level is James W. Wilkie and Edna Monzón de Wilkie, *México visto en el siglo XX; Entrevistas de historia oral* (México, D.F.: Instituto Mexicano de Investigaciones Económicas, 1969), a compilation of interviews with seven people who have played prominent roles in twentieth-century México. The Archivo de la Palabra, an oral history program based at the Museo de Antropología e Historia in Mexico City, now has an impressive collection of recorded interviews on the Revolution gathered from various parts of Mexico, including the northern frontier.

2. Investigation of Mexican Affairs, Senate Document 285, 66th Congress, 2nd Session (Washington, D.C., 1920).

3. *Proceedings of the Joint Committee of the Senate and House in the Investigation of the Texas State Ranger Force, 1919* (Texas State Archives).

4. Manuel Gamio, *The Mexican Immigrant: His Life Story* (Chicago: University of Chicago Press, 1931).

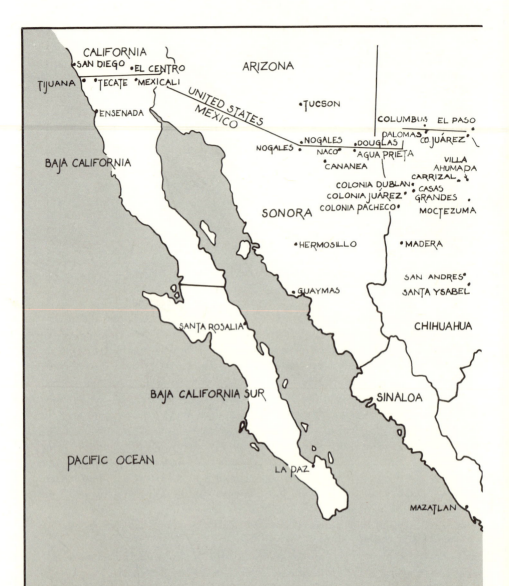

NORTHERN MEXICO
DURING THE REVOLUTION

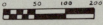

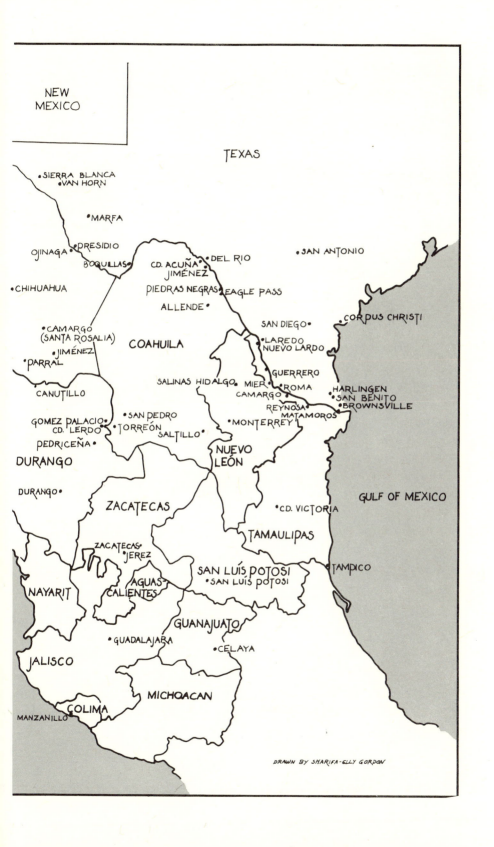

NEW
MEXICO

TEXAS

•SIERRA BLANCA
•VAN HORN

•MARFA

OJINAGA•   •PRESIDIO
BOQUILLAS•   CD. ACUÑA•   •DEL RIO   •SAN ANTONIO
            JIMÉNEZ
•CHIHUAHUA   PIEDRAS NEGRAS•EAGLE PASS
            ALLENDE•
                              SAN DIEGO•   •CORPUS CHRISTI
•CAMARGO   •LAREDO
(SANTA ROSALIA)   NUEVO LARDO
•JIMÉNEZ   COAHUILA
•PARRAL   GUERRERO
            SALINAS HIDALGO• MIER• •ROMA   HARLINGEN
CANUTILLO   CAMARGO•   •SAN BENITO
                              REYNOSA•   •BROWNSVILLE
GOMEZ PALACIO• •SAN PEDRO   MATAMOROS•
CD. LERDO• •TORREÓN •MONTERREY•
PEDRICEÑA•   SALTILLO•
DURANGO   NUEVO
             LEÓN

DURANGO•

            ZACATECAS   GULF OF MEXICO
                          •CD. VICTORIA

            ZACATECAS•   TAMAULIPAS
            •JEREZ
                   SAN LUÍS POTOSI   •TAMPICO
            AGUAS   •SAN LUÍS POTOSI
NAYARIT CALIENTES

            GUANAJUATO
         •GUADALAJARA
                    •CELAYA
JALISCO

            MICHOACAN
  COLIMA
MANZANILLO

DRAWN BY SHARIFA-ELLY GORDON

Introduction

The decade 1910 to 1920 is one of the most tumultuous periods in Mexican history. Frustrated by a generation of dictatorship and political and economic favoritism, various sectors of Mexican society united to overthrow the Porfirio Díaz regime in 1911, triggering a prolonged and violent power struggle that shook the entire republic. One of the regions most affected by the upheaval was the area bordering the United States. Along the border, political figures such as Francisco Madero, Francisco "Pancho" Villa, Pascual Orozco, Venustiano Carranza, and Alvaro Obregón emerged to lead movements of national importance. The northern frontier was repeatedly the site of key battles, and border cities were particularly active as military staging areas because of access to customhouse revenues and American munitions. At times these communities functioned as temporary headquarters for exiled governments or as the sites from which ambitious leaders who yearned to be president could issue the traditional *plan* for new insurrections. When conditions made it difficult to operate in Mexico, defeated *federales* as well as revolutionaries entered the United States to plot further incursions into Mexico. These exiles were joined by thousands of other political and economic refugees who sought asylum north of the international boundary. Inevitably fighting spilled into the United States, bringing instability to border zones from Texas to California.[1]

Such developments transformed the Mexico-U.S. borderlands into a setting for revolutionary drama that constantly drew international attention. The prevailing turmoil on both sides of the border for the years from 1906 to 1920 is reflected in Table 1.

1

TABLE 1
Major Invasions, Battles, and Other Disturbances
in the Mexican-U.S. Border Area, 1906–1920

June 1906	Two thousand workers in Cananea, Sonora, strike an American mining company that discriminates against Mexicans. Violence erupts leaving thirty-five people dead. Several hundred Anglo-Americans from Arizona participate in suppressing uprising.
June 1908	Praxedis Gilberto Guerrero leads Magonista followers in the capture of Ciudad Acuña, Coahuila, only to withdraw for lack of native support.
July 1908	After abandoning Ciudad Acuña, Guerrero's forces take Palomas, Chihuahua, but again withdraw for lack of local support.
November 1910	Francisco Madero and a small group of followers officially launch the Revolution at Piedras Negras, but return to San Antonio, Texas, when expected support fails to materialize.
April 1911	Sonorense "Red" López leads 150 Maderistas in a takeover of Agua Prieta, following a two-hour battle in which a few Americans are killed or wounded.
January–June 1911	Magonistas take Mexicali and Tijuana, but lacking arms and ammunition, retreat into U.S. territory.
May 1911	Francisco Madero's forces capture Ciudad Juárez in the first major battle of the Revolution. Porfirio Díaz agrees to resign, and shortly thereafter Madero assumes the presidency.
July 1911	Magonistas make their second attempt to capture Baja California, but are repulsed by reinforced government troops.

TABLE 1 (continued)

February 1912	Pascual Orozco captures Ciudad Juárez from Maderistas in a bloodless coup.
May 1913	Carrancistas capture Reynosa, Tamaulipas, killing thirty-one Huertistas and capturing many others.
April 1913	After several weeks of fighting, Constitutionalists triumph over Huertistas in Naco, Sonora.
November 1913	Pancho Villa takes Ciudad Juárez by surprise, defeating Victoriano Huerta's forces.
January 1914	Villa captures Ojinaga after initial setback. Both sides suffer heavy losses.
April 1914	Huertistas nearly destroy Nuevo Laredo, setting off explosions and fires as they retreat to the interior of Mexico.
June 1914	Carrancistas capture Matamoros, with hundreds dying in battle. Many others flee to the United States.
Fall 1914	Villista General José María Maytorena attacks Carrancista forces repeatedly for several months in an attempt to take Naco; fifty-eight are killed or wounded.
December 1914	Carrancistas launch unsuccessful two-day attack on Nuevo Laredo, held by Huertistas. Hundreds die.
March 1915	Villista force of 700 attacks Carrancistas at Matamoros, but, following heavy losses, retreats to Monterrey.

TABLE 1 (continued)

November 1915	Desperate attack by Villa is repelled in Agua Prieta by Carrancista forces aided by reinforcements that had traveled through U.S. territory.
November 1915	Alvaro Obregón captures Nogales, Sonora, after a battle between Villistas, who hold the town, and U.S. troops across the border. The binational encounter, apparently started accidently, decimates already weakened Villa forces. Over one hundred people die.
1915–1916	Raids associated with the Plan of San Diego keep the Texas Lower Rio Grande Valley in continuous turmoil. Raiders include Mexican revolutionaries, Mexican-American guerrillas, and bandits of various backgrounds. U.S. troops, Texas Rangers, local lawmen, and vigilantes retaliate against the attackers, sometimes crossing into Mexico to avenge losses. Hundreds die in these raids.
January 1916	Villistas kill sixteen Americans at Santa Ysabel, Chihuahua.
March 1916–February 1917	In March 1916, 500 Villistas raid Columbus, New Mexico, killing twenty American soldiers and civilians. General Pershing leads thousands of U.S. troops into Chihuahua in vain pursuit of Villa. While in Mexico, the Americans are attacked at Parral by townspeople and at Carrizal by Carrancistas, resulting in close to a hundred casualties on both sides.
May 1916	Two groups of Villistas raid Glenn Springs and Boquillas, Texas, killing several Americans. U.S. troops cross into Mexico in unsuccessful pursuit of the attackers.

TABLE 1 (continued)

May, November, 1917	Villa captures Ojinaga twice.
December 1917	A band of Mexicans attacks a ranch near Marfa, Texas, killing several people. Texas Rangers and U.S. troops retaliate by assaulting Pilares, Chihuahua, killing thirty-five people and recovering stolen merchandise. The slaying of innocent people at Pilares results in an investigation and the disbanding of a Ranger company.
December 1917	Following a raid in which 160 goats are taken from a ranch near Eagle Pass, Texas, a force of 150 U.S. soldiers, Texas Rangers, and others cross into San Jose, Coahuila, where they kill some thirty Mexicans.
March 1918	A band of Mexicans raid a ranch near Van Horn, Texas, killing one person. U.S. troops again attack Pilares; thirty-three people die.
August 1918	After someone tries to cross the border at Nogales without stopping, unidentified customs agents commence firing. A shooting battle between Mexicans and Americans ensues; U.S. troops cross into Mexico. Over one hundred persons lose their lives.
June 1919	Aided by artillery fired from the U.S. side, about 3,600 U.S. troops cross into Ciudad Juárez to help Carrancistas repel an attack by Villa.
May 1920	Obregonistas take Ciudad Juárez from Carrancistas in a bloodless coup.

Serious discontent with economic and political policies prevalent in early twentieth-century Mexico first surfaced in a border labor dispute in Cananea, Sonora, in June 1906. Mexican workers struck the American Consolidated Copper Company for better wages, improved working conditions, and an end to racial discrimination. Violent repression of the strike by the company—which included the intervention of 200 to 400 American "volunteers" who acted at the invitation of the procompany Sonora governor—created deep resentment and ignited other disturbances throughout Mexico. That same year Ricardo Flores Magón's revolutionary Liberal Party, combining labor dissatisfaction with demands for political change, made unsuccessful attempts to take Jiménez, Coahuila, and Ciudad Juárez in the state of Chihuahua. Díaz's agents seized a large amount of ammunition from the party's office in El Paso; they barely missed apprehending Flores Magón. Two years later the Magonistas tried again, directing short-lived uprisings along the Coahuila and Chihuahua frontiers as well as in other parts of México. With their forces depleted, these revolutionaries subsequently operated out of Los Angeles, California, plotting their invasion of Baja California in 1911. Later they had continuous problems with U.S. authorities, who charged them with violating neutrality laws, among other things.[2]

In November 1910, Coahuila native Francisco Madero, while living in San Antonio, Texas, officially launched the Revolution by crossing into the border town of Piedras Negras, Coahuila. Uprisings followed in various border states and in other parts of the republic. By April 1911, an estimated 17,000 people had taken arms against the Porfirio Díaz government, with more than half the revolutionaries active in Chihuahua and Sonora. In May, Madero's forces, which by then included Francisco "Pancho" Villa, from Durango, and Pascual Orozco, from Chihuahua, took Ciudad Juárez, an event that marked the first major victory for the insurgents. The Treaty of Juárez provided for an end to hostilities, the resignation of Díaz, and a new presidential election in the fall, which Madero easily won.[3]

Madero's ascension to power brought forth opposition in the borderlands. Rejected as a presidential candidate in 1911, General Bernardo Reyes of Nuevo León took refuge in San Antonio, Texas, and schemed a counterrevolution against Madero. Reyes's effort ran aground in his home state by December 1911. In February 1912, Pascual Orozco, a hero of the Madero revolt who felt his deeds had not been properly recognized and rewarded, called for the President's ouster as part of a larger counterrevolutionary movement led by Emilio Vásquez Gómez, then also in exile in San Antonio. Reyes surrendered when he failed to win supporters in Nuevo León, and Orozco fled to Arizona following his defeat in Chihuahua.[4]

The northern Mexican frontier assumed even greater importance for the Revolution after Victoriano Huerta's overthrow and assassination of Madero in February 1913. A movement to avenge the president's death and to restore constitutional government emerged in Coahuila, Chihuahua, and Sonora, led by Venustiano Carranza, Pancho Villa, and Alvaro Obregón. Carranza, as the head of the Constitionalists, led a shaky alliance of *norteños* in deposing the usurper Huerta. For a time Carranza made Piedras Negras his revolutionary headquarters, and Nogales, Sonora, his "capital" in exile. Northern cities became not only the gathering places for intellectuals, idealists, and radicals, but often the sites of spectacular, decisive battles. Villa emerged as the master of Chihuahua, demonstrating his military genius in countless victories inside and outside the state. On November 15, 1913, he triumphantly rode into Ciudad Juárez on a hijacked train that had been traveling south, taking the *federales* at the border by surprise. Along the western border, Obregón drove Huerta's troops from Sonora in a string of impressive victories.

A major tragedy of the Revolution was the development of a schism between Carranza and Villa, which led to prolonged warfare. Villa-led forces delivered the death blow to the Huerta regime in the bloody battle of Zacatecas in June 1914. Yet by that time the rift with Carranza was so serious that Villa reluctantly returned to Chihuahua while Obregón and Carranza marched into Mexico City. Carranza soon took over the presidency. Attempts to resolve the two men's differences led to the Convention at Aguascalientes, from which Villa emerged as the military arm of a new government following the delegates' decision to have Carranza resign. In December 1914, Villa entered Mexico City with Emiliano Zapata, the peasant leader from Morelos, while Carranza, with the support of Oregón, ran a government-in-exile from Vera Cruz.

In early 1915 Villa returned to Chihuahua to operate as an independent military chieftain, but his fortunes changed radically as Obregón took the offensive against him. By the end of the year, following defeats in Celaya, Aguascalientes, Zacatecas, Agua Prieta, and Hermosillo, Villa ceased to be a major military force. U.S. de facto recognition of the Carranza government and the embargo on arms destined for Villa were major factors in his decline. The arrival of Carranza reinforcements by U.S. rail ensured Villa's defeat at Agua Prieta and embittered him against Americans. In December, Villa disbanded his remaining forces and withdrew to the Chihuahua mountains to plan guerrilla actions against Carranza and the hated *gringos*. In January 1916, Villista troops killed sixteen American engineers at Santa Ysabel (today General Trías), Chihuahua, and in March they raided Columbus, New Mexico. These incidents led to the Punitive Expedition into México, commanded by General John J. Pershing. The expedition not only failed to capture Villa, it seriously strained already tense relations between México and the United States.[5] Underlying this diplomatic confrontation were continuous disturbances along the Lower Rio Grande Valley, where for years Mexican revolutionaries had raided Texas settlements. This international crisis passed, but the Revolution went on.

Villa continued his war against Carranza for the next few years, repeatedly skirmishing with the *federales* in different parts of Chihuahua. In late 1916 Villistas twice took Chihuahua City; the following year they captured the border town of Ojinaga, also on two occasions. In 1919, however, Villa's bid to take Ciudad Juárez as a hoped-for prelude to another march on central México was foiled by the intervention of U.S. troops, who crossed from El Paso to repel the attack. Thereafter, the once-powerful revolutionary chieftain was limited to minor sorties. In the summer of 1920 he finally made peace with the government (by then in the hands of Adolfo de la Huerta, following the overthrow and murder of Carranza in May), accepting a cash settlement for himself and his troops and an hacienda in Durango. Eventually Villa suffered the same violent fate of other revolutionary leaders: he was ambushed and killed in the streets of Parral, Chihuahua, in 1923. Villa's departure from the battlefield considerably lessened revolutionary activity in northern Mexico, although a few regional *caudillos* (chieftains), die-hard Carrancistas, and others took up arms sporadically to avenge prior defeats or to resist government-imposed change.

The people of the border welcomed the peace that returned to their region after so many years of violence and suffering. Lives had been disrupted, loved ones had been killed or injured, and much property had been lost. Relations between Mexico and the United States had been severely damaged, and only extraordinary diplomacy had prevented a war between the two neighbors during the peak years of instability. At the local level, the economies of the Mexican border cities had been devastated and population growth had been halted. Many localities near the border had been practically abandoned during periods of heightened turmoil, with most refugees taking asylum in the American border towns.

Viewed in perspective, the 1910s represent a tragic but also exhilirating period in the history of the border region. Armed conflict, a natural part of the area's heritage, had never before been so explosive, prolonged, and destructive. At the same time, no previous era had produced so much excitement. The years of revolutionary upheaval would be long remembered by those who lived in the borderlands.

NOTES

1. The Mexican Revolution has an extensive and rich literature, but only until recently did researchers begin to probe seriously the regional and local dimensions of this epic historical struggle. Recent regional studies are discussed in David C. Bailey, "Revisionism and and the Recent Historiography of the Mexican Revolution," *Hispanic American Historical Review* 58:1 (February 1978): 62–79. What literature there is tends to focus on descriptive narratives of revolutionary events in individual northern Mexican states, on the origin of the conflict in selected localities, on personalities, or on sensational incidents that occurred in the borderlands. A general synthesis that integrates the significant themes of borderlands history during the Revolution has yet to appear. Among the best books that deal with regional aspects of the Revolution are the following: Hector Aguilar Camín, *La frontera nomada: Sonora y la Revolución Mexicana* (México, D.F.: Siglo Veintiuno, 1977); Francisco R. Almada, *La Revolución en el estado de Chihuahua*, 2 vols. (México, D.F.: Biblioteca del Instituto Nacional de Estudios Históricos de la Revolución Mexicana, 1964); William H. Beezley, *Insurgent Governor: Abraham González and the Mexican Revolution in Chihuahua* (Lincoln: University of Nebraska Press, 1973); Lowel L. Blaisdell, *The Desert Revolution: Baja California, 1911* (Madison: University of Wisconsin Press, 1962); and Michael C. Meyer, *Mexican Rebel: Pascual Orozco and the Mexican Revolution, 1910–1915* (Lincoln: University of Nebraska Press, 1967).

2. On the Flores Magón movement, see Blaisdell, *The Desert Revolution;* Charles C. Cumberland, "Precursors of the Mexican Revolution of 1910," *His-*

panic American Historical Review 22:2 (May 1942): 344–56; Charles C. Cumberland, "Mexican Revolutionary Movements from Texas, 1906–1912," *Southwestern Historical Quarterly* 52:3 (January 1949): 301–44; Peter Gerhard, "The Socialist Invasion of Baja California, 1911," *Pacific Historical Review* 15:3 (September 1946): 295–304; Juan Gómez-Quiñones, *Sembradores: Ricardo Flores Magón y El Partido Liberal Mexicano: A Eulogy and Critique* (Los Angeles: UCLA Chicano Studies Center, Monograph No. 5, 1973); and William D. Raat, "Diplomacy of Suppression: Los Revoltosos, Mexico and the United States, 1906–1911," *Hispanic American Historical Review* 56:4 (November 1976): 529–50.

3. Madero's revolution is treated in Charles C. Cumberland, *Mexican Revolution: Genesis under Madero* (Austin: University of Texas Press, 1952), and Stanley R. Ross, *Francisco I. Madero: Apostle of Mexican Democracy* (New York: Columbia University Press, 1955).

4. The Reyes and Orozco counterrevolutions are discussed in Peter V. N. Herderson, *Mexican Exiles in the Borderlands, 1910–1913* (El Paso: Texas Western Press, Southwestern Studies, Monograph number 58, 1979).

5. For references to published works on the Columbus raid, see footnotes 1 and 2 in Friedrich Katz, "Pancho Villa and the Attack on Columbus, New Mexico," *American Historical Review* 83:1 (February 1978): 101–30.

Part I

Fighting the Revolution

People became insurgents for a variety of reasons. In the middle and upper sectors of society, political disaffection from the Díaz regime prompted many to form or join organizations that propounded revolution, while others assumed leadership on the battlefield. Among the lower classes, lack of education and confusion over the precise objectives of the various factions made it difficult to know the meaning of involvement in the conflict. Depending on circumstances, a person might be induced to become a *federal* or, just as easily, to join an antigovernment army. Through persuasion, pressure, or force, thousands upon thousands of *campesinos* (peasants) and *obreros* (workers) were integrated into the conflict. Countless died without understanding the nature of the struggle; others knew from the beginning that the Revolution presented a long-awaited opportunity to redress wrongs inflicted by abusive employers or functionaries of the old regime.

By 1910, the majority of *campesinos* lived in abject poverty, while *hacendados* enjoyed an affluent life-style. The large, fertile estates of the landlords contrasted sharply with the tiny plots of the peasants. Villagers who had lost their communal properties seethed with resentment and looked forward to the day when they could reclaim their farming, grazing, and timber lands. Throughout rural Mexico, the feeling was widespread that cheating and exploitation by the rich, both native and foreign, aided by government connivance, largely accounted for the plight of the poor. Urban workers had similar grievances against employers and allied institutions. Poor wages, substandard working conditions, inflation, bad housing, and deficient social services created an environment ripe for the embracing of revolutionary ideas by the poor.

A desire for adventure and the chance to see new places motivated thousands to enlist in the armies of insurgents, but many responded out of fear that if they declined the invitation, harm would come to them or to their families. For those who wanted no part in the conflict, the choice became to hide or leave the country. An undetermined but significant number chose the latter course, as the statistics on Mexican migration to the United States during the period confirm.

Once a man enlisted in the Revolution, his major concern became survival. Poor training, obsolete weapons, erratic leadership, inadequate clothing, insufficient supplies, negligible health care, short rations, recurring epidemics, and constant fighting—all these contributed to the soldiers' plight. Maintaining contact with loved ones was practically impossible; many parents and wives heard nothing from sons or husbands for years. Because so few physicians or medical facilities were available, caring for the wounded presented a major challenge. Frequently, unattended battle wounds resulted in death, while many men lost arms and legs in the absence of timely treatment.

Fatigue and disillusion took their toll after extended periods of hard fighting. Soldiers who could endure no more took their leave and returned home with or without permission; others escaped to the United States as permanent deserters. In some cases, defeated units disintegrated, with the survivors scattering in all directions. Many such stragglers were captured by opposing forces, to suffer punishment at the hands of their captors or switch over to fight on their side.

Participants in the Revolution included many non-Mexicans. Europeans, Anglo-Americans, Mexican-Americans, and others—whether idealists, adventurers, or money-seekers—became combatants, usually on the side of the insurgents. The accounts that follow focus mainly on the experiences of Mexican participants in the Revolution, but one selection deals with a Mexican-American who was "drafted" by the Villistas, and another with a Swedish-American who joined the Villistas for a short period. What these men describe helps us understand the feelings and attitudes of those who formed the Revolution's rank-and-file. As the reader will recognize, their memoirs have much in common with the stories of other soldiers who have fought in other civil wars before and since the struggle in Mexico.

14

"My house . . . was turned into a conspiracy against the dictatorship."
—Sra. Flores de Andrade*

Mexican women played an important role in the Revolution, participating at various levels of the conflict. Best known for their courage and dedication are the soldaderas, *who fought, cooked, washed, cared for the wounded, and offered female companionship to the men. There were also women who assumed leadership in promoting revolutionary ideology, often encountering situations which brought them personal danger. Sra. Flores de Andrade was such a woman, dedicating her efforts to the cause of the Flores Magón brothers and later that of Francisco Madero.*

I was born in Chihuahua, and spent my infancy and youth on an estate in Coahuila which belonged to my grandparents, who adored me. My grandparents liked me so much that they hardly allowed me to go to Chihuahua so as to get an ordinary education. At seven years of age I was master of the house. My grandparents did everything that I wanted and gave me everything for which I asked. As I was healthy and happy I would run over the estate and take part in all kinds of boyish games. I rode on a horse bareback and wasn't afraid of anything. I was thirteen years of age when my grandparents died, leaving me a good inheritance,

*Interviewed in the 1920s. Manuel Gamio, *The Mexican Immigrant: His Life Story* (Chicago: University of Chicago Press, 1931), pp. 29–35. Reprinted by permission of the University of Chicago Press.

15

part of which was a fifth of their belongings, with which I could do whatever I wished.

The first thing that I did, in spite of the fact that my sister and my aunt advised me against it, was to give absolute liberty on my lands to all the peons. I declared free of debts all of those who worked on the lands which my grandparents had willed me and what there was on that fifth part, such as grain, agricultural implements and animals, I divided in equal parts among the peons. I also told them that they could go on living on those lands in absolute liberty without paying me anything for them and that they wouldn't lose their rights to it until they should leave for some reason. Even yet there are on that land some of the old peons, but almost all of them have gone, for they had to leave on account of the revolution. Those lands are now my only patrimony and that of my children.

Because I divided my property in the way in which I have described (and as a proof of which, I say, there are still people in Ciudad Juárez and El Paso who wish to kiss my hand), my aunt and even my sister began to annoy me. My sister turned her properties over to an overseer who has made them increase.

They annoyed me so much that I decided to marry, marrying a man of German origin. I lived very happily with my husband until he died, leaving me a widow with six children. Twelve years had gone by in the mean time. I then decided to go to Chihuahua, that is to say, to the capital of the state, and there, a widow and with six children, I began to fight for liberal ideals, organizing a women's club which was called the 'Daughters of Cuauhtemoc,' a semi-secret organization which worked with the Liberal Party of the Flores Magón brothers in fighting the dictatorship of Don Porfirio Díaz. We were able to establish branches of the woman's club in all parts of the state by carrying on an intense propaganda.

My political activities caused greater anger among the members of my family especially on the part of my aunt, whom I called mother. Under these conditions I grew poorer and poorer until I reached extreme poverty. I passed four bitter years in Chihuahua suffering economic want on the one hand and fighting in defense of the ideals on the other. My relatives would tell me not to give myself in fighting for the people, because I wouldn't get anything from it, for they wouldn't appreciate their defenders. I didn't care anything about that. I wouldn't have cared if the people had crucified me, I would have gone on fighting for the cause which I considered to be just.

My economic situation in Chihuahua became serious, so that I had to accept donations of money which were given to me as charity by wealthy people of the capital of the state who knew me and my relatives. My aunt helped me a little, but I preferred for her not to give me anything, for she would come to scold me and made me suffer. There were rich men who courted me, and who in a shameless way proposed to me that I should become their mistress. They offered me money and all kinds of advantages, but I would have preferred everything before sacrificing myself and prostituting myself.

Finally after four years' stay in Chihuahua, I decided to come to El Paso, Texas. I came in the first place to see if I could better my economic condition and second to continue fighting in that region in favor of the Liberal ideals, that is to say, to plot against the dictatorship of Don Porfirio. I came to El Paso in 1906, together with my children and comrade Pedro Mendoza, who was coming to take part in the Liberal propaganda work. I put my children in the school of the Sacred Heart of Jesus, a Catholic institution; they treated me well there and took care of my children for me.

With comrade Mendoza we soon began the campaign of Liberal propaganda. We lived in the same house and almost in the same room and as we went about together all day working in the Liberal campaign the American authorities forced us to marry. I am now trying to divorce myself from my husband for he hasn't treated me right. He goes around with other women, and I don't want anything more to do with him.

In 1909 a group of comrades founded in El Paso a Liberal women's club. They made me president of that group, and soon afterwards I began to carry on the propaganda work in El Paso and in Ciudad Juárez. My house from about that time was turned into a conspiratory center against the dictatorship. Messengers came there from the Flores Magón band and from Madero bringing me instructions. I took charge of collecting money, clothes, medicines, and even ammunition and arms to begin to prepare for the revolutionary movement, for the uprisings were already starting in some places.

The American police and the Department of Justice began to suspect our activities and soon began to watch out for me, but they were never able to find either in my house or in the offices of the club documents

17

or arms or anything which would compromise me or those who were plotting. I was able to get houses of men or women comrades to hide our war equipment and also some farms.

In 1911, a little before the revolutionary movement of Sr. Francisco Madero became general, he came to El Paso, pursued by the Mexican and American authorities. He came to my house with some others. I couldn't hide them in my house, but got a little house for them which was somewhat secluded and had a number of rooms, and put them there. I put a rug on the floor and then got some quilts and bed clothes so that they could sleep in comfort. So that no one would suspect who was there, I put three of the women of the club there, who washed for them, and took them their food which was also prepared by some of the women.

Don Francisco and his companions were hidden in that house for three months. One day Don Francisco entrusted my husband to go to a Mexican farm on the shore of the Bravo River so as to bring two men who were coming to reach an agreement concerning the movement. My husband got drunk and didn't go. Then I offered my services to Sr. Madero and I went for the two men who were on this side of the border, that is to say in Texas territory, at a wedding. Two Texas rangers who had followed me asked me where I was going, and I told them to a festival and they asked me to invite them. I took them to the festival and there managed to get them drunk; then I took away the two men and brought them to Don Francisco. Then I went back to the farm and brought the Rangers to El Paso where I took them drunk to the City Hall and left them there.

Later when everything was ready for the revolutionary movement against the dictatorship, Don Francisco and all those who accompanied him decided to pass over to Mexican territory. I prepared an afternoon party so as to disguise the movement. They all dressed in masked costumes as if for a festival and then we went towards the border. The river was very high and it was necessary to cross over without hesitating for the American authorities were already following us, and on the Mexican side there was a group of armed men who were ready to take care of Don Francisco. Finally, mounting a horse barebacked, I took charge of taking those who were accompanying Don Francisco over two by two. They crossed over to a farm and there they remounted for the mountains.

A woman companion and I came back to the American side, for I

18

received instructions to go on with the campaign. This happened in May 1911. We slept there in the house of the owner of the ranch and on the next day when we were getting ready to leave, the colonel came with a picket of soldiers. I told the owner of the ranch to tell him that he didn't know me and that another woman and I had come to sleep there. When the authorities came up that was what he did; the owner of the ranch said that he didn't know me and I said that I didn't know him. They then asked me for my name and I gave it to them. They asked me what I was doing there and I said that I had been hunting and showed them two rabbits that I had shot. They then took away my 30-30 rifle and my pistol and told me that they had orders to shoot me because I had been conspiring against Don Porfirio. I told them that was true and that they should shoot me right away because otherwise I was going to lose courage. The colonel, however, sent for instructions from his general, who was exploring the mountains. He sent orders that I should be shot at once.

This occurred almost on the shores of the Rio Grande and my family already had received a notice of what was happening to me and went to make pleas to the American authorities, especially my husband. They were already making up the squad to shoot me when the American consul arrived and asked me if I could show that I was an American citizen so that they couldn't shoot, but I didn't want to do that. I told them that I was a Mexican and wouldn't change my citizenship for anything in the world.

The colonel told me to make my will for they were going to execute me. I told him that I didn't have anything more than my six children whom I will to the Mexican people so that if they wished they could eat them.

The colonel was trying to stave off my execution so that he could save me, he said. An officer then came and said that the general was approaching. The colonel said that it would be well to wait until the chief came so that he could decide concerning my life, but a corporal told him that they should shoot me at once for if the general came and they had not executed me then they would be blamed. They then told me that they were going to blindfold me but I asked them if their mothers weren't Mexicans, for a Mexican isn't afraid of dying. I didn't want them to blindfold me. The corporal who was interested in having me shot was going to fire when I took the colonel's rifle away from him and menaced

19

him; he then ordered the soldiers to throw their rifles at the feet of the Mexican woman and throw themselves into the river, for the troops of the general were already coming. I gathered up the rifles and crossed the river in my little buggy. There the American authorities arrested me and took me to Fort Bliss. They did the same thing with the soldiers, gathering up the arms, etc. On the next day the authorities at Fort Bliss received a telegram from President Taft in which he ordered me to be put at liberty, and they sent me home, a negro military band accompanying me through the streets.

At the triumph of the cause of Sr. Madero we had some great festivities in Ciudad Juárez. The street car company put all of the cars which were needed for free transportation from one side of the border to the other.

Afterwards Sr. Madero sent for me and asked me what I wanted. I told him that I wanted the education of my six children and that all the promises which had been made to the Mexican people should be carried out. The same man told me to turn the standards of the club over to Villa who told me that they weren't good for anything. I afterwards learned that Don Francisco was trying to cajole Pancho by giving him those things which we wanted to give to Pascual Orozco.

During the Huerta revolution I kept out of the struggle, for I considered that was treason, and little by little I have been separating myself from political affairs and I am convinced that the revolution promised a great deal to the Mexican people but hasn't accomplished anything.

"Villa said, 'Listen, boy, will you come
with me?'"

—Pedro González (1899–   )*

*Thousands of teenagers became part of the revolutionary
forces when manpower needs required it. Some joined of their
own volition while others were "drafted" on the spot. Perhaps
starting as errand boys for the soldiers and officers, it was
not long before most of these youngsters became full-fledged
fighters. The story of Pedro González, native of Guadalajara,
illustrates how a boy perceived his involvement in the Revolution and how older comrades and enemies viewed him. González found moments when he could enjoy activities common
to his age group. Ultimately his youth saved him from execution as he struggled to return to a normal life.*

In 1913, when I was fourteen years old, I joined some federal troops
that were going from Guadalajara to Torreón with the intention of con-
quering Villa. Since I was an orphan, I wandered around with them,
just to see what was going on. I gave the officers shines and ran errands
for them whenever they needed something, and they would give me a
quarter, a dime, twenty cents. Then some other people gave me food
to eat, and that's how I earned my living. I had a good friendship with
those people and they treated me very well. From Torreón we went to

*Interviewed in El Paso in 1976 by Oscar J. Martínez. On file at the Institute of Oral
History, University of Texas at El Paso. Portions published in *Password* 25:1 (Spring
1980): 29–37. Reprinted by permission of *Password.*

21

Durango, and from there we conducted a search, looking for Madero's followers in towns controlled by the federalists.

It turned out that the Maderistas attacked Pedriceña, where I happened to be at that time. At that point I went with the revolutionaries because there was more food and excitement with them. A man gave me a short 30-30 rifle and that's how I became a revolutionary against the federal government. I joined General Calixto Contreras' troops, and they must have liked me because they treated me very well. I went along with the colonel who took me under his wing.

One day there was a meeting of generals and colonels, and Villa was one of them. When they finished talking about the attacks that they were going to carry out, Villa said to me, "Listen, boy, will you come with me?" I told him that *I* couldn't say—that he would have to talk to the colonel that I was assigned to, and if *he* allowed me to, then I would. I was afraid of Villa since he was the head of the Revolution. Then he left me entrusted to the colonel and to General Contreras. He told them, "OK, I leave you in charge of this boy; take good care of him." They said, "We will." A little later Contreras and Villa got together again and that's when I became a part of the *División del Norte* [Villa's troops]. At that time Villa only had about 200 or 300 men. He picked me up and I went with him.

I enjoyed being where there was fighting going on, probably for the simple reason of just being young. Most of the generals appreciated me a lot and they all wanted me to go with them. But since I was working for Villa, I couldn't. If the general gave me permission to go to another brigade with another general I went; if not, I didn't go. The general saw how clever I was in doing jobs which were a little difficult. He sent me to certain cities that he was going to attack so that I could find out how many troops there were and which positions were strong. For a week I would go all through town and the outskirts where the federal troops were, selling cigarettes, candy and other things, so that I wouldn't be suspicious looking.

In November of 1913 we captured Ciudad Juárez, and we were there until the federal troops started to come to attack us from Chihuahua. When we were in Juárez, the mayor of El Paso and a general from Fort Bliss came over to talk with the general. They asked him to please not fight in Juárez because the bullets could go over to the American side and there could be accidents involving civilian families. Villa told them that they didn't have to worry—that he didn't like to fight among the houses, that he always liked to fight on the open plains.

We left Juárez and went about 10 kilometers toward the south to Tierra Blanca. The federal troops started to come in trains, but they couldn't get to Juárez because we were already waiting for them. We were there several days, and they distributed to us that sausage that the American government gave out at Fort Bliss—a big piece—and a square piece of bread which was also American. At that time the American government helped Villa a lot. Finally, one daybreak, Villa gave the order to attack and the battle began. There was a lot of shooting and I had to retreat to a little hill where our infantry was continuing to fire. While I was trying to get rapidly into a hole with a fellow soldier, they wounded me and I lost my horse. The federal troops kept advancing, and there I was, hurt. I climbed down the hill to a little stream, hoping that if the federalists came they would pass me by and not kill me. Then I heard a horse coming and saw that it was one of my compañeros [fellow revolutionaries]. I told him, "Compáñero, pick me up, get me out of here." He returned, put me on the horse and we left. My condition was really quite bad with a wound in the shoulder and the back right next to the spinal column. The shower of bullets whizzed by us on one side and the other, and we were the last ones to get out of there. I told my comrade, "Make this horse go faster because they're going to kill us both right here." Well, he hit the horse a little more but I began aching badly and I told him, "Friend, don't hit him any more," and he stopped the horse for a while.

Finally we were out of danger and then we found the general. Villa recognized me and said, "Boy, is it you?" I answered, "Yes, sir." He ordered the first lieutenant who had gotten me out of the battle: "Take this boy to the train for me and assign soldiers to take care of him until they get to Juárez, so that he can be cured in the hospital." Well, the officer took me to a train where there were a lot of wounded people and we left.

When I got to Juárez I found lodging in a hotel where many people were recuperating. There were two other people with me in my room and a nurse from El Paso came and took care of us. After two weeks I could get up and go to the bathroom myself, but the nurse didn't want me to get out of bed because she was afraid it would do me harm or something, and it embarrassed me [to go to the bathroom in the room].

23

Then they spoke with the hospital, and they were moving some of the wounded people over there. Since Villa had left money at the hotel and they had given me clothes, I took advantage of the opportunity that presented itself during this move, left, rented a bicycle, and took a ride around the plaza. The nurses were looking for me, saying, "That boy! Where could he have gone?"

When the hour was up for the bicycle rental I went to the hospital and arrived about 1 p.m. I realized that the nurses had been worried since they couldn't find me, and when I saw them, I gave them each a hug. When the person in charge of the hospital saw that, he didn't like it and he sent a report about me to the general's barracks where General Aguirre Benavides was in charge. I went to the barracks and the general told me, "Listen, young man. You should know that I have a complaint that the nurses at the hospital can't put up with you, that you arrive there hugging and kissing them." I told him, "Sir, you know that they all like me. They were running around looking for me and they couldn't find me, so when I returned to the hospital all the nurses were surprised and they came to hug me and everything. And really, the administrator of the hospital is very ugly. Which one of the girls is going to hug him? No one! I think *that's* part of the problem." And since the general of the barracks liked me—on one occasion he had even invited me to go along with him—he told me, "OK, boy, get out of here." I was very lucky. From there I went to a store where they had pinball machines. I wasn't in a hurry and there wasn't anything I had to do. I played for a while but then the machine broke down; the result was that I just pulled the handle and six or twelve (or more!) nickles came out. Since I had so many nickles in my pocket, I was afraid that the owner of the store was going to realize what had happened. I left right away and returned to the hospital.

Some days later a train was leaving Juárez with some of Villa's soldiers, and since I liked to hang around the station, I climbed up on the top of the train with the soldiers. But Villa noticed that I was up there and he told me to get down. I got down and then he gave some money to one of the brothers of Luz Corral de Villa (the general's wife who was sick in El Paso at the time) and said, "Take this; take the boy to El Paso and take him to the movies." Well, we went to El Paso, but since Luz's brother had a girlfriend, he left me at the theater and he left with her.

I frequently went to see Luz because I was always going back and forth from the hospital in Juárez to El Paso.

Time passed, I got well, and we left Juárez to fight in various places: Ojinaga, Chihuahua, Torreón, San Pedro de las Colonias, Saltillo, Monterrey, and Zacatecas. The battle at Zacatecas was rough because the whole federal army reassembled there. I happened to be at the battle on the side of the Cerro de Coronel. We attacked one afternoon, but they forced us back to the bottom of the hill. When it was darker we attacked again and this time we managed to make it to the top, forcing the enemy back into Zacatecas. We were fighting that whole night and all of the next day when the order came from Villa for us to enter the city. Our group had to enter by way of the station where the enemy had a cannon and two machine guns. We were lucky enough to overcome them, and that allowed us to go into the station where we found other revolutionaries who had entered from the other side. We joined together and went into the town, except that you couldn't walk very well because there were so many corpses. On the corners there were entrenchments of soldiers, and in the streets were dead men and horses. We had to advance the best we could, trampling dead people and horses, crushing them. Some of the federalist prisoners made ditches in which to bury the dead. They filled mule-drawn carts with cadavers and dumped them in the hole, until they cleaned up the city and everything was all right. We were there about two months.

My last expedition with the Villistas was in 1915–1916 in Sonora. We were going to go towards Hermosillo but it wasn't possible because the Carrancistas had joined together with the Mexican troops that had gone over to the American side. Because of that, Villa couldn't seize the border. We fought for a while in Agua Prieta and from there we went to Guaymas to take over the port, but we couldn't because it was already full of Carrancistas. Little by little we retreated until we reunited with the people who had stayed at the foot of the Cañon del Púlpito near Colonia Dublán, Chihuahua.

We were only there for two days because there wasn't anything to eat. I got a hold of a can of salmon and a little bit of wheat that had been left at the edge of a mill, and that's what I ate. We decided to climb the Sierra del Púlpito and go down to Old Casas Grandes. It was winter at the time and there was a lot of snow in the mountains. I was on foot because they had killed my horse. There wasn't a road, and the snow came up past my knees. We fell in holes and everything. Finally we got out to the plain and we arrived in Old Casas Grandes where General José Rodríguez was with a few people who had arrived a little earlier. There wasn't anything to eat there either.

The next day General Rodríguez told me, "Listen, boy, do you want to join General Villa quicker?" Well, I told him that I did, although I was sorry later. He said, "I'm going to send a group of five men towards Chihuahua to find him so that he knows that here in Casas Grandes the people who left for Sonora are reuniting." They gave me a horse and saddle, and it seemed like an easy job to me. Six of us left under the command of a lieutenant colonel—five who were commissioned, and I only went with them to join the general. We traveled all that day toward the south and we reached a farm where the colonel had some relatives. After we were there about two-and-a-half days I asked the colonel, "What's going on? Are we going to continue with the search for the general?" He said, "Yes, boy, we're leaving tomorrow."

The next day we continued our journey but now we went toward the north, and I realized that we were more or less heading toward Juárez. That worried me, but I didn't say anything. On the road we came across a man who was carrying two large demijohns of *sotól* [poor man's alcoholic beverage], and two of our comrades asked him if he would give or sell them a little bit. Well, they emptied one of the demijohns and they began to drink and drink while we were traveling along. We arrived at a ranch near Carrizal, and we asked the person in charge if he would give us a little fodder for our horses. He gave us fodder and we went into the hills to camp. The men continued drinking, and it occurred to them to return to the ranch where we had gotten the fodder because there were two women there. A little later we heard a shot from the ranch and the colonel said, "This is bad business. Who knows what they're doing there!" When the two drunk men came back, each one had a woman with him. Then the colonel talked with the women and one said, "Sir, I came because I wanted to, but this other girl—I think they shot her husband or her father." Then the colonel told the two women to go back to the ranch, but they were afraid that the soldiers were going to follow them. The colonel assured them that they wouldn't, and the poor ladies left. I spent that night worried, fearing that the two

26

drunks were going to start a fight because the colonel had deprived them of the women, but nothing happened.

The next morning it seemed to the colonel that things weren't going very well and he decided that the best thing would be to stop being revolutionaries. After traveling for a little while, we stopped and he said, "Boys, wait here two or three hours while I go to Villa Ahumada to arrange an armistice for us." He left and those two kept on drinking, and the rest of us were without food or anything. In a little while one of the men who was drinking said, "We've been waiting a long time. Let's go see what happened to the colonel." Well, there we went and we arrived in Carrizal [15 kilometers from Villa Ahumada]. The two drunks went into a large corral and the rest of us went to get something to eat. I went to a home and asked a lady for some food; she gave me some and I paid her. On my way back to rejoin the others I saw a cloud of dust and I thought that the Carrancistas were coming. I got to my comrades and told them, "You know what? Here come the Carrancistas!" But they said, "Ah, those aren't Carrancistas." Well, I left them and went to blend in with the townspeople. I had already changed clothes; I looked like a civilian. It turned out that they captured my companions and a little later the Carrancistas came to where I was. They noticed the Texan hat that I was wearing and one of the officers asked me if I was a revolutionary. Right away I thought that if I said that I wasn't, someone might tell on me and then they would treat me even worse. I told him that I *was*, and they took me to where they were keeping the others.

The Carrancistas searched us and took everything that we had. I had one of those cartridge pouches that the American Army uses around my waist, and I had hidden around 250 pesos in silver inside. Well, every-thing was lost there—money, blankets, clothes. Then they tied the five of us together in a row, one behind the other, and made us march in front of the horses until we reached Villa Ahumada, where they put us on a railroad car. We were very tired, without sleep and our arms ached because they had tied us so tightly. Sleep overcame me and I slept for a little bit, but then I woke up and saw that one of my companions wasn't there. I thought, "Well, who knows?"

A little bit later we got out of the car and joined the rest, and a sergeant told me, "Listen, friend, put yourself in God's hands because

27

the train is going to take you now."* I answered him, "One day it's going to take you, too." Well, he hit me with the rifle and he made us walk to an old shed where we saw our companion who had been taken out before, thrown on the floor. I thought that maybe they had killed him and I looked at him to see if he were breathing or anything. One of the Carrancistas told me, "The same thing is going to happen to you." Then they tied our hands and feet behind us and put a rope around our necks. Four or five men pulled it upwards and upon feeling that they were strangling me I said to the captain, "Why are you punishing us this way if we're not murderers, bandits or criminals? That's why you have rifles— to shoot us."

They let the rope loosen a little and they began to ask us questions about how many Villistas there were and how many were on their way to that place. We answered that we weren't the leaders and that we didn't know. Then they kicked the man who was on the floor and he turned over. He hadn't been strangled; he was just pretending because they had told him that if he breathed or moved, they would kill him. Because of that, it looked like the poor man wasn't breathing. He got up right away. Then they took us to the railroad car again.

The next day in the morning they put us in a barracks. Things got complicated for the pair who had taken the two girls from the ranch, because the Carrancistas learned about the incident through complaints that the people had made. They threw them in a basement, and they left the rest of us in the barracks. We were there two days without food—just watching all the soldiers eat! I felt the little pocket in my pants to see if there happened to be some coins left there, and it turned out that I found a fifty-cent piece. For two days I hadn't thought to look in that little place, and then I said, "Thank God." Right away I asked a Carrancista to do me the favor of buying me some bread with those few cents, and he said that he would. Each piece of bread was worth five cents, so I expected ten pieces. But the soldier returned with only five. Well, I shared them with everyone else and we ate them with water and had a halfway decent lunch.

That afternoon they took us to where the head of the garrison was and he told us, "Well, boys, here is some paper so that you can write

*Popular expression meaning, "You're really going to get it," that is, punishment is forthcoming, with an implied possibility of death.

letters to your families if you want, because tomorrow you're going to be shot by the firing squad." I thought, "Well, who should I write to?" None of the others wrote to anyone either, except one man who was older. He wrote his letter, and when he finished, they took us back to the barracks.

The next morning around eight o'clock I saw that there were already people there watching and that the soldiers were beginning to put on their cartridge belts and get their rifles, and I said, "Who knows what's waiting for us now?" The soldiers got in formation and they took the three of us out. Then they brought the other two who had been locked up in the basement and they reunited the five of us. Then they decided that they would carry out the execution behind the church, and they took us over there. The townspeople were already there and the soldiers got into firing formation. Then the captain read us the verdict (according to them), and asked, "All right, men, do you want to be blindfolded?" One in the group said, "No, sir, none of us want to be blindfolded." They were going to shoot us when one of our comrades said, "By any chance do you have some cigarettes that you'll give us?" The captain came back, gave each one a cigarette and lit it, and then we smoked them.

The captain returned to the line of soldiers and gave the order, "Load!" I thought, "Hey, stop!" I was dying there and just then a train passed full of Villistas who had just been discharged, and upon seeing them I thought, "If only God had allowed me to go on that train to my house, to see who I could find in my family." And then from the other side: "Load! Aim! Fire!" They fired, and so I wouldn't see, I turned to the side. What a surprise to see that everyone else had fallen except me! The comrade who had been next to me fell beside my feet, and I turned to look at him. He was hurt and tried to get up, but the captain came and pow!—he shot him in the head and killed him. The captain was next to me with his pistol in his hand and I thought, "Well, since he shot that poor guy in the head, he's going to shoot me, too!" I looked to see if the captain was raising his pistol. There was a very calm silence as if there were no people there; not even the dogs were barking. Some time passed, and I thought that according to the rules of execution, if an accident happens and the one who's being executed doesn't get shot, well then he's saved. But I said, "What are these people going to know about that?" Everything was very serious for about ten minutes, but

29

then the people started to move and the atmosphere changed. The soldiers got in marching formation and the people began to go to their houses. They took me back to the barracks again. It must have been that they decided not to kill me because I was a boy or that it just wasn't my time to go yet. Only God saved me from death; I've always considered it a big favor that they did me.

In the barracks the first lieutenant realized that I had been a leader in Villa's army and one of Villa's adopted sons, and he was always on my back. He didn't like me; that man didn't trust me very much. Either he or one of the others was always guarding me and I couldn't do anything, just stay there being punished. I was there like that for two or three days; there wasn't a chance to do anything. Then I went to see the head of the barracks and I told him that now that they had done me the favor of not killing me, I wanted them to do me a last favor and let me go. I told him I didn't want any more fights, that I wanted to try to find my family. He said to me, "OK, boy, if you want to go, leave." But I didn't believe what he had told me, so I went to talk to a first lieutenant that I trusted because he had also been a Villista at one time. He advised me not to go. He told me that I should wait until they moved me from that place on the train within three days, and that I should escape on the way.

I stayed until that train came although I didn't have any money or food. But I made ten pesos by getting ahold of a horse that the Carrancistas had left in a corral when they put the animals on the train, and I sold it to a soldier. The horse wasn't mine; I was only cleaning it, but since no one claimed it and a soldier offered to buy it from me, I took advantage of the opportunity. After I got on the train I was hoping that the horse wouldn't start to buck because he was hard to handle and if someone pulled on his reins he became angry and uncontrollable. I was getting anxious when the train didn't leave because I thought that the soldier was going to come and take back his ten pesos. Finally the train left and I calmed down.

We traveled from Villa Ahumada toward Chihuahua City, and I couldn't get off the train because they were always guarding me. In Chihuahua City I got off at the station but there wasn't any chance of hiding myself. We got on the train again, and there we went. I was near the back of the train with a soldier that started to talk to me, and I couldn't get him to go to sleep. Finally he fell asleep and started to snore. In the darkness of the night I got close to the ladder on the car and let myself fall. I fell, rolling around on the track, but I didn't get hurt at all. I got up, brushed myself off, and began to walk. But like a fool I walked toward the south instead of going toward the border. I could hear wolves and coyotes howling and I threw stones toward where it seemed the closest animals were. At daybreak I sat down to rest, when I saw a train that was going towards the south. I managed to get on it because it stopped to let another train pass which was going in the opposite direction. At that place there was a railroad siding.

I think that the guard saw me climb aboard, because he came to where I was hanging on and told me that I would have to pay two and a half pesos. I told him that I didn't have any money and asked him to allow me to stay aboard anyway, but he got very mean and hit me on the head. I had to get off, and there I went again. I walked and walked and walked and in the afternoon I saw another train that was also heading south. Once again, as luck would have it, *that* train stopped and I could get on board, but this time I was more careful to make sure that no one saw me. I climbed in a freight car and got as far as Gómez Palacio where I had a good opportunity because I knew some people there. I went to the home of a family I knew, dying of hunger and everything. It was dark already and when they saw that I was all filthy and my clothes were all torn, they didn't want to open the door. It turned out that the father was in Durango at the time and he had told the family, which included two girls, that they should be very careful with the Carrancistas because they were going around robbing people. Since they didn't recognize me, I began to explain to them who I was and they opened the door a little bit. Through the opening I could see that they were eating; there were refried beans, bread, milk, and it made my mouth water. When they opened the door wider they recognized me and pulled me inside, locking the door behind me.

We chatted for a while, but I could hardly talk since I was so hungry and kept staring at that food. One of the girls asked me if I had already had dinner and I was going to tell her that I hadn't eaten for two or three days, but I just told her that I hadn't had dinner yet. Then she told the maid to serve me, and she brought me beans, tortillas and milk. I ate that and the girl asked me if I wanted more. Of course I was still

31

hungry and yes, I wanted more, but I thought that if I ate more I would get sick. As it was, I wasn't sure how I was going to feel after having eaten what I had just finished.

We talked until midnight, and then it was time to go to bed. I had noticed some large sacks that were in an empty room and I thought I would sleep there, but the girl had already made up a bed for me in another room with one of the boys. I told her, "No! How am I going to sleep in a bed in these filthy clothes, even if it's just for one night? I'm going to sleep here on these sacks." I even had bugs, and I insisted so much that I got my way and she went to bed. About an hour later my stomach began to ache; my insides were churning. Well, it was embarrassing because I had to go to the bathroom and I couldn't find a place to go. The patio was very pretty, all fixed up, and I couldn't do it there. I had my underpants down; I got to the gate in the fence and as soon as I opened it, I went to the bathroom. I was like that all night; I had diarrhea until 5:00 a.m. Before everyone got up, I covered up what I had done, just like a cat. In the morning we ate, talked and then, embarrassed, I took a bath and put on some of the boy's clothes which they had given me. I saw myself in the mirror and I looked very different from when I had arrived!

Some time passed and I was still there with that family. One day one of the girls sent me to the market on an errand, and I ran into one of the soldiers who had captured me in Carrizal. He was dressed as a civilian. We greeted each other and he said that he had left the army, but when I left I had a heavy feeling that they would be looking for me. The next time that I was asked to go to the market, I told them about my fear and they didn't send me any more.

After being with that family two months it seemed like a lot of time to me, so then I went to stay with a man who had a ranch near Gómez Palacio. I knew him because of his sons, who had been with our troops in Sonora when we were defeated. I asked the man to lend me some money because I was thinking about starting a business, but he told me that the only money that he had right then was in 100 peso bills and that Carranza had suspended the use of that kind of bill because they were going to be replaced with new bills. But he told me not to worry; he said that within two weeks he would have fruit in his orchard and I could pick whatever I wanted and sell it. He also gave instructions to his maid to give me something to eat whenever I was there. Therefore, if I couldn't eat in one place, I ate in another, and now I had the possibility of doing some business.

A little later I had the bad luck of being captured again. I was at the Fifth of May celebration in Torreón and someone recognized me; I was arrested by an officer and a soldier. They took me to the barracks and that night they harassed me, but finally they left me in peace. The next morning they undressed me and gave me some cut-off undershorts and also a cut-off undershirt. Then they took me to a big corral and there they beat me with a steel sword. It hurt a lot because I was almost naked. Then I remembered that it isn't hard to break a sword; if one puts his elbows back, they hit in the hollow space between the elbows and the sword breaks. That's what I did and "pop," the sword broke in two. I said, "Let's see you beat me now." Well, it was worse, because then they brought another sword and they hit me twice as much. They laid open my whole back, rear end, and arms. I couldn't bend over or even lay down. I had to stand up almost all the time for eight days. At night when my legs were aching, I got as comfortable as I could and little by little I reclined.

Finally I got better and they made me learn how to play the bugle because they needed a bugler. I didn't want to make the effort and one of the officers hit me in such a way that my mouth swelled. Then I told the captain that I couldn't play with a swollen mouth and he gave orders to the one who had hit me to leave me alone. When I got better I could play the instrument.

One day I ran into an acquaintance who told me that the Villistas were going to attack Torreón, and if they caught me with the Carrancistas they would kill me. He advised me to leave Torreón, but it was impossible. When the attack began I was sleeping. An officer who didn't like me gave me a kick which hurt a lot: "Come on! Go get a rifle and ammunition so you can fight." Well, I didn't want to fight because I knew that if the Villistas caught me they would kill me, but I went to get a Mauser rifle and I loaded it. I spent that night in a big horse corral, and since it was dark no one noticed if I had gone to fight or not. I prayed to God that that officer wouldn't return because then he would have realized that I hadn't fought and he would be a worse enemy and cause me *more* difficulties. The next afternoon the ones who had gone to fight came back and I realized that that officer was among those who had been killed. I said, "Good heavens! Poor thing! May God forgive him, but at least now he won't punish me any more."

I decided that I had to escape, but I thought that it was going to be difficult. In order to get out of the barracks I would have to jump over a tall wall that faced the street. One night I felt the impulse, and with much difficulty I was able to jump over the wall to the street. I hurt one of my feet a little, but I was able to walk all that night until I reached Gómez Palacio where I had a friend who had told me that if I escaped, I could stay with his family. We had agreed that he would look for me in the Plaza de Armas every day. At daybreak we saw each other there and he quickly took me to his house. I stayed with that family a few days. The father went to work and I stayed at home with the children. In order to earn the food that they gave me, I watered the patio and cleaned the place. The food consisted of two or three tortillas filled with beans and a little broth made of nothing but goat bones—it had no substance—and that was all. The other kids ate the same thing. I was always hungry because I was physically active all day, but I lived through it.

It turned out that the Carrancistas found out that I was around there and they asked my friend's father some questions; they told him that if he were helping me, they were going to kill him. The soldiers said that they were going to look for me until they got me either dead or alive. I didn't find out about that until later because the father didn't come home for several days, and when he returned he told me. He said that it would be better if I left and that he, too, was going to go to Durango and that he wasn't going to return.

A little later a man selling firewood came to the house, and I asked him if he needed a helper. He said that he did and the next day I went with him to his little ranch on his burro. We arrived at night and I was extremely hungry, but his family was very poor. They offered me a little pitcher of *champurrado* [a corn-based chocolate drink] which had been recently made; it was salty and I thought that if I drank it I would get diarrhea because my stomach was empty. I was stirring it and stirring it and the man said to me, "Come on, young man! Drink up! It's very good!" I replied, "Yes, sir, it *is* very good, but it's hot. I'll drink it in a little while." I never did drink it and I went to bed without having eaten anything.

In the morning his wife ground a little bit of corn and made three tortillas, of which she gave me one. I ate it with a few beans, and that was all. There wasn't any coffee, or cinnamon, or anything. Then we went outside and the man told me to bring water that he needed to make some adobe bricks because he wanted to build on another small room. Well, there I was—drawing water from the well, transporting it, stirring the mixture for the bricks, and he was just sitting there! My back was still hurting, but I put up with it—I didn't say anything. After two days the work was getting too much for me and I thought that it would be better to go to Gómez Palacio and try to earn a living there. I thought, "If even Jesus could hardly endure the cross, how can I, a mere human, put up with this? I'm going and if they catch me and shoot me, well, at least I'll have some rest." I told the man that I was leaving and he said that it was all right. He gave me two pesos, and I left.

I entered Gómez Palacio with caution and I began to sell fruit. I sold grapes to the people who were getting off the streetcar at a peso per kilo to the average person and a little less to the poorer people. After two days I had gotten together a little money and I bought half a dozen glasses so that I could sell fruit drinks. In the mornings I sold fruit, at noon I sold fruit drinks and ice cream, and in the evening I sold sweet bread which I bought in a bakery. I walked through the streets and yelled, "Sweet bread, sweet bread." Then a fellow from Durango came along and set up a place to sell cigarettes, sodas, candy, and things like that, and he invited me to be his partner. I accepted, and he sold at the stand and I sold on the streets.

One day he decided to sell one of his stands for 500 pesos, receiving half of the payment in the form of shoes. When I saw them, I thought that they looked very small for the people who lived in Gómez Palacio because it seemed to me that everyone there had big feet. We decided that in order to sell them we would have to go to the surrounding ranches. My partner left one of his nephews in charge of the business and we walked from ranch to ranch; but we didn't have very good luck— we didn't sell anything. In one ranch we exchanged a pair of our shoes for another one, and in another ranch they gave us corn or beans for a pair. We got tired of walking back and forth out there, so we returned to the business. While we were gone, the nephew had bought some very green watermelons and my partner got angry because it was going to be difficult to sell them. He kicked the boy out and then it was just the two of us with the business.

35

A little later I ran into a man who had seen me when I was a prisoner in Torreón, and he invited me to go with him to Ciudad Juárez and I thought that that was a good idea. I left the stand to my partner and we left. When I arrived in Juárez I was very dirty because I had traveled in the coal car of the train. We arrived in the middle of the night and at sunrise we went to the market to eat whatever we could buy with the few cents that we had. We decided to cross over to El Paso and at the bridge they made us take a bath. There were showers for men and for women; while one was bathing, they disinfected your clothes. I came out clean, but my clothes were all wrinkled. The man got a job right away because he was a railroad man, but I still couldn't do heavy work, and that's why he went on to New Mexico and I stayed in El Paso. I didn't have any relatives or friends here and my situation was pretty bad. I earned a dime or a quarter however I could, and that's how I lived.

On the first of January 1917, I went out to see the military parade that they have in downtown El Paso. I ran into a boy more or less my age and since it was cold, he invited me to watch the parade from the window in the building where he worked. We watched the parade very comfortably and we continued chatting until nightfall. Since that place was the YWCA, there were beds where the ladies did their exercises and rested, and the boy told me that I could spend the night there. In the morning we got up, ate, and I helped him clean up. I became a friend of the director of the place and I was able to live and work there until April, earning five dollars per week.

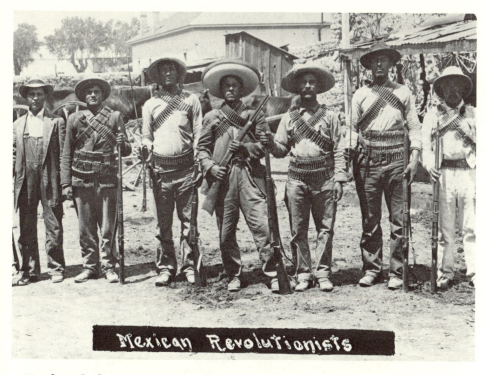

Unidentified Mexican revolutionaries. (Courtesy, El Paso Public Library, Photograph Collection)

Women revolutionaries prepare to meet General Antonio Rabájo, a follower of Pascual Orozco. (Courtesy, El Paso Public Library, Photograph Collection)

Unidentified children revolutionaries. (Courtesy, El Paso Public Library, Photograph Collection)

Explosives destined for use by revolutionaries in the battle of Casas Grandes, Chihuahua, in 1911. (Courtesy, U.T. El Paso Library, Aultman Collection)

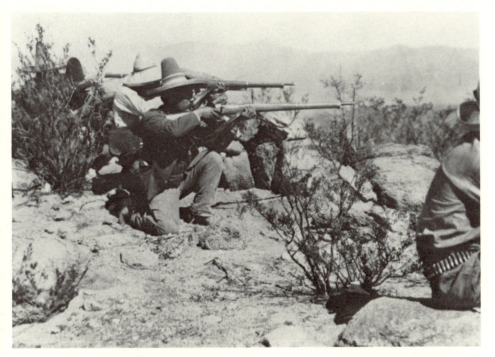

Revolutionaries fight the battle of Juárez, 1911. (Courtesy, U.T. El Paso Library, Aultman Collection)

Revolutionary fires while partner takes a break from the action, c. 1911.
(Courtesy, U.T. El Paso Library, Aultman Collection)

Revolutionaries watch the capture of Ojinaga, Chihuahua, in 1911.
(Courtesy, U.T. El Paso Library, Aultman Collection)

Venustiano Carranza's soldiers cooking *tortillas* at Agua Prieta, Sonora, in 1915. (Courtesy, U.T. El Paso Library, Aultman Collection)

"I encouraged my comrades to go
with me to drive out the filibusters."
—Angel Ruiz*

*Many Mexicans living in the United States involved them-
selves in the Revolution to varying degrees and for different
causes. Angel Ruiz was prompted by patriotism to join the
federales in Baja California in their fight against an invasion
launched by Ricardo Flores Magón. Because of suspected
backing from American businessmen and the presence of non-
Mexican soldiers of fortune in the Flores Magón ranks, many
viewed the invasion as a filibustering expedition that, if allowed to succeed, would result in the annexation of Baja California to the United States. (In later years, this perception
changed, and Flores Magón's movement is now seen as a genuine attempt to bring about revolutionary change in Mexico.)
Later Ruiz fought on the side of Victoriano Huerta.*

In referring to the notorious events which occurred in Tijuana, Lower
California, of which the national as well as the international press took
notice, I might say that I was working in 1911 on a farm in California
about 12 miles from Bakersfield together with eight other Mexicans.
Being informed of the events in a newspaper from the Capital *El Im-
parcial,* I encouraged my comrades to go with me to drive out the

*Interviewed in 1920s. Manuel Gamio, *The Mexican Immigrant: His Life Story* (Chicago: University of Chicago Press, 1931), pp. 36–40. Reprinted by permission of the
University of Chicago Press.

filibusters who were invading the rich territory of Lower California. They didn't want to go on account of obstacles which most of them saw in the way, but I found a way by means of which I got them to go. I kept telling them that they were unpatriotic and that they weren't Mexicans, so that they began to get angry at me, but I kept on with my arguments until I convinced them. One of them told me that they couldn't accompany me on account of lack of finances. I told them that I had $300.00 and what was coming to me for the few days that I had been working, so that they didn't need to worry on that account. But my companions weren't satisfied with what I had told them about the passports and the expenses of food and shelter as well as of tobacco, until I actually showed them the $300.00, and they knew that it was the truth that I had been telling them. We then started on our way to Los Angeles. I took the first step there by going to the Consul of Mexico and telling him what we wanted, which wasn't anything else but to throw out the filibusters who were in our country. He said that he didn't have instructions from the government to send men, and that in addition he didn't know whether we were going to send men to the government or to the revolutionists. I told him that we weren't asking for our passage or for expenses of any kind and that all we wanted was a recommendation to the government. Having given us a letter to the Consulate in San Diego, he refused to help us, even refusing to send a telegram to the governor of the state, who was Colonel Celso Vega. He told us that it cost money to send a telegram to the commander. But I said that I would send a telegram myself no matter how much it cost, saying that I and five Mexicans wished to give our services to the forces as volunteers, as we were Mexicans and had the right to do so.

The commander replied that he didn't have arms or ammunition. So then I, as leader of my four companions, told him that we would take arms and ammunitions. After we had been accepted we immediately went to several hardware shops, where I got them. We then took an auto to Tijuana. There the Mexican authorities received us and showed us where we should stay and the next day put us on day duty in front of the customs office. This was the 28th of April 1911, and the place was taken from us on the 10th of May, after two days of fighting in which I lost one of my five companions. I was taken prisoner by the filibusters together with a soldier of the federal army. But after a hard fight that I had with the guard who watched us two yards away, I freed us both.

He had a rifle and I had a knife, for we were disarmed when we were taken prisoners. I came out on top and as soon as we saw ourselves free we re-enlisted, after finding nine of the defenders of the customs. Among them was the brave lieutenant Miguel Guerrero, who was badly wounded. The *jefe politico* was killed, and since we were all without ammunition we had to abandon the place and cross the border. Here the nine who crossed over were taken prisoners. My pal and I didn't cross the line (so as not to fall into the power of the American soldiers). We hid in the forest along the river and crossed the line four days later, after being lost and not taking food or water in that time. We went to San Diego and went to the Consul and told what had happened to us. He said that he had known about that and that he couldn't give either my pal or me a single cent. I was penniless and had one hand wounded, which had been bandaged by a Red Cross doctor in Tijuana. Without being able to work, I somehow got thirty-five cents and we went to a ten-cent restaurant and got some food and bought a little pouch of Bull Durham tobacco and went on to Los Angeles, where I found a friend who helped us out and we organized a committee with directors and we collected money for expenses. I telegraphed to my chief in Ensenada who sent us a ship called the "Bernardo Reyes" in which 300 men sailed for Ensenada. There we were given a banquet and we were all armed with Remington-Mausers, only single shot, but very good. They used 7 millimeter cartridges. At the same time we received military orders for fifteen or twenty days and marched towards Tijuana. When we got to Aguascalientes we were ambushed by all the men under Prye Bocro, the leader of the filibusters. There were 450 of them on a train of the Southern Pacific lines. A number of them were killed, and we burned them the next day under the orders of Colonel Celso Vega. We entered Tijuana triumphantly where we forcibly tore down a number of red flags that had been raised on different buildings and hoisted that of the eagle and the serpent. I stayed several days in Tijuana and then the colonel sent me with 100 armed men to a port that is on the border called Tecate where Major Esteban Cantú was. At that time he was a major. He later received other promotions.

Knowing that my family was short of funds, I decided to return to where I could work in order to get together some more money for the support of my family. I began to work and in a short time saved a small amount and prepared to leave California for my country. It was at the time of General Huerta. I took the ship "Benito Juarez," which was taken by surprise by the war-ship "Guerrero" that escorted it to the Islas Marias, where it was taking food for the prisoners. Our ship was then taken to Mazatlán where some 370 passengers were landed. All of us without any cause were sent to Manzanilla where a body of troops were waiting for us. We were then sent on to Mexico City to a recruiting barracks called "La Canoa" where there were thousands of recruits. A companion and I paid one of those in charge of locating the recruits to send us at once to our posts, for we were trying to pay for substitutes by writing a number of times to the president of the Republic. Since that was denied us we left for Vera Cruz with the 18th Infantry Battalion. We were there only ten months, having been defeated in Zacatecas. From there we went to Minillas, a few of us, and we joined the men of General Orozco and kept on towards Aguascalientes after having blown up a bridge about thirty-five kilometers from Minillas, called "De la Soledad." We kept taking up the rails as far as Chicalate. As soon as we got to Aguascalientes, I was transferred to an artillery division where I was promoted from a private to be first sergeant, only that we were disbanded in Toluca on 15 August 1914. I gave all of these services to my country while now I am here in a land where I can make no money in order to go back [to Mexico] with my family, which is made up of my wife and three children whom I have in school. I am very short of money because I am out of work.

> "Convinced that Madero . . . had reneged on his revolutionary promises, my brother led a popular revolt."
> —Serafina Orozco Vda. de Blanco
> (1895–   )*

Pascual Orozco, Jr. was one of the prominent leaders of the Revolution in its early stages, serving as a general under Francisco Madero, but later leading a rebellion against him. Orozco was a native of rural western Chihuahua, where sentiment against Porfirio Díaz and his wealthy regional supporters ran strong. In the following account, Pascual's sister Serafina Orozco Vda. de Blanco describes how the family was affected by her brother's involvement in the conflict. The Orozcos were one of many "activist" families who found it necessary to seek refuge in the United States.

The night of November 19–20, 1910, was bitterly cold. I was fifteen years old. Our home was in the agricultural community of San Isidro in the foothills of western Chihuahua's Sierra Madre Occidental. The village had suddenly become unusually active, what with the mysterious arrival of friends and relatives from various locales throughout the region.

We resided in a large house built of reddish adobe brick that had been plastered over and whitewashed. A particularly spacious adjoining

*Written memoir; first place winner in the 1980 Historical Memories Contest of the El Paso County Historical Society. *Password* 25:1 (Spring 1980): 11–16. Translated by Richard Estrada. Reprinted by permission of *Password*.

41

room served as the town schoolhouse. We heard voices emanating from there late that night. It was easy for Sara, Transito, and me to stack some wooden crates one on top of the other, climb them, and peer through the transom. Little did we realize that a dramatic moment in the early stages of the Mexican Revolution was unfolding before us.

Agustin Estrada was there. He would later become a famous general. Francisco Salido from the lower sierra was an educated man who would soon die a violent death. And there stood my father, Pascual Orozco Sr., and my eldest brother, Pascual Jr. The men chose my brother to be their leader. My father began to speak and it was then that we learned of the purpose of the meeting. He said that they were about to undertake a venture from which there would be no turning back, and that they would either destroy the tyranny of Porfirio Díaz "and his 60,000 bayonets" or die in the attempt. We girls were proud of our father and "Pascualito," but we knew the imminent danger they faced, so we began to cry softly. The meeting broke up. We continued to cry. Within a few hours they attacked the hamlet of Minaca. Later in the day they returned to take complete control of San Isidro. By the following morning they were besieging Ciudad Guerrero, our district seat. The Revolution had begun.

A ranchero and merchant, my father was a portly man whose gregarious ways, respectability, and kindness earned him the special fondness of the *peones* and *muleteros*. Pascual, my brother, was best known as a *conductor de metales*, the owner of an outfit that transported precious metals—mostly silver—by mule-back from the mines deep in the mountains to the state capital at Ciudad Chihuahua. He was unlike my father insofar as he was laconic and very formal, like my mother, Amada Vasques de Orozco. But Pascualito was similarly respected for his efficiency, his scrupulous honesty and sincerity, and his excellent riding skills and marksmanship. He was over six feet tall, lanky but strong, mustachioed, of light complexion, with reddish-brown hair and penetrating green eyes.

Some of my memories have dimmed. However, those events which touched my family stand out clearly in my mind. I recall the visit of Francisco I. Madero himself to our home about the spring of 1911. Short, bearded, nervous, and not especially inspiring, he was a loquacious man who commanded our respect not because of his personality, but rather because he was the nationally recognized leader of the Revolution. Our menfolk were generally quiet and humble, but far from meek; they proved themselves decisive and tenacious at critical moments. Madero was quick to refer military matters to my brother. Pascual commanded several small revolutionary groups. They engaged the federal forces in various battles and skirmishes. They had suffered a terrible defeat at Cerro Prieto because they made the mistake of fighting a formal battle against the *federales*, who won the day with their artillery. The revolutionaries soon became guerrillas. Many of our friends and relatives had been killed. Our father and brother and their forces fought with that much more resolve. We remained in San Isidro during this time. Pascual eventually led his forces northward. In the second week of May 1911 we were notified that he had taken Ciudad Juárez.

The success of the Madero movement changed our lives. My brother was lionized in Chihuahua and throughout the rest of Mexico. He was even a hero in El Paso. He was named chief of the Chihuahua state militia. Pascual summoned us to live in Ciudad Chihuahua. Important people began to seek him out. My brother took an active interest in politics and became a gubernatorial candidate, but eventually withdrew.

Convinced that Madero, who was now president, had reneged on his revolutionary promises, my brother led a popular revolt against the *Maderistas* in the early spring of 1912. Thousands of men joined him. But he suffered ill-fortune and by the summer he had retreated to Ciudad Juárez, where we lived with him in an annex to the customhouse, or *aduana*. I recall one incident that happened there particularly well. We were dining one evening with Pascual and his staff when someone suddenly hurled a metal object into the room. Leaping to his feet, Pascual seized it and flung it out the window. The bomb or hand grenade immediately exploded, destroying the front porch.

Continued reverses forced Pascual to send us to El Paso to live. Dozens and perhaps hundreds of prominent families poured into the city to live in exile. For a time we lived on Second and then on Third Street. Later we moved to 1218 Montana, across the street from where the El Paso Museum of Art stands. The extreme heat of El Paso was unbearable to those of us who were natives of a cool mountain country. Later, at another house, we learned to take refuge from it by napping in our basement in the middle of the afternoon.

In early 1913 Huerta revolted in Mexico City and Madero was killed. My brother allied himself with the new government and we returned to Chihuahua. Huerta soon thereafter summoned my father to the national capital and entrusted him with a peace mission to Morelos state, where the intractable revolutionary Emiliano Zapata operated. We were all heartbroken when we found out several months later that Zapata had imprisoned my father and had finally executed him.

In the fall of 1913 our enemy, Pancho Villa, took Ciudad Juárez. Federal General Salvador Mercado feared our forces would be caught in a pincer movement by revolutionary troops moving in from the north and south. He retreated north-eastward to the Texas border at Ojinaga-Presidio. Many of us who were civilians joined him, afraid as we were of *Villista* vengeance. The Terrazas and Creel families also accompanied us. We started out by train but only got as far as San Sóstenes. There was a lack of coal. Worse, many of the trainmen, also afraid of Villa, deserted. We were lucky to be able to ride in my brother's Cadillac automobile, but thousands of others had to march across the cold desert. It was a sad spectacle. Huge clouds of dust hung over our paths. We parted company with Pascual at Ojinaga and went to San Antonio, where we rented a house on Skinner Street. I was particularly impressed by the beautiful and elegant Mexican girls who lived there. Perhaps they, too, were exiles.

We did not hear from Pascual for months. I believe he wandered with a few followers throughout Coahuila and Chihuahua until he joined the government forces in the interior.

My mother decided that we should move back to El Paso a few months later. We rented a home at 1319 Wyoming Street.

Villa was able to defeat Huerta in the summer of 1914. About a year later Huerta, my brother, and their friends were converging on El Paso, in order to jump off into Mexico and launch their new revolution. Before they could do so, U.S. authorities arrested them at Newman, Texas, and brought them to the federal courthouse in El Paso. Huerta was jailed at Fort Bliss. He died of natural causes toward the end of that year.

Pascual was placed under house arrest at our home on Wyoming Street. Military guards were posted outside. We were thrilled to see my brother but pained by the circumstances. One July afternoon as the rest of the family enjoyed a *siesta* in the basement, I happened to go up the stairs to the kitchen for a glass of water. Pascual was donning his black hat, his well-known trademark (my father preferred Stetsons). I

44

quietly asked him where he was going, but he put his finger to his lips, signalling me to hush. I did so. I was seized with fear. He was calm and deliberate. The soldier out back had been drinking beer and dozed off. Pascual silently opened the door. He stepped gingerly over the guard. He took long, slow strides toward the alley. Pascual looked one way, then the other, made up his mind instantly, pulled the brim of his hat down slightly over his forehead, and strode away. It was the last time any of us saw my brother alive.

Pascual's escape was front-page news in El Paso. Soldiers and officals interrogated us demanding to know his whereabouts. We simply did not know. About two months later a friend of ours brought us the crushing news that Pascual was dead. Ranchers and Texas Rangers had slain him near Sierra Blanca under mysterious circumstances. His body was returned to our new residence on Montana Street. We held a wake there. We placed Pascual's body in a mausoleum at Concordia Cemetery after one of the largest funerals in El Paso history; thousands attended.

My mother and siblings were thus left without the guidance and support of our beloved brother. Coming so soon after the loss of her husband, the death of her first-born was a terrible shock to my mother, who died in 1918 at the age of fifty-two.

"He gave me a choice of joining Villa
or of dying. I joined."
—Blas Rodríguez (1891–   )*

*In time of war, unfortunate individuals are pulled into the
conflict simply because they find themselves at the wrong place
at the wrong time. Blas Rodríguez, a native of Presidio, Texas,
had no idea when he crossed the border that from that moment
on he would have to abandon his life as a* vaquero (*cowboy*)
to become a Villista.

One day when I was in my twenties I crossed into Mexico [from
Presidio] to gather our stray cattle. Sometimes our cows would wander
away and we would have to find them. I was busy looking, when I saw
some riders coming toward me. The leader of the band, whom I later
learned was Hipolito Villa [brother of Pancho Villa], asked me if I had
ever heard of Pancho Villa. I told him that I had. He then gave me a
choice of joining Villa or of dying. I joined. They needed men to fight
Carranza.

I remember after my first battle at Moctezuma we went to get supper.
There were five Chinese men there and they waited on us. Since they
were so good to us we gave them the opportunity to leave. We told
them to get out of town because Villa would be coming soon. But they
said Villa was their "compadre" and "amigo" and that they were not

*Interviewed in the Lower Rio Grande Valley in 1975 by unidentified researcher. On
file at the Institute of Oral History, University of Texas at El Paso. Used by permission
of Professor Rodolfo Rocha of Pan American University.

46

leaving. After awhile, Villa arrived, rounded up the Chinese, and the next day shot them. He hated the Chinese because in a battle against Carranza forces, a good number of Chinese fought against Villa. This angered Villa because it was not their land or their Revolution. He believed the Chinese had no business in Mexico.

As we rode through the countryside we were always getting involved in skirmishes and battles, but there are a few battles I remember more than others. One day at about seven in the morning the Carrancistas attacked Parral, Chihuahua. We put up a fight but it was to no avail; they had too many men. During the battle I was wounded. A bullet shot through one side of my neck and came out through the back. I thought I was going to die. I was bleeding and hurting and I had no medical attention. That night we slipped out of the city. For two days we rode until we came to a village that was safe. I'll never forget those two days. Only God saved me from death. Riding in the hot sun with all the pain and with my neck puffed out was pure hell. Even now I still don't know how I managed to live through that wound. Only God knows.

In 1919 the Villistas and the Carrancistas fought at Ciudad Juárez. The fighting was heavy and both sides suffered many casualties. After two days, however, the Carrancistas let the Americans come into Juárez after Villa. We were weary and exhausted and the American troops were fresh and there were too many of them. Villa told us to get out of Juárez as best as we could. The Americans almost caught Villa on this occasion but he somehow managed to escape. We retreated to a remote camping place. It was there that I saw Villa cry; perhaps it was that he felt responsible for so many civilian and soldier deaths, or frustration and anger at the Americans. It was a sad moment for us.

The last battle in which I fought was at Villa Ahumada. A Carrancista general attacked us. We were routed badly. After this battle I went to the border with general Aranda. I was tired of fighting and I wanted to go home, but General Aranda wouldn't let me go. One day I just couldn't wait any longer so I left the camp and headed home. I was afraid they would track me down and shoot me, but I managed to get home safely. When I got to Presidio my parents were really happy to see me. They cried and the rest of the family just smiled and hugged me.

"Long live the Revolution."
—Severo Márquez (1891–   )*

For small town young men, the prospect of adventure offered a real enticement to join the Revolution, even if the reasons for the fighting remained clouded. Severo Márquez, a native of Coyachic, Chihuahua, was one such recruit.

In December of 1910 I was working with a Mormon in San Pedro de Madera, Chihuahua. A good friend of my father's, who found out that there had been some fighting in Chihuahua, began to recruit people in that town. Since he was my godfather and from my part of the country, some other boys and I got all fired up. "Let's go with Che Delgado. Long live the Revolution!" And several of us boys joined with him. Then we attacked and took over an American's ranch who lived near Madera and we got ahold of his horses.

We young people didn't understand anything, although we knew that it was a revolution. As far as I'm concerned, I think we went to fight because we liked the idea of an adventure. We went around giving speeches, saying that Porfirio Díaz's government wasn't worth anything, that the landholders weren't paying, and so forth. And there we went, speaking against Porfirio Díaz.

We fought in Casas Grandes and then at a mine between Casas Grandes and Ciudad Juárez. On the 8th of May, 1911, we arrived in Ciudad

*Interviewed in Ciudad Juárez in 1974 by Oscar J. Martínez. On file at the Institute of Oral History, University of Texas at El Paso.

Juárez. I didn't have to fight very much when we took over Juárez, but the other soldiers who had entered the city on the other side had to fight a lot because it was a big battle.

After the victory I remember that I wanted to go over to the other side to see what the United States was like. But an uncle of mine came and convinced me that I should return to Chihuahua City where we would be mustered out of military duty. And that's what happened. When we got to Chihuahua City they gave each soldier 100 pesos in addition to horses and arms.

I was working in Chihuahua City when a faction of revolutionaries in Coyoachic began to make trouble for my father. They demanded that he give them arms, horses, and saddles, which he didn't have. They went to search my parents' house, but my brother shot at them and didn't let them get in. My brother had to go to San Andrés. Then they took my father prisoner because they wanted my brother to turn himself in. I went to Coyoachic, and when I got there my friends asked me what my plans were. I told them that I was going to get my father out of jail, but I couldn't, so I went to another town where there was a district judge. But that didn't help either. I couldn't get my father out.

I went to my parents' house and then some revolutionaries came to unarm me. I quickly got out of the house and found a good place to hide among some trees. When they got to the house, I had my carbine ready, pointing it at them. My mother told them that I had gone. I thought about killing the leader, but I decided that it would be better not to. I told the leader to come alone to where I was, but since he came with the whole troop I shot at them. Finally I ran them out of there and they went toward the river. Then I went to San Andrés, joined with my brother and the rest, and became one of Villa's followers. Later my father got out of jail and my brother died in the Revolution.

I fought in the capture of Zacatecas and Torreón, and in several battles along the border. Besides the battle of Ciudad Juárez, I also fought in Agua Prieta and in Nogales. In Agua Prieta we fought for three days and we would have captured the city if the trains hadn't arrived from the American side. Seven trains stuffed with federal soldiers arrived. General Villa couldn't do anything else but say, "Let's get out of here!"

Then we had a shoot-out near Nogales. In Cananea they had named me as the one to go on the train to Nogales to bring back provisions. We went armed with machine guns; we loaded the train and were returning, but halfway back, in a place called Estación Tortilla, they were waiting for us. We put two machine guns on a flatcar in the front of the train and got the train going, but they destroyed a bridge and we had to return to Nogales. Villa had a meeting of his officers and we agreed that we should leave toward Guaymas along the American border. We traveled along where the wire fence is. On the American side there were a lot of black soldiers, but that time they didn't interfere with us at all.

Villa still resented the Americans' betrayal in Agua Prieta, which is mainly why we lost there. But I think that where the Americans are concerned, Villa wasn't the lion that they painted him to be. One time in Sonora I had the luck to be near him when he called a meeting of generals, among whom were Medina and Angeles. They got together under a large mesquite tree, which was very close to the American border, where the fence had fallen down. Then we saw two cars that were coming from the American side. They were four doctors who came to offer Villa bandages and other medical supplies—first aid equipment that would help him. The people were distrustful. Only one of the Americans spoke Spanish; the others needed interpreters. I clearly remember that I heard Villa say, "I don't want anything from the Yankees; I don't want anything." He ordered that they be shot. The biggest American cried like a baby, begging us not to shoot them; he was very frightened. Villa said that those medicines were probably something to finish off the wounded men. But the doctors explained that they were offering them because they sympathized with him and his soldiers, and that they were doing it for humanitarian reasons. Finally Villa didn't accept anything and he let the doctors go.

> "By getting drunk, the influenza
> didn't harm me."
> —José Victoriano Avila Escobedo
> (1895–   )*

Confusion, idleness, food shortages, lack of pay, and illness were recurring concerns for many common soldiers like José Victoriano Avila Escobedo, a native of Jalisco. Here Avila Escobedo recalls the Battle of Juárez (1911) and later incidents.

In the camp while we were waiting for orders to attack Juárez, Villa put everybody to work because we had officers from Sonora and from other parts who stood around with their arms crossed, not knowing what to do. He walked around ordering everyone, "Do this and do that. Give water to the horses; give them something to eat; make them rest so that they will be ready if it's necessary to run. Get them ready, try to oil your weapons, your rifles, your carbines." We didn't have any good pistols. We had to fight a lot—thirsty, hungry, and only sleeping during a short break that they gave us the second night. The fighting lasted three days, from the 8th until the 10th when we won and General Juan Jose Navarro's troops surrendered to us. This general was a very large Indian; he wore a black overcoat with a white silk lining underneath, a military cap with an eagle on it—one of those eagles which is sitting down with its wings outstretched.

*Interviewed in Ciudad Juárez in 1975 by Teresa Jimarez and José Torres. On file at the Institute of Oral History, University of Texas at El Paso.

51

After the victory, almost everyone in the city got together to get drunk. Men and women yelled in the streets: "Long live the Revolution! Long live Madero! Long live Orozco! Long live Villa!" But that was all. There wasn't any food here; you had to go to El Paso in order to get something to eat. And we still hadn't received the payment that Madero had promised us.

One year there was an influenza epidemic and many people died, to the degree that they carried the dead people on mule-drawn carts without even being in boxes. They took some to the cemetery and left them there, unburied. When they returned to the ranch or to the town where they lived, there was already another car full of bodies. People died day and night. A person's head began to ache and the next day he was a corpse. The doctors, who thought that this was the way to stamp out the disease, sprayed poison in the houses where people had influenza, believing that "once the dog is dead, the rabies are done away with."

During that time my head began to ache, and I and some other soldiers got drunk on tequila which was very sweet and good. One didn't even get a hangover; you woke up the next day feeling fine, just hungry. I think that by getting drunk, the influenza didn't harm me. Many poor people left their small children as orphans, some here and others there, very small boys who later grew up among the soldiers, shining their boots and eating now with one, having dinner with another, and having lunch with still another. They were without father, without mother, without anything.

"He proclaimed me as his 'Chief of Artillery' with the rank of first captain."

—I. Thord-Gray*

Present among the insurgent ranks were foreigners from various nationalities who joined the fighting for adventure or other reasons. I. Thord-Gray, a Swedish born citizen of the United States, began his colorful military career in 1897 with the British in Africa, and later served various other European armies throughout the world. In the fall of 1913 he left China for Mexico "to have a look" for himself after hearing about the Revolution. He arrived in El Paso just after Pancho Villa had taken Ciudad Juárez in the famous surprise attack of November 15.

No vehicles were allowed to cross over the International bridge into Mexico without special permit. I had to proceed on foot, but was detained by the U.S. Border Guard. They advised me to remain on the American side, as the Mexicans hated all foreigners and would soon despatch me to the Happy Hunting Grounds. It took some time to convince them of my firm intention to go over and I was allowed to do so after showing the Mexican Consular permit from Shanghai. Once over the Rio Grande, it did not take long to reach General Villa's headquar-

*I. Thord-Gray, *Gringo-Rebel (Mexico, 1913–1914)* (Coral Gables: University of Miami Press, 1960), pp. 21–29. Reprinted by permission of the University of Miami Press.

ters, but many people seemed to follow my movements with suspicion and by their scowls it was evident that foreigners were not particularly trusted or wanted in this land.

After announcing myself, and waiting for half an hour, I was ushered into a large room and stood before Villa. My first impression of Pancho Villa, the reputed outlaw, bandit, murderer of hundreds, and general extraordinary, was not very bad in spite of his unsavory reputation, and his unshaven and somewhat unkempt appearance. He was powerfully built, forceful looking, robustious, with a roundish large head and slightly bloated face. The lips were large and strong but sensuous. The upper lip was covered with a heavy stumpy mustache. The eyes were bloodshot as if in need of sleep. The hair was out of sight under a sombrero which was tilted back. He wore soft leather leggins reaching above the knee. His face was dirty looking but a gorilla-grin, not at all unkindly, illuminated his countenance which otherwise seemed hard and coarse.

As the great Villa did not condescend to look my way, there was time to observe that the unventilated room stank with noxious human exhalations, stale sweat-soaked clothing, and cigarette smoke. A bunch of pretty hothouse flowers stood in front of Villa, stuck in an expensive blue Chinese jar from the Ming period, a beautiful museum piece.

Eventually Villa looked but when he saw me his face turned into a scowl, almost of anger, associated, it seemed to me, with arrogance or contempt. His whole attitude was a challenge, startling though not altogether objectionable. But, for the moment, it reminded one of a bull-ape beating his chest in the African or Malayan jungle. I couldn't help feeling this was a pose or a show put on for the benefit of his staff to cover up some idiosyncrasies or, perhaps, not unlikely, to scare me.

When introduced by a staff officer, I saluted and presented my credentials from the Mexican Consul in Shanghai. General Villa did not return the salute nor did he in any way acknowledge my presence. In fact, he seemed completely oblivious of my existence which nettled me perhaps a little. He took the document from the officer and read it carefully, upside down, and then I realized Villa could not read. After "reading" the permit he passed it to an aide with a remark, which in Mexico, I found later, is equivalent to son-of-bitch, or worse.

The staff officer, a thin, undersized, sallow-faced, half-breed Indian, looked at the letter and asked in good English, "Where did you obtain this permit to enter Mexico? Why are you here?" When I explained that my trip across the Pacific was for the purpose of archaeological research work in Mexico, but that I wished to join the revolutionary army, he looked incredulous and unconvinced but told his chief.

Evidently Villa did not believe my answer either, as he appeared enraged once more and the words, "*Gringo* spy," came from his almost frothing mouth. It was evident that this hard man's nerves were on edge. He was caught off his guard and looked repulsive. I seemed to have met baboons in South Africa better looking than Villa at this moment. He turned to me with blazing bloodshot eyes, shouting orders for me to get out of Mexico.

When requesting the return of my permit, Villa tore it up with some more insults and accused me of being an American agent, sent to spy on him for Huerta in Mexico City.

There was nothing more for me to do. Not wishing to lose my temper, I walked out without saluting, to return to El Paso. It was obvious my long trip from China had been in vain, but I had not lost my bet with Bradstock* which consoled me a little, perhaps. There was, of course, the Mexican Federal Army to be considered, but I dismissed the evil thought. Then it flashed through my mind to return to China and more friendly people.

On my way back through Villa's camp, however, I noticed two field guns by which stood a handsome but dejected looking officer, obviously not a Mexican. Having been through a course in Horse Artillery while in Pondoland, I became interested naturally and wanted to see what kind of guns they had in Mexico, and stopped.

I found the man to be an American, keen to pour out his trouble to someone, not a Mexican. He had been a sergeant in the U.S. Infantry, and got into trouble over a woman by hitting an officer and had skipped into Mexico rather than face a court-martial. He offered his services to Villa who, possessing no artillery officer, made him captain of his artillery, taking for granted that the American sergeant would know something about guns.

The captain informed me he was in trouble as he knew very little about artillery, but thought the guns had been tampered with by the federal gunners before they abandoned them. I examined the breech-

---

*An American journalist who had made a bet with Thord-Gray that the revolution would be over and lost before Thord-Gray could get to Mexico.

blocks, found that the firing pins had been broken, and suggested he make ones. The possibilities of making temporary pins astounded the man, and he admitted he didn't know how. Personally, I wasn't sure either, but was willing to try and offered to do so, at which he brightened up but was horrified when told I needed to take one of the blocks to El Paso.

At this point, the officer straightened up like a ramrod and ordered me to move on. But, it was too late as Villa with a few men was striding toward us. When he spotted me he roared out an order at which four men, armed with guns, machetes and long knives, closed in and grabbed me. I was under arrest. There was a tall, swarthy-looking man standing close to Villa who constantly kept his eyes on me in an unfriendly manner. Afterwards I found out it was the much feared Rodolfo Fierro, better known as *El Carnicero* (The Butcher), because of his unscrupulous killings.

The officer intervened and spoke to Villa explaining that this foreigner, pointing to me, was an expert on artillery. I had never said anything of the kind, but it worked wonders. My arrest was suspended for the moment. Villa's stern and angry face became relaxed and transformed into an open-mouthed grin and looked me over with some interest. When the conversation led to the necessity of taking a breechblock out of Mexico he flared up in anger but calmed down and asked, "Why can't you fix them in Juárez?" The outcome was obvious, he needed the guns desperately, and I could not fix them without one of the blocks and a good machine-shop, so he gave in. But, while this conversation was going on, misgivings had entered my mind as to the possibility of the breechblock being confiscated by the United States on the bridge into El Paso. It was heavy and it would take two men to carry it between them on a pole, in a gunny-sack, and therefore difficult to smuggle past the boundary guard on the other side of the Rio Grande. Besides, Villa had stipulated that the block must be back in Mexico within two days, so there was no time to maneuver around farther up or down the river.

It was therefore necessary to dismantle the block in Juárez. A machine-shop was found to which the gun was moved. It was not an easy operation. Luck was with us though for the firing-pin was, in fact, merely broken at the point and, consequently, fairly easy to copy on a lathe. With this pin in my pocket I began to walk toward the bridge when the captain impressed upon me that he would be imprisoned or sent back to the States if the pin was not back within the specified time. I then went over the bridge to El Paso.

Due to my newly acquired relationship with the revolutionaries, I thought it prudent to keep my own counsel and began looking for a trustworthy owner of a machine-shop, and to get further information about the trouble in Mexico. I moved about and listened to conversations in bars where usually one obtains most valuable information.

To my surprise there was a decided mixed feeling for and against the revolution. Some were downright hostile, others felt sorry for the peons' desperate struggle for freedom and wished them luck. No one seemed to like Pancho Villa, his reckless shooting of prisoners and confiscation of cattle, especially cattle and horses. He was severely censured yet many admired his ability.

Eventually a machine-shop was found with an owner in sympathy with the peons. This man wished them luck but did not think they had a chance to win because the United States and Great Britain were against the rebels, and besides, there was a large well-trained Mexican army moving northward against them.

I returned to work at the machine-shop the following morning and after several tries we had two fairly good looking firing-pins cut on a lathe, and with these I again crossed the bridge into Mexico on the afternoon of the second day. My appearance was a great relief to my new friend, the captain in charge of the guns. He almost pulled me to the shop to see if the pins fitted. They did.

With my firing-pin mission completed, I wished the captain good-bye and luck with his guns. As I was about to leave, an officer marched up with four armed men and informed me that General Villa had commanded my detention until further orders as he wanted the presence of the *gringo* at the gun trials the following day. I protested vigorously as I had an appointment in El Paso that night, but to no avail. The order had come from Villa himself.

Thus I was under arrest once more. I was allowed to walk around, but four armed soldiers were detailed to see that no harm came to me in their words. Resigned to my fate, I took this opportunity to inquire into the artillery pieces that had caused so much trouble. They were Montregon guns, so named for a Mexican artillery general who served several years in the French army. When asked about the gun-sights and instruments, my new friend simply remarked, "There are none."

57

Early next morning Villa turned up with his staff and off we went galloping along a very dusty road for the gun trials. As speed was required, the so-called gunners were all mounted. On a low ridge a few miles south of Juárez, Villa pulled up his horse and pointed to a small bush-covered ridge standing out clear, thus making a good target, and ordered the guns to be trained on it.

I calculated the distance to be some 12,000 yards and informed him it was too far. Villa seemed embarrassed but gave a new target, a little shack, and called out, "Hit that house." He appeared extremely impatient and annoyed, but it was my unpleasant task to enlighten this bandit general that it was difficult, if not impossible, to hit the house, or even come anywhere near it, without a range-finder or a gun-sight of some kind. Having become a little irritated myself at his attitude, and at being forcibly detained the day before, I reminded him that I had only promised to try to fix the firing-pins and that this had been done.

I fully expected Villa to fly off the handle but was agreeably surprised when he looked at me hard for a few seconds, dismounted, and came to the unlimbered guns. He petted them in a gentle carassing manner with both his big hands and asked almost humbly, as in a prayer, "Is there no way in which these cannons can be used against that usurper Huerta in this our fight for land and freedom?"

There was something so pathetic about this hard, flea-bitten roughneck showing such deep sentiment that I felt sympathy for him. Then I told him they could be fired without sights or instruments by guessing the elevation, but only as a temporary measure, as the shots would be erratic and ineffective. The guns might act as a surprise to the enemy, however, and I suggested that we fire one shot per gun to make sure the firing-pins worked.

When the interpreter had explained these points, which I could not express intelligently enough in Spanish, Villa frowned, shook his head doubtfully but remained silent. This gave me the opportunity to study the man and I came to the conclusion that he considered the suggestion of range-finders and other instruments silly and superfluous, or a subterfuge on my part. Then again he might be pondering what to do with this *gringo* who had told him, Pancho Villa, what he could or could not do.

Suddenly, Villa straightened up and called out, "All right, let us try the firing-pins, but hit that house!" Pancho Villa was himself again, ignoring everything said about sights. Without any further comment I guessed the range to be about 5,000 yards, and gave the order, "Fire!"

The gun went off, thank goodness, but the shell was over one thousand yards short and to the left kicking up sand and dirt. The shell from the second gun did not hit any nearer. It went high. To everybody's surprise, four men were seen running from the house and disappearing over the ridge beyond. Then came the unexpected. Villa walked up to me and, to my amazement, gave me a Mexican embrace (*abrazo*). Words shot from his lips like bullets from a gatling-gun; I had suddenly become his friend (*amigo*) and companion (*compañero*).

A few minutes later he proclaimed me as his "Chief of Artillery" with the rank of first captain (*capitan primero*). My command consisted of two 75 mm field guns, no officers, no noncoms. There were a few half-wild Apache gunners who knew nothing about guns and some could not speak but their own language, except a little pigeon-Spanish.

"I felt my soul was being scratched."
—Justino López Estrada (1888–   )*

Soldiers wounded in battle often faced the misfortune of receiving little or no medical attention because of shortages of trained personnel, facilities, or supplies. At times improvisation became necessary to relieve pain, as is evident in the case of Villista Justino López Estrada.

The *federales* shot me through the leg. At first I just felt the force of the bullet but not the pain, so I paid no attention. While mounting my horse I hurt and then saw a stream of blood. Villa noticed that I had trouble getting on my horse and said, "Muchacho, you are wounded!" I mounted with difficulty and put my sarape around me. I was very weak and rode slouched over because of the hemorrhage. They took me to an aid station where doctors were caring for the wounded, both revolutionaries as well as *federales*. They put me in the operating room and undressed me. Then I heard the doctors say that they had run out of anesthesia, that they would not be able to operate on me. The leg was infected and they would need to cut it. I said to the chief medical officer, "No, general, operate on me however you can!" He said, "But that would be a tremendous operation!" Just then a patient, a sergeant whose leg had been cut off who was there recuperating, came over and said, "Jefe, give him what you gave me!" The sergeant took out a bottle

*Interviewed in Mexico City in 1973 by América Teresa Briseño. On file at the Archivo de la Palabra, Instituto Nacional de Antropología e Historia, Mexico City. PHO-1-49.

of *sotol* and I grabbed it from him and started drinking! The doctor said, "Hold it, don't finish it; otherwise you'll die of alcoholic congestion!" *Sotol* is a tremendous drink, even stronger than *tequila*. I drank half a bottle and got very drunk.

I lay there half-conscious and muttered some incoherent words. They asked me if I felt anything and I said, "No, I don't feel anything! Send the bull after me, you bastards!" They waited a while until I fell asleep, and then they operated. I felt my soul was being scratched. They cleaned me up, and the bullet came out. It was one of those Japanese bullets, very pointed. It didn't hurt the bone. Thank God! I was so lucky. I saved my leg. I was able to leave the hospital after ten days because the wound healed quickly.

"Villa gave me a hard look."
—Dr. Alfonso de Gortari (1904–)*

After Pancho Villa settled his differences with the government in 1920, he retired to an hacienda in Durango known as Canutillo, where he established a school. With a recommendation from José Vasconcelos, the famous educator and philosopher, Dr. Alfonso de Gortari was invited to teach there. De Gortari, a native of Michoacan, recalls the school and Villa's interest in education.

When I arrived in Canutillo they received me well, but in the first conversation with General Villa he really gave me a hard look with an expression that made me think. He said, "Look, little boy, in this hacienda I want no other chiefs but myself." I answered, "Yes sir." That was my initial meeting with him. It might have been my attitude, or the fact that I also gave him the same kind of look, or . . . I don't know why.

The school in Canutillo was really rustic. It had a large patio with classrooms all around, a sort of auditorium, and the house where the teachers lived. We didn't even have beds, just some boxes, and blankets. We hired people to come in and do the cleaning for us.

The kids who attended the school were of peasant families who lived

*Interviewed by María Isabel Souza in Mexico City in 1973. On file at the Archivo de la Palabra, Instituto Nacional de Anthropología e Historia, Mexico City. PHO-1-90.

in that hacienda as well as in surrounding farm communities such as Las Nieves, La Haciendita, and Torreoncito. The school was completely free. Villa's own children attended the school: Celia with her sad look, Juana María with her frightened face, Micaela, the oldest, who always had her hair done in a fancy way, and various boys, Agustín, Octavio, and other children who were born later.

There were plenty of adults who attended the school at night, some from Villa's troop, people from the farms, and anyone else who wanted to go. At that time Mexico did not have a national educational system. Each state had its own programs. The hacienda itself provided paper and pencils. On occasion the Secretaría de Educación would send us paper products, but not books. Villa was good at getting materials for us, because the kids had no money. In spite of that, few of the kids went to school without shoes. In the north people didn't walk around barefoot; they wore *huaraches* or shoes, but of course very few dressed well.

The teachers were influenced by our own Revolution and we were also aware of the Russian Revolution. We already know about Marx, about Engels, and we knew that social justice was fundamental to the development of a people. Thus, we talked a lot about those things, without mentioning communism. We talked about the rights of man, liberty, democracy, and dictatorship. The people there understood these things perfectly. Northerners are pretty alert people. Villa had heard of Marx, but it was not something he would talk about. I don't remember his mentioning Marx. When the subject of the Russian Revolution came up, he would just meditate about it. He *felt* the weakness of the poor; he always remembered that he had been a victim of the old haciendas, and he hated the rich.

General Villa would go to the school to find out what we were doing, and he listened attentively. We would then exchange opinions and impressions. When we talked about the education of children, the hope of Mexico, he would be moved extraordinarily. He would take the baton and launch into his opinions. He would say that the children were his brothers by race and by blood. He was moved to such a degree that he would cry, with tears running down his face.

The people of the hacienda got along well. In spite of the fact that the men were warriors with a bellicose spirit, there were no disputes. The respect people had for the *jefe* (Villa) was enough to impose discipline on everyone. There were no drunkards, because Villa did not allow the making of alcohol. Once a few individuals went outside the orders that had been given and tried to bring *sotol* into the hacienda, but Villa confiscated it and warned them that if they came near the place again with alcoholic beverages they would be in trouble. Those people never returned.

Part II

Excitement Along the Border:
Early 1910s

In the early phase of the Revolution, the Mexican border area played a key role in the fortunes of the contending factions. Francisco Madero's initial movement against Porfirio Díaz in the Coahuila frontier in late 1910 quickly ignited revolts by supporters in Chihuahua and Sonora. By spring 1911, the offensive launched in Chihuahua focused international attention on such communities as Ciudad Juárez-El Paso. Because of its location and importance in the regional economy, this binational center would become a strategic point for revolutionaries and federals alike.

By the turn of the century, Juárez–El Paso had assumed great importance in the trade between northern Mexico and the U.S. Southwest. A key crossroads for centuries, since the 1880s Juárez–El Paso had enjoyed railroad connections with central Mexico as well as all major regions of the United States. Agriculture, ranching, commerce, manufacturing, and mining provided for steady local growth. Moreover, the area served as the most important border recruiting center for U.S. employers seeking Mexican workers.[1]

The presidential meeting between William Howard Taft and Porfirio Díaz in 1909 in Juárez–El Paso attests to the area's significance. Juarenses used the occasion to beautify their city, decorating the historic customs building, the principal meeting site, with expensive tapestries and other ornamentation.[2]

Rebel activity first reached this region in 1906, when the Liberal Party plotted to capture Juárez, hoping to establish a base from which to organize incursions into central Mexico. The plan was discovererd and many rebels were arrested, but Ricardo Flores Magón escaped to the United States, where he continued to plot the overthrow of the Díaz regime. Six months after Francisco Madero proclaimed the Revolution in November 1910, Juárez played "host" to the first significant battle. Using arms smuggled from El Paso, Madero, aided by "Pancho" Villa, Pascual Orozco, and American soldiers of fortune, overran the government forces during May 8–10, 1911. Perhaps 200 died, including several El Pasoans hit by stray bullets while watching the battle from the river bank and rooftops. The battle led to the resignation of President Díaz and Madero's ascension to power.[3] In 1912, Juárez was again embroiled in conflict, although this time there was no bloodshed. Pascual Orozco, who had broken with Madero, captured the city on February 27. Orozco then advanced south toward Mexico City, but within months his movement collapsed.[4]

The most colorful capture of Juárez took place on November 15, 1913 when Villa unexpectedly arrived at 2:30 A. M. on a hijacked train. Thought to be 200 miles to the south attacking Chihuahua City, Villa showed up in Juárez with 3,000 troops and quickly defeated the defending Huertistas. Juarenses and El Pasoans were rudely awakened by the boom of cannons and the rattle of machine guns. Many residents of Juárez scurried for cover across the Rio Grande. General Francisco Castro, the Huertista commander of the garrison, fled so swiftly that he left behind his uniform, decorations, and sword, all of which Villa happily took as souvenirs. Villa then set up headquarters in the customshouse, established friendly relations with influential El Pasoans, and began gambling operations to build up his war chest. This victory considerably enhanced Villa's stature as a leader and military tactician.[5]

As the setting of constant military and political activity, other border areas played important roles in the Revolution. Mexicali and Tijuana served as key battlegrounds for the ill-fated 1911 invasion of Baja California by the forces of Ricardo Flores Magón. Following the assassination of Francisco Madero in February 1913, Venustiano Carranza led a revolt against Victoriano Huerta from the Coahuila frontier. Carranza declared the town of Piedras Negras the revolutionary capital of the state and converted the local customshouse into the "Palacio de Govierno."[6] Later that year Carranza shifted his headquarters to Sonora, where local leaders had organized a strong anti-Huerta movement. Led by Alvaro Obregón, who later became president, the Sonorans had taken control of much of their state, including such border towns as Agua Prieta, Nogales, Cananea, and Naco.[7] With the support of the Sonorans, Carranza became the leader of the Constitutionalist forces.

After 1913, the border communities continued their involvement in the revolutionary struggle, as described elsewhere in this study. The reminiscences that appear below focus on incidents that occurred along the Sonora-Arizona, Baja California–California, Chihuahua-Texas, and Tamaulipas-Texas borders between 1911 and 1913.

NOTES

1. Oscar J. Martínez, *Border Boom Town: Ciudad Juárez since 1848* (Austin: University of Texas Press, 1978), pp. 35–36; Mario T. Garcia, *Desert Immigrants: The Mexicans of El Paso, 1880–1920* (New Haven: Yale University Press, 1981), pp. 9–36.

2. Armando B. Chávez M., *Historia de Ciudad Juárez, Chihuahua* (México, 1970), pp. 343–59.

3. Richard Estrada, "Border Revolution: The Mexican Revolution in the Ciudad Juárez–El Paso Area, 1906–1915" (M.A. thesis, University of Texas at El Paso, 1975), pp. 54–89; Chávez M., *Historia de Ciudad Juárez*, pp. 369–99.

4. Estrada, "Border Revolution," pp. 90–110; Mardee Belding de Wetter, "Revolutionary El Paso: 1910–1917," *Password*, 3: 3 (July 1958): 107–12.

5. Estrada, "Border Revolution," pp. 117–20; William Weber Johnson, *Heroic Mexico: The Violent Emergence of a Modern Nation* (New York: Doubleday, 1968), pp. 170–71.

6. Johnson, *Heroic Mexico*, pp. 149–50.

7. Charles C. Cumberland, *Mexican Revolution: The Constitutionalist Years* (Austin: University of Texas Press, 1972), pp. 24–25.

"I explained to them very carefully
and fully the neutrality laws."
—Captain J. E. Gaujot*

*Americans had two principal concerns with respect to rev-
olutionary intrigue and fighting in the borderlands: enforcement of U.S. neutrality laws; and protection of American lives
and property. These objectives, however, were not always easy
to carry out, and difficulties arose repeatedly when trouble
touched U.S. territory. Although minor in the context of the
Revolution, the battle at Agua Prieta in April 1911 is an early
illustration of how federals and insurgents used the border
for their own ends. Captain J. E. Gaujot, Commander of K
Troop, 1st U.S. Cavalry, relates his involvement in that skirmish when the safety of Americans seemed threatened.*

On the afternoon of April 13th at about 3:25, the corporal of the guard
notified me that he had received a telephone message for me to the
effect that a trainload of insurgents had attacked Agua Prieta. I immediately ordered the troop to saddle up and proceeded to the international
line, arriving there about 3:45, with Lieutenant Moore and about forty
men. Major Schreiner followed with some Hospital Corps men and the
ambulance.

I deployed the troop along the International line from east to west

*Statement given on May 4, 1911. Records of the Department of State Relating to
the Internal Affairs of Mexico, 1910–1929, 812.00/1840.

from Bonita Avenue to a point about 200 yards west of the American Customshouse. Lieutenant Moore was in charge of the west end of the line. There were a great many spectators along the line on the American side—men, women, and children. I rode along the line from one end to the other giving the men instructions and observing the engagement in Mexico between the Mexican federal troops and the insurgents. The fire was continuous and very heavy from both sides, and a great many projectiles were striking in American territory. During this stage of the engagement, the majority of the bullets that struck in Douglas were the result of the federal fire from the *cuartel* and vicinity at the insurgent position along the railroad just south of the American customshouse, and the insurgents returning the fire from their position south along the railway at the federals behind guardhouse No. 2.

At about 4:00 I cautioned the insurgents stationed close to the international line against firing into the United States. At about 4:30 the federal commander, Captain Vargas, called across to me from his position behind guardhouse No. 2 that one of his officers had been wounded and asked me to stop the insurgent fire so that he could send the wounded man to the United States. I called to him that I would try and stop their fire but feared that it would be impossible. Before I could act in the matter, Captain Vargas with three other officers and twenty-nine men crossed the International line at a point north of guardhouse No. 2, and surrendered to me. At this stage of the engagement the insurgents had worked around to the south and east of Agua Prieta and, moving from west to east, occupied guardhouse No. 2, thereby completely surrounding the federals remaining in the town. As a result of the firing, projectiles from both insurgents and federals struck in the United States.

Captain Vargas, in the presence of Lieutenant Moore, requested me that if possible to get word to that part of his command remaining in Agua Prieta, to tell them that he directed them to surrender to the insurgents as their case was hopeless; that they were completely surrounded; to prevent further useless slaughter and to save their lives, to discontinue the fight. At about this time I was informed that there were some neutral Americans in Agua Prieta on business when the fight commenced, and consequently in danger of losing their lives. I was also informed that there had been Americans in Douglas killed and wounded by the fire of the Mexican combatants. I realized that the only way to save the federal garrison and the Americans in Agua Prieta and to stop

71

any further killing in Douglas was, if possible, to stop the engagement. At about 5:00, accompanied by Mr. Charles McKean of Douglas, I crossed the International line and proceeded towards the federal *cuartel*, passing through the insurgent lines.

After considerable parley with the federals, those in the *cuartel* and vicinity stopped firing. Mr. McKean stayed with them and I attracted the attention of the insurgents in the vicinity and persuaded them to suspend hostilities. After the combatants had quieted down sufficiently to make it possible to safely negotiate, I informed the federals that their commanding officer had directed them to surrender. This they refused to do, stating that if they did they would be murdered by the insurgents and that they could not surrender unless their captain was there in person to order them to do so. During the parley that ensued the engagement continued, and two men were killed in the immediate vicinity during the negotiations. A squad of federals came in from the southwest bringing five Americans whom they held as prisoners. These Americans were neutrals casually in Agua Prieta, and I liberated and sent them to the United States.

The federals, fearing death at the hands of the insurgents, would not surrender, so deeming it the only possible solution, with the consent of both federals and insurgents the federals turned their arms, ammunition, and equipment over to me. Having sent for Lieutenant Moore and a squad of troopers, upon their arrival at about 6:00 I sent eighteen federals under this escort to the United States. I turned the rifles, ammunition, and equipment over to the insurgents. Five or six federals elected to join the insurgents. All the wounded, both federal and insurgent, were taken to the United States and cared for in the hospitals of Douglas by the local physicians and Major Schreiner, Medical Corps, U.S. Army. The casualties, both sides, numbered about twenty killed and thirty wounded, evenly divided. There were about fifteen Americans fighting with the insurgents.

A few days before the engagement I had a talk with Captain Vargas, the federal commander, and my only requests were that if possible in event of an engagement he would avoid firing into the United States and that he would notify me in case he were attacked or expected an attack. I am positive that during the engagement there was no violation of the neutrality laws with reference to either federal or insurgents by any Americans along the line patrolled by my troop. After the engage-

72

ment I warned the insurgent leaders that they would be held responsible to maintain good order and to respect lives and property rights.

On the night of the 14th of April, I, with Mr. Greenway and Foster of Bisbee, Mr. Coll of Douglas, and an interpreter, had a conference with the insurgent leaders in Agua Prieta. Among those present were Belasario García, Rosario García, and Antonio Rojas. I explained to them very carefully and fully the neutrality laws as I understood them and directed them in the event of future engagements in the vicinity of the United States to make such dispositions of their forces as to positively preclude the possibility of endangering lives in the United States. I directed them also to take such precautions as might be necessary to keep their commands in Mexico.

The fight on the 17th began at about 6:30 A.M., and I arrived near the International line with Colonel Shunk shortly afterwards. In the patrolling to enforce the regulations, our troops were assisted by the city and county officials and United States marshals. On arriving on the International line, I proceeded along the line from east to west from A Avenue to the American customshouse. There were a great many projectiles striking in American territory all along the line and at the U.S. Customshouse. A hail of projectiles was striking on the American side of the line with a continuous regularity that indicated machine gun fire. I stayed at the customshouse nearly an hour and this fire continued practically all the time.

During the remainder of the day I observed the engagement with a powerful pair of field glasses from the roof of an adobe house north of the line. The insurgents were occupying a line of trenches which ran in a curve from about D Avenue a few feet from the International line southwest to the bullring. They also had some entrenchments running north and south, but these were not engaged by the federals during the fight. The federals were attacking from the south, southeast, and east. Their attack from the south was heavy and machine gun fire was used during the earlier stages of the action. This part of the attacking forces could not be seen on account of the intervening buildings in Agua Prieta and the configuration of the ground, but the attack from the southeast and east was plainly visible throughout the day.

At dark the federal lines were close to Agua Prieta on the east, southeast, and south. At about 11 o'clock Colonel Balsario García, insurgent leader, surrendered to me. At about 2:00 A.M. on Monday, I went to

73

the International line with Colonel Shunk, where he had a conference with insurgents Rosario García and Antonio Rojas. Colonel Shunk warned them against further endangering lives in the United States. Rojas told me that it would all be over in less than four hours, that the greatest part of the insurgent command was drunk, and that he was gathering together his command preparatory to evacuating Agua Prieta.

By daylight on the morning of the 18th the insurgents had completely deserted the town and the federals were in charge. The insurgents left by the west, which was not covered by the federals. I had my troop deployed along the International line by 4:45 A.M. on the 18th, the federals posting on their side a similar guard line about 5:30. From my observations the insurgent evacuation had been a panic, as saddles, rifles, blankets, and cartridges were scattered along the line in Mexico to the west for miles, and the positions previously occupied by them were plainly marked with abandoned rifles, articles of clothing, and cartridges. Also distributed along their trenches were thousands of empty bottles. All armed insurgents crossing into the United States were apprehended by our troops.

"Certainly not."

—Aloysius Coll*

An employee of the Douglas, Arizona, Chamber of Commerce, Aloysius Coll witnessed the contact between Captain Gaujot and the insurgents during the Agua Prieta troubles in April 1911.

I accompanied Captain Gaujot to Agua Prieta, and was present at the conference on April 14. It was held in a side room of the *comisario* headquarters. Captain Gaujot had difficulty in gathering all the rebel chiefs together, but finally succeeded, with the possible exception of one or two. He spoke in English, the interpreter being an official of the American Customshouse. Captain Gaujot, in emphatic language informed the rebel chiefs present that the United States had instructed him to give warning to the *insurrecto* commanders that in defending Agua Prieta against expected federal attacks the rebels would have to dig their trenches and conduct the battle in such a way that American lives in Douglas would not be in jeopardy. He also instructed them that they should instruct the scouts firing outside Agua Prieta to make every effort to have the battle outside the town of Agua Prieta. He warned the rebel chiefs that they must keep the soldiers of their several commands on the Mexican side of the International line, and that if they came across into Douglas they would be arrested. The rebel commander

*Statement given on May 4, 1911. Records of the Department of State Relating to the Internal Affairs of Mexico, 1910–1929, 812.00/1840.

promised to entrench in such a way that the injunction might be obeyed, and also that they would advance outside the town to meet the federal forces, thus removing the danger from fire close to the American town. "But," said the rebel chief, "we may be driven back into our entrenchments by the federal fire, especially if the federal machine guns are used effectively."

The interview, or conference, closed with these assurances on the part of the rebel chief.

That same day I went to the line in an automobile, left the auto at the line, and went forward with a rebel passport to the first Mexican guardhouse. At this guardhouse stood on American *insurrecto* holding a 30-30 rifle. Captain Gaujot stood just at the American line a few feet north of the guardhouse. The American *insurrecto* approached Captain Gaujot with the gun showing him that it was out of order and asking permission to send the gun over to Douglas to have the firing pin repaired. "No," said Captain Gaujot. The American *insurrecto* then asked that he be permitted to send into Douglas only the firing pin. "Certainly not," said Captain Gaujot, turning away. I then went over into Agua Prieta, and later returned to my automobile, when the same *insurrecto* came forward to the machine and started to get into it. The troopers of the American cavalry immediately ordered the *insurrecto* back from the line and he obeyed.

"Don't shoot! We are Americans!"
—Thomas Henry Elvey*

A chauffeur who worked on both sides of the border, Thomas Henry Elvey recalls how he and other Americans got caught in the crossfire during the troubles at Agua Prieta in April 1911.

I was in Mexico standing by my machine out in front of the depot waiting for the train to come in and hardly before the train stopped they commenced shooting toward the town. I ran under the train and through the depot and got with a lot of other Americans and several Mexicans into a ditch alongside the railroad grade. I do not remember exactly, but it was about three-quarters of an hour we stayed in the ditch to get out of the way of the fire.

This Mexican boy who was killed later said that the *federales* were coming. We all commenced waving white handkerchiefs. Some of the Americans shouted that they were passengers on the train and all the rest of us hollered, "Don't shoot! We are Americans! Don't shoot!" Some of the boys spoke good Spanish and talked to the Mexicans. But the Mexicans said, *"Chingen su madre! Maten los gringos!"* About eight or nine ran up as close as they could, one of them within twenty feet of me. He shot down into the bunch of us. The rest stood at the end of the ditch and fired a part of the time into us and a part of the time at

*Statement given on May 4, 1911. Records of the Department of State Relating to the Internal Affairs of Mexico, 1910–1929, 812.00/1840.

the *insurrectos* in the grade that led toward the American customshouse firing straight north toward Douglas. They fired at us for probably ten minutes. I looked up and seen [sic] this Mexican boy was shot and killed and that this Dickson, this British subject, was shot through the legs. We felt it was best to get out of there, so we got up and asked the federal soldiers if we could get behind an adobe house alongside of the track. They said yes, and we got out. They threw their guns down on us, took us prisoners, and then took us to the opposite side of the railroad grade and stood us around there a while. A switch engine came up and they drove us out of there at the point of their guns and lined us on the opposite side of the track. The *insurrectos* got busy and commenced firing on us, so presently they took us along the southern limits of the town.

We stopped three or four different times behind adobe houses in the southern limits of the town and from there the federal soldiers fired out through the town to the north and in the direction of Douglas. They took us into the east of the town, about two hundred yards northeast of the bullring in the open fields to these trenches. They made us lay down and got behind us and fired over us into Agua Prieta. They also fired in a northwesterly direction toward Douglas. They kept us out there about fifteen or twenty minutes while they were firing volleys into town. Then they told us we could go, so we got up and started for the bullring as fast as we could run. They put us in the bullring with a guard over us at the door with fixed bayonets. The rest of the federal soldiers went up above and kept shooting. After they took us prisoners, they cursed and abused and poked us with the butts of their guns. They even refused water to us when the women brought water to the bullring while they were still fighting.

"It is a beautiful sight to see the shrapnel bursting up in the air."
—Judge Joseph U. Sweeney
(1875–?)*

The battle of Juárez in May 1911 attracted considerable attention throughout the United States. Witnesses to the fighting proudly related what they had seen and heard of this important encounter. Ex-County Judge Joseph U. Sweeney, a native of San Antonio, Texas, wrote this letter to his brother in Richmond, Virginia, on May 12, 1911.

Dear Jack:

I presume you have been deeply interested in the events transpiring in Juárez. . . . The *insurrecto* army under [Francisco I.] Madero had been lying in the foothills across from the smelter for the past three weeks, but on Monday last early in the morning a small detachment of insurgents were fired upon by federal troops with the result that it precipitated a battle.

When the battle opened, I was anxious to observe its prosecution as closely as possible, so Dr. [James B.] Brady, Dr. [Henri] Letord and myself went to the Union Depot and secured positions on the roof. The

*Password, 17:2 (Summer 1972): 68–73. Reprinted by permission of Password.

fight was then in progress across the river and rapidly approaching Juárez, so we went down to the water works plant on the river bank opposite the Santa Fe Coal Shoots and took positions on box cars along the levy line.

We found that we were in the line of fire, and then went up the canal bank following the fight as it progressed toward Juárez until we reached Seventh Street. We then secured positions on top of the El Paso Laundry which is located on the north bank of the canal on the corner of Santa Fe and Seventh Streets, distant about 250 yards from the point where a very stubborn, several hours' fight took place.

Immediately opposite from our position on the Mexican side, you will recollect the grove of trees along the river front with a few scattered adobe houses north and west of that point. In the most westerly house, a detachment of federal soldiers had taken refuge after having retreated from their line of entrenchment.

The insurrectos came in single file in squads of fifteen or twenty, keeping the bank of the Mexican *acequia* [irrigation ditch] between them and the house, and took positions about 150 or 200 feet east of the house. They then proceeded to try and dislodge the federals. Three insurrectos approached the rear of the house and dynamited it. About thirty-five or forty federals evacuated the position, running southeasterly toward Juárez. They were required to cross an open field for about 300 feet before they could secure shelter in other houses. I saw a number of these federal soldiers shot down. Some were killed while others were wounded. The fight raged at this point for possibly two and one-half or three hours.

After dislodging the federal soldiers, the insurrectos then advanced into Juárez through the big alfalfa field immediately west of the Santa Fe bridge. They used the Mexican levy constructed of rock and timber as a breast-works, and in a very short time obtained possession of the Mexican guardhouse at the south end of the bridge. They then advanced across to the Mexican Central [railroad] bridge, and there to the Mexican Northwestern [railroad] bridge, and from there to the Stanton Street bridge, taking each one in turn. Up to this time, I should judge that there were not more than 150 or 200 insurrectos engaged, and they were slowly but surely driving in the federal outposts.

Along about three o'clock, a large body of insurrectos approached from the west in the same manner, and went to the support of those in front. They then commenced a determined advance on the city, advancing from house to house toward the center of Juárez. All the fighting up to this time was being done with Mauser and 30-30 rifles, no machine guns or rapid firing guns or artillery yet being in use.

About four o'clock in the afternoon, large numbers of the insurrectos had penetrated Juárez, and you could hear the rattle of the machine guns and the rapid firers. They sounded very similar to steel hammers on your big steel frame buildings in the city. About five or six o'clock in the afternoon, large reinforcements of insurrectos were deployed over the hills and in the ravines approaching Juárez from the extreme west.

Then the federal artillery, which was located up immediately in the rear of the federal barracks, commenced action. The federals had two cannon which consisted of a two and one-half inch bore and a three inch bore which threw solid shot. They also used two mortar guns which threw shrapnel into the approaching insurrectos. The artillery fire was directed in a northwestwardly direction, the shells falling and exploding abut two and one-half miles from the barracks and on the hills and in the ravines immediately opposite the [El Paso] Santa Fe Depot. It was a beautiful sight to see the shrapnel bursting up in the air and scattering its death-dealing missiles on the hills and in the valleys surrounding. The artillery fire was well directed and did considerable execution which resulted in compelling the insurrectos to mask their approach back of the hills and required them to come in on foot instead of on horseback. The machine guns were also directed toward the approaching insurrectos. The guns were located in the vicinity of the church [Nuestra Señora de Guadalupe] in the heart of the city on some of the buildings. You could hear the incessant pounding of these guns and could see the dust rising out across the top of the mesa and in the valley where the bullets were skipping about.

The insurrectos used two smooth bore, three-inch cannon in reply to the federal artillery. These cannon were located at a point in the hills and the other at the gate of the Mexican *acequia*. These guns were made by the insurrectos down in Pierson, Mexico, in the machine shops. They were constructed out of piece shafting. They did some execution, but not very much. Early in the fight, the breach of one of the guns blew out, putting the gun out of action, but the other kept pounding away for a couple of days. Its fire was directed on the barracks and at the church.

81

Night came on and the insurrectos were scattered all over the eastern, southern, and northern portions of Juárez. The small arms kept up a continuous rattle. It was interspersed occasionally with the boom of heavy artillery issuing from the center of the city. This was caused by the insurrectos using dynamite and throwing hand grenades. The fight did not conclude at sunset but continued throughout the entire night.

Tuesday morning, practically the entire insurgent army consisting of from 1,600 to 2,000 men, had gained access to the city. The federals were massed at Cowboy Park, at the bullring, in the church and municipal buildings, and in the barracks, numbering in all about 700 regulars and about 300 volunteers. At this time early in the morning, artillery firing became very heavy in the city by reason of the insurrectos making combined assaults on the various positions held by the federals. Along about noon, the insurrectos under Col. [José] Garibaldi captured the bullring, but were unable to sustain their position by reason of the fact that artillery and federal reinforcements were brought to that point and dislodged them. They were also running short of ammunition, and as a consequence, fell back to the river. Cowboy Park was then attacked and machine guns were brought into service and did effective work in behalf of the federals. The pressure of the insurrectos on all sides was entirely too much for the federals and they slowly commenced to fall back from the bullring and Cowboy Park toward the church and municipal buildings.

Col. [Manuel] Tomborel of the federal army met his death in the execution of this maneuver. He was shot in one leg, through his sword hand, through the breast, and through the head almost immediately between the eyes.

The next general assault took place in the vicinity of the church. A large body of federal troops took possession of the church and fought from the roof thereof. They were dislodged by the insurgent fire and retreated westerly toward the barracks where the main body of federals were located under the direct command of General [Juan J.] Navarro. The insurgents then massed in the vicinity of the barracks and directed their fire against same, using what artillery they had captured. After sustaining a heavy fire for a considerable period of time, General Navarro hoisted a white flag and surrendered to Colonel Garibaldi and General [Benjamin J.] Viljoen, the Boer general. Navarro surrendered with approximately 480 men. The dead and wounded on both sides will approximate 250.

The insurrectos are now in complete control of Juárez. Madero is organizing his provisional government, and they are seeking to place the city in order and restrain lawlessness. On Thursday afternoon, El Pasoans were permitted to visit Juárez. The papers estimated that 10,000 men, women, and children went over to Juárez on that afternoon.

The wounded are being cared for in improvised hospitals in Juárez and El Paso. Practically every surgeon in the city tendered his services and was busily engaged with the wounded. The insurrectos are removing the dead, burying some, and burning the bodies of others. John O'Keeffe told me this afternoon that he was over yesterday and that he saw an entrenchment in the western portion of the city filled up with creosoted railroad ties on which were many bodies being burnt. Cattle, dogs, sheep, goats, and horses killed during the battle were also being burnt.

Excellent order prevails, taking into consideration the conglomeration of humanity in Juárez. The responsible officers among the insurrectos are bending every effort toward preserving and protecting property. They have placed guards over practically every house in the city containing any valuables, and are exhibiting admirable efficiency as administrators. Their conduct toward their captives has been admirable in the extreme. No cruelty or unnecessary severity has been inflicted upon the vanquished federals or their sympathizers.

I want to state that what was called "The American Legion" in the insurrecto army consisting almost entirely of Americans was in the forefront of the battle and was the first to penetrate the heart of the city.

The insurrectos captured about a thousand Mauser rifles and many thousand rounds of ammunition. They have control of the most important part of the northern frontier and are rapidly recruiting an army. During the battle, the southern portion of the city of El Paso was under a hail of lead almost constantly. The majority of the people here are now very familiar with the whistle of high power guns in action, and it was really amusing, forgetting the tragic scene being enacted, to see people dodge as a bullet whistled by. Certainly, you realized that when you heard the bullet, it has already passed, but as a matter of form, you were entitled to a dodge.

The people of this city have had an opportunity of seeing the first battle ever fought in the world wherein all the arms in use were modern, high power guns.

Your brother,

(signed) Jo.
(Joseph U. Sweeney)

"It was a great day for liberty, equality, and justice."

—Norman Walker*

Newspapers carried stories about the 1911 Juárez battle long after its occurrence, usually at anniversary time. Interest about this epic event lingered not only at the border but throughout the United States, since media coverage had been extensive. In recalling the battle, American reporters highlighted the unusual and the sensational to feed the curiosity of the readership. Associated Press correspondent Norman Walker wrote the following piece in 1922.

Bells in the old church clanged, rebels fired their rifles in the air, plate glass windows were broken, impromptu parades passed through the streets and everybody was happy except the poor devils who were being put underground by burial squads of federal prisoners.

Juárez had been captured for the Madero revolution. It was the afternoon of the historic Diez de Mayo—May 10, 1911—following the surrender of Juárez, after three days of fighting by federals and rebels—and rubber-necking by El Paso's gallery on the river bank. Navarro and his officers were prisoners. Colonel Pueblito sat in the Three B store with his woman, awaiting the coming of the El Paso medicos, while he nursed a bullet wound in the jaw. Federal soldiers from the Díaz garrison walked up and down Comercio Street in their B.V.D.'s, as animated

El Paso Times, May 11, 1922.

85

white flags of surrender, having divested themselves of their blue uniforms, piped in red.

It was a wild afternoon in Juárez, long before the coming of the wild women of the cafe period. Victorious Maderistas gave vent to their enthusiasm by smashing windows along the main street, helping themselves to the pink silk shirts and 10-gallon hats therein.

One boy from Coyame wore five hats ricked one on top of another, a couple of bilious shirts, and a pair of African yellow shoes. He fairly squeaked with his recently acquired newness. An old woman carried a piece of white chinaware plumbing past on her head, a revoltoso passed on horseback with a pocket size sewing machine under one arm and a phonograph under the other. It was great for the victors until guards from Madero's headquarters arrived on the job.

Dead sprawled on the streets where they had fallen during the fighting. A Chinese merchant had been killed in his doorway, his face to the east, like all good Orientals wish to die. A woman camp follower of the federals had fallen as she crossed the open ground of the Plaza of Peace (more Mexican paradox) and had been buried where she fell, with her right arm protruding from the ground. On the roof of the municipal hospital, where a machine gun had been operating industriously, under the protection of a Red Cross flag, the machine gunner was draped over his piece, dead. In the back of the old Tivoli, where the cars turn, two federals had been shot from ambush. Burial squads of federal prisoners, guarded by rebel soldiers, went from place to place, digging shallow graves and throwing the bodies of the federals into less than the six feet of earth to which every man is supposed to be entitled as his last due.

There is a two-story brick house on the street going over to Juárez. The bullet marks may still be seen in the face brick. A blond American boy was found dead in one of the upstairs windows. No identification marks were to be found in his clothes and he was buried in the adjoining lot, with no more ceremony than is given a man in the potter's field, although he had given up his life fighting for the Madero cause. Only recently a story was printed locally that, while excavating for a new bungalow adjoining this brick house on the north, the bones of a human body had been exhumed. No "rest in peace" for that blond boy.

About 3 o'clock that Wednesday afternoon, Madero rode into town on a little bay mule, accompanied by Mrs. Madero, Abraham González, governor of Chihuahua, and preceded by an overfed El Paso policeman, who proudly carried the banner of liberty. This started the bells clanging again and more of the product of Mr. Winchester's well known factory was wasted on the desert air.

It was a great day for the souvenir seekers. Most of these swarmed over from the El Paso side and carried off everything movable, but the figure of Benito Juárez on the monument. Someone started to carry off an image of Jesus from the old church, but abandoned the effort in the churchyard, where the sacred statuette remained during the afternoon to receive the homage of the passing revolutionists. An American attempted to steal some ritual vessels from the altar of the old church, but was caught and hustled off to jail. Pieces of federal equipment, bayonets, canteens, bugles, and even tunics and uniform caps were toted back to the American side by a souvenir-mad mob. The fact that typhus fever was found in the federal hospital and many of the uniforms were covered with typhus-carrying vermin failed to stop the souvenir weevils until an El Paso boy died from typhus contracted while souvenir hunting in Juárez. Then a memento embargo was slapped on at the bridge and no more uniforms not entirely of metal were permitted to be brought over.

At the old Porfirio Díaz hotel, the name of which was changed overnight to the Hotel Francisco I. Madero by a politic proprietor, war in all its horror was revealed. Men who had had their wounds undressed for three days lay on the operating tables in this improvised hospital and submitted to operations by American and Mexican doctors. One man had his shoulder shattered. He had received not even first-aid since the battle opened. Infection had set in and he died of blood poisoning. Another federal had been blinded by a bursting shell. A boy lost his leg in the Madero cause. A mother carried a baby into the hospital, wounded through the body, she said. When she unwrapped her shawl the doctor found the baby had been dead for hours. Such was the seamy side of the battle picture.

On the main streets the parades continued, bands played, and everyone shouted "*Viva Madero*," "*Viva Liberdad*" and *viva* for everyone and everything connected with the revolution. It was a great day for liberty, equality, and justice. Every man was his own commander-in-chief. For a brief hour it looked as if the revolutionary dream of a mule and a farm for every man was about to be realized. But the *vivas* did not restore the boy blinded by a shell or resurrect the baby. Bullets kill whether fired in the name of liberty or oppression.

Had anyone who participated in the celebration in Juárez on that memorable May 10th known the years of suffering and misery, the lives to be sacrificed and the lands desolated, there would have been less celebrating and more sober thinking that afternoon—"*Es guerra,*" professional soldiers say. But war is war wherever found and none the less terrible when waged between brothers of blood.

"I figured that to be in at the kill, if there was to be one, I had better find Navarro first and wait where he was."

—Timothy G. Turner*

After the victory in Juárez, insurgents Pancho Villa and Pascual Orozco intended to execute General Juan Navarro, the defeated federal commander, in retaliation for the previous shooting of rebel prisoners. Newsman Timothy G. Turner happened to be on the scene as Navarro, aided by Francisco Madero, fled to safety across the border. Turner included his recollection of the incident in a memoir published in 1935.

When I returned to Juárez after my sleep, a good solid twelve hours of it, I ran right into a lot of excitement. Orozco's and Villa's men were running around yelling, "*¡Muera Navarro!*" and it was sure that if they had found the old federal commander they would have killed him then and there. They had been drinking and were worked up into a fury, paying no attention to those *insurrecto* officers who tried to calm them.

I figured that to be in at the kill, if there was to be one, I had better find Navarro first and wait where he was. So I borrowed an automobile

*Timothy G. Turner, *Bullets, Bottles and Gardenias* (Dallas: South-West Press, 1935), pp. 66–69.

and driver from some El Paso women who were over to nurse the wounded. I learned that Madero had taken Navarro to a house in the eastern part of the town where Madero had spent the night.

This was a fine big house, what they call a "palacio" in Mexico, and we drove through the open gates into the courtyard. I told the young *insurrecto* officer who met us what I had heard the *insurrectos* yelling and he went directly to tell his chief. Madero immediately came out, bareheaded and with a napkin in his hand.

When I told him about the men wandering around the streets yelling "muera Navarro" he became very excited.

"General Navarro is my prisoner but also my guest; I will defend him with my life," he said.

But the men were drunk, I told him, and with this he decided it was best to get Navarro out of town. I offered him my car, thinking to keep things in my hands as much as possible. Madero started in to fetch Navarro, but soon returned alone.

"I have decided not to let him go," he said, "I will make them a speech."

I pointed out that this whole business might cause a mutiny against his orders, which it was more politic to avoid, and so he agreed and went into the house again, soon returning with Navarro.

The old general had on a neat civilian's suit and a derby hat. He gave me a curious look, for he had never been friendly to me. He got into the car and with us went Colonel Roque González Garza, one of Madero's staff. We told the chauffeur to drive fast and to start out on the Fabens road to the east. Our first thought was to get over the bridge at Fabens. But González Garza thought we might run into *insurrecto* troops which had moved out into the countryside and that it was best to get the general over as soon as we could. Navarro himself wanted this. He said he was sorry to cause so much trouble. Before we left the house he had offered to do anything rather than cause Madero embarrassment. It was gentlemen's warfare so far as those two were concerned.

The old man sat very stiff beside me, never speaking a word.

We put in at a fine house a few miles out of town, the home of Max Webber, the German consul at Juárez. He was in town at the consulate, but Frau Webber met us. I explained the situation to her and she at once asked us all in. She was an upper class German woman, cultivated and very good-hearted.

90

A horsewoman, Frau Webber had ridden all over the country, and told us that we could go down the river road from her estate and find a fordable place in the Río Grande, which was then running pretty high, although she thought the general would have to swim his horse in some spots. The general thought that that would be easy.

Frau Webber ordered her groom to get out her best horse, and a fine animal with an English saddle was soon at the door. Navarro mounted and, with Mrs. Webber in the car, we all drove down the road to the river to see him off. He asked us to go back before he started into the river. This, I later learned, was because he wanted to take off his clothes which he did not want to do before the lady. So we left him.

I got back to Juárez to find the mob still running around looking for Navarro. They had already been at Madero's house. He merely had assured them that the general was not there, and they went away. The newspapermen in Juárez and El Paso had sent out bulletins about Navarro's danger, which, since nobody knew where he was, made it all the more exciting. It was ideal for what is called a second-day story.

Newspapermen can fancy my youthful complacency as I made my way through all this hullabaloo to my office in El Paso and, sitting down at my mill, wrote about Navarro's escape, just what had happened except, of course, keeping Frau Webber's part out of it, for that would have embarrassed her husband's position as consul.

This business had a strange sequel. I no sooner had finished my story than I was called to the telephone.

"This is A. Schwartz speaking," said a voice in gutteral tones. A. Schwartz was the owner of the Popular Dry Goods Store in El Paso.

"General Navarro is here," Mr. Schwartz continued, "and he asked me to tell you to please come to see him. He is in chinaware in the basement."

When I arrived they had Navarro in a little stock room in "chinaware." Some of the Mexican clerks were getting abusive. The old man embraced me when I entered and told me that I had saved his life.

His suit, the same he had worn in Juárez, was as dry and well pressed as when I had left him. He explained that after we had left him he had taken off his suit, strapped it on his back with his suspenders (rare old campaigner that he was), swam his horse over and then put on his suit in some brush on the El Paso side. He had come to the department store to get some dry socks and underwear.

91

They sent Navarro to Hotel Dieu, the sisters' hospital in El Paso and, under an assumed name, kept him there in bed until the feeling against him calmed down. The old man hated to hide that way but submitted to the plea of the American officials who felt responsible for him.

"Oh, it was a carnival here."
—Aurelia Phillips (1901–   )*

Memories of the 1911 Juárez battle:

We lived in a small house close to the river. At the time we had relatives in Juárez, and twenty-one of them came over to stay in our house! They didn't have anywhere else to go; their houses were being burnt. Somebody poured some coal oil or something on my great uncle's house and set fire to it. They all had to leave because the government forces were waiting for Madero to come in and fight on the street, from one house to the other. The Maderistas advanced by the river, and the Porfiristas were all shooting toward El Paso, and there were a number of people that were wounded, and some were killed. There were quite a few tourists who came from elsewhere to see this. They would stand up on the two- or three-story houses, up on the roof, and they could see the fighting! I didn't see any fighting myself, because we were kept at home. But we went to Juárez immediately after Madero took the place, because my Mexican relatives were all Maderistas. So we saw everything that was done, the destruction on the streets.

The Maderistas took a cannon that El Paso had next to the city hall. It was a little cannon with two wheels, and I guess it must have been about eight to ten feet long. It was quite something. Nobody stopped them and nobody objected to it; all the Americans in El Paso were for Madero.

*Interviewed in El Paso in 1975 by Oscar J. Martínez. On file at the Institute of Oral History, University of Texas at El Paso.

93

While the Maderistas were stationed at the river, they built a bridge, one of those floating bridges, and we went over there. I went with my grandmother and I shook hands with Madero, Villa, Orozco, and I don't know who else. I was very small then. Americans were taking them food and all kinds of things. They established a hospital in El Paso and people took cots and the Popular Department Store gave them bedding and other things.

Later on, the *federales* took Juárez again. There was another big to-do. Oh, it was a carnival here!

"They would stand there and watch
like damn fools."
— Pete Leyva (1894–   )*

*A native of Presidio, Texas, Pete Leyva, as a teenager, met
some of the insurgents who took part in the 1911 Juárez battle.
Later he had some interesting dealings with Villa.*

Both my father and grandfather were involved in the Revolution. My
father was a major and my grandfather a general with Pancho Villa's
army. My grandfather lived in Ojinaga right across the river from my
father's ranch in Presidio. When the Revolution broke out my father
joined my grandfather's troops on the Mexican side, although he was a
U.S. citizen. However, my mother was from Ojinaga, so we felt very
Mexican.

My first exposure to the Revolution was before the battle of Ciudad
Juárez in 1911. As a boy I was there when the Americans and the Indians
from Sonora joined the revolutionaries. I was impressed by this Indian
chief from Sonora, Mansuo. He was big and good-looking, a mean son-
of-a-gun. I also saw General Felipe Angeles, who was a military man
with a college education, a very smart man. He was the chief artillery
man; he could handle any kind of gun, cannons, or anything. I used to
watch him at the camp next to the river opposite the American smelter
plant. I used to take lunch to my brother after he joined the revolutionaries. I took a bunch of bread, sandwiches, stuff like that.

*Interviewed in El Paso in 1976 by Oscar J. Martínez. On file at the Institute of Oral
History, University of Texas at El Paso.

One time they began to holler, "The troops are coming." There was a detachment of federal soldiers along the river, so one of the revolutionary generals chased them off. I was on the other side of the river and could hear everything.

A lot of people would go alongside the river and watch the fighting. They would stand there and watch like damn fools. They killed a little boy who was standing right close to me. He got hit and started crying, and I knew goddamn well he got hit! Deader than hell, a little boy about six- or seven-years-old, standing there watching them. And them goddamn people wouldn't get out of the way! Finally the American soldiers from Fort Bliss went down there and sent all the people back downtown.

On one occasion my mother and I went to see father and grandfather in Torreón. Once there we ran out of money. Villa had all kinds of money, so my mother said, "Go tell your father to give us money to buy some groceries." I went over where the troops were and came to this railroad car and a guard stopped me and asked me where I was going. I told him I wanted to see my dad. The guard, who was one of my father's troops, told me to wait while he called him. I was then told to enter Villa's private car and I saw Pancho sitting there talking to all those generals and newspapermen. Pancho asked, "Who is that boy?" My father answered, "He's my son. I want to give him some money to get groceries." Pancho took out a bag and said, "Let the kid take some money out of that." I took a bunch of money (don't know how much) and left in a hurry to give it all to my mother.

Later I did some interpreting for Pancho during visits to father and grandfather. Once this American cattleman, a man named William Benton,* was arguing with Pancho because Pancho's men were taking his cattle. Pancho and the others could not understand what this *gringo* was saying. So my daddy said, "Let's get my boy." I had been waiting outside. Pancho said, "What's this *gringo* want?" Then I asked Benton, "What is it you want to tell Pancho?" "Well," he said, "I'm missing a lot of cattle and I want him to pay me for them." I told Pancho, so he thought a little bit what to do about it, and said, "You tell that *gringo*

---

*Benton was a Scotsman who owned considerable ranching land in northern Chihuahua. Later he was killed at the hands of the Villistas under uncertain circumstances. Villa explained that Rodolfo Fierro clubbed Benton with a gun butt. The Scotsman's bad fortune caused an international furore.

we'll pay him later." But Benton stayed there arguing, so Pancho told him, "Get out or we'll take you out." So Benton went out.

Pancho had this fellow named Rodolfo Fierro, "the killer," they used to call him, a big Mexican. I was afraid of him. All he knew was to kill people. He'd kill you in a minute just over nothing. He was a mean son-of-a-bitch, ugly looking; couldn't read or write, but he could ride a horse and shoot. I never saw him shoot anyone, but one time in Juárez I heard shots behind a building and later found out Pancho's people had taken a paymaster from the post office or the bank to the backyard and had killed him because he wouldn't cut loose.

On one occasion when Villa was in control of Juárez, his brother Hipólito came to El Paso to deposit some money and I showed him where the bank was and interpreted for him. He wanted me to carry the money, but I said, "No, you get somebody else to do it, 'cause I don't want to get shot." You see, I thought someone might kill me just to get the money. Pancho's brother was a little guy who didn't know how to read or write. One time on our way to make a deposit I started to tell him, "Look, you're young, I'm young. Why don't we put away some of that money? Leave it here with me." I started to tell him, but I was afraid. There must have been millions of dollars in those sacks since they contained Mexican gold pieces.

I met this guy who got $100,000 from Pancho to buy ammunition, and the son-of-a-bitch took off. Later I saw him at a big beach hotel in Los Angeles. We said, "Hi," that's all. If Pancho had'da got him, he would'da hung him, 'cause you couldn't steal nothin' from that guy. Pancho had a lot of eyes, you know.

After Villa quit fighting, the paymaster who worked with my father gave me a box full of money Pancho had had printed up. I went to California on vacation, and I took a bunch of the stuff. I met a fellow on the beach and he asked me if I had any of Villa's money. So I gave him, oh, hell, a bunch of it! He took it and sold it to people on the beach for 25 cents apiece. He made money and I got nothing! I didn't care, 'cause I had a lot of it. I don't know what the hell I done with it; I guess I gave it away.

American sightseers view Francisco Madero's camp on the Rio Grande, El Paso–Juárez, in 1911. (Courtesy, El Paso Public Library, Photograph Collection)

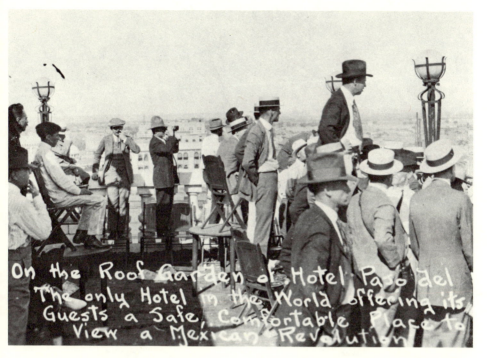

On the Roof Garden of Hotel Paso del
The only Hotel in the World offering its
Guests a Safe, Comfortable Place to
View a Mexican Revolution

Americans view the battle of Ciudad Juárez from the Paso del Norte
Hotel in El Paso, 1911. (Courtesy, El Paso Public Library, Photograph
Collection)

Pascual Orozco and townspeople at an unidentified place in Chihuahua. (Courtesy, El Paso Public Library, Photograph Collection)

"Pancho" Villa, Pascual Orozco, and a friend enjoy ice cream at the El Paso Elite confectionery. (Courtesy, U.T. El Paso Library, Aultman Collection)

"Pancho" Villa tries out a motorcycle, 1910s. (Courtesy, U.T. El Paso Library, Aultman Collection)

Music was an important part of revolutionary lore and recreation. (Courtesy, U.T. El Paso Library, Aultman Collection)

Railroads were a principal means of transportation for revolutionaries. (Courtesy, U.T. El Paso Library, Aultman Collection)

Proud display of revolutionary attire and small arms. (Courtesy, El Paso
Public Library, Photograph Collection)

"I had seen enough—and too much!"
—Margaret L. Holbrook Smith*

On June 22, 1911, the Madero forces defeated the followers of Ricardo Flores Magón at Tijuana, ending a movement made controversial by the presence of many foreigners in its ranks. The battle occurred only three weeks after some of the adventurers abandoned the original plan of a socialist-anarchist revolution and chose instead to proclaim their own "Republic of Lower California," presumably hoping to eventually gain annexation to the United States. Flores Magón repudiated that action, sent a new commander to Tijuana, but the Maderista troops prevailed. Similar to what El Pasoans did during the battle of Juárez, Margaret L. Holbrook Smith and other Californians witnessed a major rebel victory at Tijuana in May, 1911 from American soil.

"Watch him whip up his horses!" "Just look at the clouds of dust as they plow through that dry riverbed!" "Do you suppose they'll get here all right?" "See the federals riding close to the stage to protect them!" These were the words we uttered as we stood close to the international boundary that morning last May and watched some Americans as they rushed toward us and—safety. They were a few tourists who, half an hour previous, had ventured into Tia Juana and had just reached the town when the word came to them: "Get out of here as quick as ever

*Overland Monthly, 58:1 (July 1911): 1–7.

98

you can." We found it exciting enough to watch those stage drivers as they frantically made their horses plunge through the heavy sand, and I think it is safe to say that never did Uncle Sam's domain look more attractive to those Americans than it did that day, as they scurried toward "Home, Sweet Home."

For years the little town of Tia Juana (Aunt Jane) has been known to thousands of tourists as the gateway to Old Mexico. Lying just over the border, it has been the objective point for those who wish to visit a foreign land with the least exertion. One could find in it Mexican curios, could wander among the adobe houses, witness a real bull-fight and partake of a genuine Spanish dinner.

Today it is much changed, for on May 8th or 9th occurred there one of the fiercest fights of the Mexican revolution. The tourist trade was the chief business the town had, but the *insurrectos* wanted to hold the spot as a base and possibly also thought to use it as a recruiting station.

As it happened, we were stopping at San Ysidro, a tiny village on American soil, only a mile from the international boundary. On Sunday (the 7th) we were allowed to enter Tia Juana, for we were anxious to behold—in the age of peace—a town actually prepared for seige. We were advised not to snap our cameras nor to comment on the breastworks thrown up nor to make laughing criticism of anything that we should see. This last warning was most unnecessary, for no one with a ray of humanity could have felt anything but sympathy for the band of federals and *rurales* prepared to fight for their homes. For months they had been awaiting the attack, and it was pitiful to see their strained and anxious faces. The Mexican Customhouse, the administration building and the huge bullring were the main points of defense, and were surrounded by barricades of sand bags. Almost all of the women and children had been sent on to American soil, so only the defenders were left in the town. These men, clad in their white uniforms, paced back and forth through the streets, the sun poured down on the hot sand, and the Mexican flag (red, white and green, surmounted by the eagle) floated lazily in the noonday breeze. We could see the *rurales* up on the hills and in the canyons riding hither and yon. They were acting as scouts— keeping sharp outlook for the invaders. Everywhere the air was tense with expectation.

All that night they kept watch, and with morning came the word that the rebels were marching from the springs, only two miles distant. We

99

were at the American camp when the news arrived. This camp—part of the Thirtieth Infantry commanded by Captain Wilcox—was close to the American customhouse, and to the granite monument which marks the boundary line between the two countries. This border line, by the way, is no imaginary one these days, for a high wire fence has been erected, and during the battle was patrolled by our troops. From the camp and the monument we watched the advance of the enemy. When the bullets began to come our way and whizzed too near us, we retreated to the canyons, and by lying down on the hillside, could continue our vigil through the glasses. These bullets, I am told, were the dum-dum bullets, which spread or flatten out as they strike.

At first it did not seem possible that it was real war. The rapid shots sounded to me exactly like quail shooting, and the volleys as if some target practice were in progress. It was only when I saw a line of men run crouching behind the sage brush, drop on their knees and open fire—or a woman running in terror for her life, carrying her two children—or one poor fellow stagger and fall from his horse, that I realized what war meant. Then I handed the glass to someone else. I had seen enough—and too much!

All that day and night the fight continued, and it was after eight o'clock on Tuesday before the rebels had captured the town. Then the Red Cross doctors and nurses crossed the line. They were ably assisted by a few volunteers, and they all did splendid work. Several houses were at that time burning, and also the bullring, which was famous in the Southwest.

By afternoon, the Americans were flocking in. They found a strange sight. The odor of liquor was everywhere. This was because the rebel commander—Rhys Pryce—had ordered that every bottle in the town should be destroyed, and his orders were obeyed. It made no difference—champagne or whiskey, all were smashed and the contents ran down on the counters and floors and even trickled out into the streets. Of course the victors were in high spirits and many were busy "shopping"—that is, ransacking the stores and helping themselves to whatever they fancied. Others decked themselves in gaudy Navajo blankets and sombreros, and promenaded through the streets, or raced their horses through the village. That this guerrilla band should loot and plunder was to be expected—it was war; but sad to relate, their behavior compared favorably with the actual robbery that was committed by a few of the visiting Americans. Fortunately the customhouse put a stop to the situation as soon as possible.

And in the midst of this spectacle lay the dead and wounded. Many of the federals were brought into San Diego for burial. The rebels had twice as many men as the federals, but their losses were small, and those few were placed in one trench in front of the Mexican customhouse, while Captain Rhys Pryce read the burial service. He, it seems, is a Welshman, and has served in African wars for nine years. He did not look very soldierly, clad in his khaki trousers, green coat and gray felt hat. Strangely enough, only one-tenth of his band were Mexicans—the others being from various countries, Germany, France, Sweden, America—even negroes. Some of the Americans were college men from Harvard, Yale, and Princeton. These gave fictitious names, not caring to disclose their identity. One amusing incident was told by an onlooker, who overheard the following remarks made by a German sergeant as he tried to line up his men from night guard: "I vant you rascals to know dat ven I calls, you come. I don't run my legs off hunting you. Ven I vants you, I vant you. Ve haf no bugle in dis army, but ven I blows dis whizzle it means you are vanted, and see dat you get here."

On the American side close to the customhouse many federal wounded were cared for. These showed much fortitude while being treated. One man had both arms so horribly torn that he could not move them. He begged the doctor to put a lighted cigarette between his teeth, and then told him to go ahead, for he could bear anything if he only had a smoke. This was done—it was the only anaesthetic used—and the fellow never made a moan.

On our side, also, was the refugee camp. Poor things! their condition was pitiable—often whole families herded under one bit of canvas stretched out to shelter them. One man, unable to fight, came to the inn where we were stopping—"where could he get one room—only one room—no mucho familee—only wife, mother-in-law and five children!" Many poor women walked all the eighteen miles in to San Diego, carrying babies in their arms. Others fled toward Ensenada, which lies on the coast eighty miles to the south.

Whatever the merits of the Mexican struggle may be, we can only admire the pluck and courage of the federals who fought, as they did at Tia Juana, for their homes; and we cannot fail to regret that it is our American "soldiers of fortune" who have largely swelled the ranks of the rebels, and therefore have helped to demolish those homes. The situation has been especially serious in Lower California. Conditions similar to anarchy have prevailed in certain portions for a long time, and it looks as if many months would elapse before an absolutely peaceful solution of the problem could be reached.

"If you go to Juárez they'll shoot you."
—Ignacia Delgado (1889–   )*

*Shortly before declaring open rebellion against Francisco
Madero, Pascual Orozco took over Juárez in February 1912.
The anticipation of a big battle that did not materialize kept
the local population on edge. During the disturbance some
families found themselves split on one side of the border and
the other, as Ignacia Delgado's reminiscences show. Delgado,
a native of Cusihuiriachic, Chihuahua, also relates how Villa's
attack on Juárez in November 1913 traumatized her family.*

In 1912 there was a time when very frequently we heard that the
colorados—the troops of Pascual Orozco—were going to arrive, that
they were going to attack Juárez. A friend of the family from El Paso
came for us in his car and took us to the American side. At that time
there weren't those passport requirements like there are now; no one
had to have any type of documentation at all. We went to our friend's
house and when things calmed down we returned to Juárez.

The day Orozco attacked, my father had gone to El Paso to participate
in a wedding as the godfather. In the afternoon the bride and groom
were going to go to México for their honeymoon, but neither the new-
lyweds nor my father could cross the bridge because they were fighting
in the center of Juárez. A boy crossed, but he returned hurt, although

*Interviewed in El Paso in 1977 by Oscar J. Martínez. On file at the Institute of Oral
History, University of Texas at El Paso.

not seriously, and he said to my father, "You can't cross. If you go to Juárez, they'll shoot you." So my father stayed on the American side. I was working in El Paso in a store that was called El Globo. I was working because the Revolution forced us to. Many times my father didn't have the means to live. My father came to the store at closing time and told me, "Daughter, we can't go because they are attacking Juárez. Your sisters are there, but I already called the Petits' house [where his friends got together] and it seems that the lawyer Ceijas [a friend] will take care of them."

That's how it was. The next day Mr. Ceijas brought the poor, frightened girls to El Paso. They said that the moment the fighting began a Don Mesta arrived at our home to talk about business with my father. There Don Mesta got caught by the shooting and he had to stay in the house all night. At least he was good company for my sisters. After that we stayed in El Paso for a while.

Later we returned to Juárez and then the revolutionaries offered my father employment. He, in order not to get on their bad side, accepted. But they began to see that he had pro-Díaz ideas, that he had always worked under the jurisdiction of President Díaz. We saw that everything that was happening was very bad.

On the 14th of November 1913, General Francisco Castro, commander of the military zone in Juárez, was visiting in our house. He was waiting for his battalion to arrive the next day; they were already on their way. When we were eating he received a telegram from Chihuahua which informed him that they had turned back Villa's forces. The general said to my father, "Ah, this is very good."

That day one of Castro's officers got married to a friend of ours. They invited us and we went to the wedding. That night there was a precious moon and it wasn't the least bit chilly. On the way home I was supposedly guarding my father's back. I thought that since he was a judge he must have had a lot of enemies. The four of us sisters were going along with my father and when I turned around I noticed that someone was crouching down and hiding. I said, "Look, Dad. There's one." He answered me, "Let him alone." Nothing happened; the suspicious one must have just been curious.

In short, it didn't take us long to get home. My room was on the second floor of the house, facing the barracks of Juárez. I went up and

104

noticed that they were firing. I said, "Dad, they're firing at the side of the barracks." My father said, "Yes, Castro's battalion must have arrived." "No," I answered, "they look like lights from very big cannons." My father came up to the second floor and said, "You're right. Yes, this *is* strange."

The house was fairly big and my father had rented several rooms to some employees of the customs service. Father called everyone and told them, "It seems like something is happening. They are shooting cannons at the barracks, and that indicates that either Castro's battalion has arrived or only God knows what's going to happen to us. If you want, get dressed and get your documents together." Well, that's what they did. Everybody got together in the living room and father said, "Turn out all the lights, hide the weapons and hide the documents."

They hid the documents underneath a rug. They put a few of the weapons inside the oven of the stove in the kitchen. Father had horses behind the house and we were there a while when a large group of people filled the street like an immense troop. And then one screamed, "Who lives?" "Pancho Villa!" "Whose troops?" "Carranza!" Father said, "That is very bad. I didn't expect that."

There were some small stores in front of the house. With the rifle butts they opened them, took out the liquor and began to disperse everywhere. They came in our house and took the horses. Since the moon was so pretty, we could see everything very well. Our maid, Francisca, said to father, "Mr. Delgado, you have to take yourself and your daughters away from here because only God knows what is going to happen. Now with Villa's troops in charge, we're not going to have any security or peace." Well, we were there for a while; we all got dressed, we put on black overcoats. There were about eight of us. About 4 A.M. the maid said, "Mr. Delgado, get out of here. I know what I'm telling you."

Well, father decided to leave and head toward the river. On the way we could see in the distance where they were fighting. Since all of us were dressed in black, I think that we were mistaken for soldiers and they began to fire machine guns at us. Father got very frightened and he pushed us into a cultivated field so that some bullet wouldn't do a terrible thing. We all got full of mud, from top to bottom.

Upon arriving at the river we saw that it had lots of water. There we ran into a man whom we knew who had an old mule wagon and we crossed the river in that although the wheels were almost breaking apart. Some of us crossed first and the others came afterward. Then some American immigration agents came and we told them what had happened. They thought it was funny how we had crossed and they let us enter to the American side. Since it was now getting light, people from around there came out and we told them also what had happened. One very nice lady said, "Goodness! But look how you are, all covered with mud. Let's go to my house." Well, she took us and gave us something to eat. We didn't have anything except what we had on our backs. The only thing of value that we brought were the documents of the mining property that father had in Chihuahua. I had carried them.

From that lady's house we took a streetcar to downtown El Paso, and then went to the house of a Mrs. Schuster because we knew that she rented places where we could stay. Upon arriving she told us, "Yes, in the front of my house is a very large parlor. Take it. It seems to me that there are going to be more refugees." Well, we went to that parlor, on the second floor of the building. There we were, we didn't have any furniture, nothing for us to use. Later my father was able to get in touch with our maid in Juárez, but Francisca said, "Don't even come here for a moment, not even one of your daughters, not for *anything*, because they've already asked about you. If I can, I'll send you something."

We were still in this situation when three other families arrived who had also left Juárez. Since they were looking for a place to stay, they ended up staying with us. Now there were more than twenty-five of us. Father said, "We have to find a place to live. Let's see what we'll do. How can we stay here like this?" We didn't have anywhere to sleep or anything.

My father went downtown and ran into a friend from Juárez who, it turned out, had come to El Paso with his family across the bridge. This man told my father that when they crossed there were many people from Juárez and Chihuahua wanting to do the same thing, including General Castro. He said that he and his family had found a big house in South El Paso, and since there was room, he invited us to go there. So that's what we did, but even there we still didn't have anything. Father said, "OK, I feel like seeing if I can get to Juárez to bring some furniture or at least *something* we can use." But no, Mrs. Schuster

106

wouldn't let him. She told him, "Don't go, because something bad will happen to you. It's better to sleep on the bare floor than to return to Juárez. Right now Villa is committing atrocities."

After some time we went to Juárez and we found that none of the people whom we knew were there. Many were in El Paso and others went to different places. General Castro also ended up living in El Paso.

> "The Service detailed me to make
> contact with Villa and work out
> arrangements."
> —Clifford A. Perkins*

*Inevitably when a border city fell during an attack, reper-
cussions extended across the political line. U.S. agencies,
charged with border screening and maintenance, got involved
with matters such as refugee flow. Clifford A. Perkins, an
immigration official, found it necessary to work directly with
the Villistas following the famous capture of Juárez in November 1913. Perkins had some interesting experiences that he
remembered in considerable detail, as the following account
illustrates.*

After three years as a Chinese Inspector in Arizona, I was posted by
the Immigration Service to El Paso, Texas, effective May 15, 1913. I
arrived just in time to take a hand in one episode of the Mexican Revolution. El Paso, as the largest city on the border, was a focus of undercover revolutionary activity, and Juárez was the scene of some heavy
fighting. The Service could not help being heavily involved, and I was
involved too as the newest man on a force of well over fifty people at a
large and active port, headquarters for the entire border at that time.

Pancho Villa's forces were moving northward through Chihuahua at

*Memoir written for *Password*, 22:2 (Summer 1977): 61–69. Reprinted by permission
of *Password*.

the time of my arrival, and in mid-November they occupied Juárez. As they progressed toward the border, they commandeered all railroad rolling stock, including locomotives, loading equipment onto freight cars on top of which the women and children traveled and even built fires. A couple of passenger cars would be hooked on for the officers and their women, and a caboose for the train crew would bring up the rear. The crew worked under the guns of Villa and did only as they were told. Altogether, the train was pretty much self-contained and occasionally even included a stock car full of cattle so there would be meat for everybody.

The Villistas raised considerable hell as they progressed northward, and a great wave of refugees poured across the line ahead of them. These frightened and often destitute people became the responsibility of the Immigration Service. They included a wide variety of human types—merchants, housewives, children, workingmen, along with prostitutes, criminals, beggars, and street scum. Villa's men enjoyed killing Chinese of all varieties, and they too fled to the United States to save their lives: tradesmen, cooks, laundrymen, and gardeners. Each fugitive brought whatever he could with him, especially food, clothing, and household goods, with some miscellaneous livestock and pets.

Among the earliest arrivals, when actual fighting broke out, was the entire mounted police force in a body and in a hurry. Villa had been known to cut off one ear of a captured *federal* (for future recognition), telling him as he did so that if he ever caught him again, he would kill him. And he meant it. Provision was made for turning the horses of these *federales* over to the United States Army and placing them under guard. The men themselves were paroled to the Mexican consul in El Paso. In due time the better-known individuals and others who could establish their good character were freed on their own recognizance. The rest quickly swamped the Immigration Service.

Without available facilities for housing, feeding, and sanitation, the government people had to put them up in a temporary camp behind the railroad embankment near the river, where army guards could patrol the area to keep them from escaping and where field kitchens could be used to feed them. The beggars and street people were a particular problem. Mexico had not yet made provision for the care of the indigent and many of them had become beggars, often grotesquely crippled and always pathetic.

Once some semblance of order existed in Juárez, repatriation of individuals ineligible for parole was mandatory. The Service detailed me to make contact with Villa and work out arrangements. The fighting had tapered off, but gun battles were still going on in various sections of Juárez and traffic was nonexistent as I left the office and headed for the international bridge. It was usually crowded at that hour of the morning, a streetcar on the elevated track along one side, foot traffic on the walkway along the border, and a line of horsedrawn vehicles plus an occasional automobile in the center. Today it was deserted, except for one barefooted Villista in ragged pants and high-crowned straw hat with two banderillas across his chest containing not more than eight or ten cartridges. Under his supervision I crossed to the Mexican side of the river.

I was in difficulties at once. Several rag-tag soldiers armed with assorted weapons quickly closed around me and my idea of walking alone through their ranks, hoping they would be more amused than upset by such temerity, began to seem more foolhardy by the second. I explained my intention of talking with El General. A prolonged serio-comic debate followed which ended in their drawing aside, but as I moved off, a steady stream of sneering jibes about *gringos* and American "peegs" followed me, calculated to make me mad. I would have been, too, had I not been so acutely aware of the exceedingly vulnerable area between my shoulder blades.

When I reached the customs building on Avenida Juárez, I was passed on to the officer of the guard and obtained his permission to proceed to Villa's command post in the police station on Calle Comercial. As I continued my progress, I encountered more soldiers, and it was not consoling to observe that they were in a festive mood, for I well knew it would take very little to change bantering vulgarities to bullets. There was sporadic shooting all along Calle Comercial. The sidewalks were littered with broken glass and merchandise that had been taken or thrown out of the stores. There were more dead soldiers and horses than I wanted to count and several bullet-riddled cars and wagons had been abandoned along the gutters.

Everywhere I looked was evidence that while the officers had been appropriating the better houses for themselves and their women, the Villista soldiers had been on a drunken rampage—looting, burning, and killing. Order of a sort had been restored, but more than one *soldado*

110

leaning against the wall of a vandalized saloon, liquor store, or office building, was too drunk to fire the gun he waved at me so threateningly.

About the time I started debating the wisdom of reaching my destination by some other route, a man wearing the racing commissioner's full-dress uniform staggered out of an alley. I knew him well. He was, or had been, a ticket seller at the racetrack who answered to the name of Luis. As this resplendent figure rounded the corner onto Calle Comercial, a loaded peon, seated in the corner doorway of a ruined liquor store, observed him. The soldier's rifle was propped against the side of the building so he could more easily consume the contents of two bottles of tequila which he had confiscated. At sight of the uniform he carefully settled his bottle between his thighs, saluted and called out, "Hola, mi capitán!"

Since Villa was well acquainted with the racetrack personnel, it was obvious that Luis knew his general. I realized that this could be opportunity knocking, but at the same time I wondered how Luis would react to me in his new situation. I could only wait to find out. Weaving in my direction with a bemused smile on his face and a bottle of *tequila* in each hand, he stopped every so often to take a drink from one bottle or the other, apparently indifferent to the occasional bullets whistling by. Within a few feet of me he stopped, frowned uncertainly, rocked forward to search my face, then threw both arms around my shoulders with an exuberant greeting, offering me a drink from either, or both, of his bottles. Under the circumstances I was happy to accept.

On his inquiring what business brought me to Juárez, I explained that my purpose was to obtain permission from El General for the return of some poor people who were being held in El Paso with no roof over their heads and no food to eat. I made the story as pathetic as possible and he became increasingly sympathetic. At the conclusion he offered to go with me to the police station to make sure all arrangements were worked out immediately. When we arrived, he brushed past the guard on duty with a wave of his hand and escorted me straight to the officer of the day. As a result, a messenger was dispatched immediately to the general.

After only half an hour (though it seemed much longer) the messenger returned with the necessary clearances. The two bottles were nearly empty by then, but Luis could still move under his own power when I stood up to leave. Nor was he about to allow his good *amigo* to walk back to the bridge alone. He presented me with one of the bottles and put an arm around my neck as we started for the river, staggering and swaying along and singing at the tops of our voices, though mine could not have added a thing to his rendition of "La Golondrina." In the middle of the International Bridge my almost paralyzed escort bade me a tearfully affectionate farewell, made an exceedingly sloppy about-face, and started back toward Juárez while I went on thankfully to the office to report a mission completed.

By the time word got around that permission had been granted by El General for Juárez residents to return, they had been divided into groups according to their need for detention under American statutes and the problems they, or their possessions, presented. The first group ushered back into Mexico under guard included all horses, burros, livestock, and wagons. Next went the cripples, beggars, prostitutes, and the rest of the human refuse that had been filling the jails. The more or less responsible refugees were allowed to move out when ready, although many of them did so reluctantly, having a good idea they would find their homes and stores in ruins. None of them displayed much emotion, although there was no food immediately available in Juárez and little water. Electricity was still shut off by the El Paso supplier, and they had almost nothing to look forward to but hardship and probably slow starvation. Residents of consequence sent servants back to check on the condition of their homes, most of which had been completely stripped or taken over by high-ranking officers, their friends, and their women, and the furnishings wrecked. Many who had suffered severe financial losses or were afraid to go back remained on the American side until notified by the Service either to return to Mexico if they wished to avoid deportation or apply for permanent residence, a simple procedure at the time since visas were not required.

El Paso residents reaped one unanticipated benefit from Villa's triumph. That summer the Villistas had taken over control of practically the entire state of Chihuahua, had seized the treasury to get money for guns, ammunition, and supplies, and had occupied many of the large *haciendas*. Villa's men rounded up the cattle on the larger estates, making deals with the *hacendados* at something like five dollars a head for signing the papers legalizing sale in the United States. While the fee was tantamount to no payment at all, the owners had little choice; it was that or nothing, and trainload after trainload of cattle arrived at the line and were sold through one of the El Paso banks, Villa collecting all but the head fee paid to the owners. Slaughterhouses were set up where the beef was butchered, and it was sold retail or given away to the poor, probably in an effort by Villa to make himself popular with the element that represented his principal backing. El Paso residents who were in a position to do so bought Villa money, which had no real value but had to be accepted in the towns he controlled, and used it to purchase meat in Juárez. And the meat was every bit as good as it should have been, coming as it did from the best cattle the ranchers had been able to produce.

Almost every day while Villa held Juárez, situations arose that necessitated reaching his top command, most of them having to do with the actions of Villistas at the line. Soldiers on guard at the bridge wouldn't pass anything or anyone on their own initiative; permissions had to be obtained for the entry into Mexico of aliens being deported, and so on, and two or three times a week, at least, there was some matter which had to be cleared with Villa personally. Probably because of my successful negotiations concerning the refugees, and the fact that I spoke the language, the Immigration Service assigned me to act as go-between with Villa and his officials.

The general was a chunky, powerfully built man, with the slender legs of a horseman, tiny, close-set eyes almost buried in a round, full face, and a thin-lipped mouth overpowered by a heavy drooping black mustache. Though he seldom raised his voice, and was not at all bombastic, he was extremely alert and quick, and his speech as well as his manner reflected his abrupt, determined attitude toward everything and everybody. All sorts of stories have been written about the general, but in the main my personal dealings with him were very satisfactory. Sometimes it was difficult to convince him about something, but when he finally agreed, he could be depended upon. I don't know whether he was dedicated to anything more than power and fame for himself, but he ran the show and accomplished his purpose. He gave everybody trouble, but you could look him in the eye and if he was a friend, fine; if not, you'd better watch yourself from then on.

Villa never consulted with his officers about a matter presented to him and brooked very little interference, but although he was crude, he always treated me with courtesy, shaking my hand when we met, and again when we parted, giving me a firm, hearty grip. He was a

113

dangerous, vindictive enemy when crossed, but I found the best way to get along with him was just to stand up to him in the belief that if I dealt fairly with him, he would do the same with me. It worked out that way, too.

After several weeks of almost daily contacts with the general, and just about the time conditions in Juárez appeared to be reaching a semblance of normal, somebody took a pot shot at me during one of my trips to Villa's headquarters. As I passed in front of a saloon near the *comandancia*, there was a sudden commotion around the corner; then a shot rang out and a bullet shattered the saloon window right above my head. There wasn't time to be frightened, or at least the excitement of the situation overcame physical fear. It was the same at other times in my life when I had equally close calls, but three or four hours afterward, I would let down and sometimes actually become weak. The only times when I experienced cold creepings of fright was when there was time to think about the possible danger ahead.

About a week after the bullet broke the plate-glass window, a Mexican customs officer told me that a drunken Villista officer had spotted me less than ten feet away and had decided to kill himself a *gringo*. Jerking his gun, he pulled the trigger just as another customs officer recognized me and slammed the drunk's arm upward, deflecting the bullet to a spot over my head. He also told me that when Villa heard about it, he busted the officer and put him in jail.

Villa seldom left his office in Juárez, and I don't recall ever seeing him in the United States. Not only would he have been arrested for violating our neutrality laws, but the *federales* had undercover agents in El Paso, any number of whom would have risked killing him, given the opportunity. Most of his affairs were handled through his staff, primarily by Rodríguez, his buffer, personal aide, and secretary. Rodríguez was a slender, neatly dressed young man in his mid-twenties who spoke English well and had the ability to be courteous yet not allow everyone who came to see the general to do so. Once while I was at headquarters on a routine matter, Rodríguez asked me to step into the general's office to discuss something of a confidential nature. Villa was waiting for me with a proposition.

He wanted to get around the embargo against selling munitions to forces opposing the party in power in Mexico. President Wilson had forbidden this traffic in order to cooperate with the seemingly stable government in Mexico City, thereby giving rise to considerable smuggling of guns and ammunition west of El Paso where there were few barriers to such activities. After considerable beating about the bush, Villa said that he had checked me out and decided I could be trusted to undertake a commission for him. He told me he had $50,000 in gold and wanted me to go to Canada to purchase guns and ammunition for his men, a difficult task made doubly so by the varying calibers and gauges of the guns they used. Since the general had, in a manner of speaking, paid me a compliment and was not a person who took kindly to having his requests turned down, refusing him presented a real problem. I declined, however, as gracefully as possible, but as a result we never got around to discussing what he would have paid me for the job. It would no doubt have been well worth my while financially, as agents in such dealings usually received a kickback from the seller in addition to the commission from the buyer. Before we parted, Villa did tell me that he had given $50,000 to another American for the same purpose and had never seen the munitions nor heard of the agent again.

Such incidents, as well as the assistance given by our government to those the general considered his enemies, undoubtedly accounted for much of his antipathy toward *norteamericanos*.

Americans did have their place in his scheme of things, however, for while he held Juárez, he insisted that Luz Corral de Villa, his legal wife as far as was generally known, spend her nights in a house he rented for her in El Paso. The general was accompanied from place to place by innumerable women and referred to several of them as his "wife." He would not have been averse to going through any number of wedding ceremonies if it suited his purpose, but whatever the status of the women with him, he did not want Luz in Juárez overnight because he anticipated an attack by the *federales* at any time.

Luz was a woman of about twenty when I first met her as I was relieving an immigrant inspector on the International Bridge. She dressed unpretentiously with a *rebozo* over her head and was gracious, soft spoken, and very much on the quiet side, but she loved the diamonds Villa gave her and wore lots of them. Her skin was lighter than average for her people, but she was rather heavy set and there was nothing in her manner to distinguish her from any ordinary Mexican housewife.

She would leave El Paso for Juárez in the morning in a large, black chauffeur-driven car, occasionally accompanied by another woman, and would return about sundown or shortly thereafter following dinner with Villa. One day I learned from a friend that a detective on the El Paso police force was planning to take Luz into custody the next evening when she returned from Mexico. His intention was to shake her down and relieve her of the diamond rings and earrings she usually wore, plus the large sum of money it was her habit to carry. The detective figured that since the United States government did not recognize Villa or his army and authority in Mexico, the general wouldn't be able to do a thing about it, and nobody in the U.S. would care.

As soon as I heard what was in the offing, I called Villa's office. When I got through to Rodríguez, I said, "You tell Luz when she comes over tonight to leave all her diamonds and her money in Juárez." When he wanted to know why, I answered, *"Por que sí!"* (just because). That evening when Luz' car crossed the bridge, it was stopped by two detectives. They climbed into the limousine and directed her chauffeur to drive to the police station. A friend told me several days later that the detective nearly had apoplexy when he discovered that Luz was wearing no diamonds and had only small change in her purse.

Villa returned the favor a few weeks later, following a shooting on Cordova Island, a silt deposit along a wide loop on the north side of the Rio Grande [that was] left as the river shifted its course farther and farther into Mexico. Trees and shrubs had found a foothold in the loose soil, offering a measure of protection from observation, especially at night. A screen of brush and cottonwoods dotted the Mexican side of the one-time riverbed, and a densely populated maze of Mexican shanties on the American side gave immediate shelter to *contrabandistas*. Smugglers gave us more trouble here than any place else in the vicinity of El Paso.

While Jack Belcher and I were patrolling the Island one afternoon, we noticed a mounted Mexican officer who forded the river and rode directly toward us. We made no effort to conceal ourselves, but when he was forty or fifty yards away, he suddenly dismounted, raised his rifle, and started pumping lead at us. We dropped to the ground immediately and returned his fire. When no more shots came from his direction, we cautiously stood up and walked toward him, finding that two of our shots had reached their mark. As we stood there reviewing what had happened, I took off my hat and discovered that one of his bullets had gone through it. This was probably my closest call in the service, for some of my hair, which was cut fairly short, had been clipped off and was still clinging to one of the two holes through the crown of my Stetson.

If a smuggler was killed at night and fell in the river, we forgot about the body unless it showed up downstream on the American side. Then, as with a smuggler killed north of the river in the daytime, we called the police to dispose of the remains, which was usually by burial in a potter's field, for the bodies were seldom claimed. Villa had to be notified about his dead officer, however, so Jack and I left the man there and returned to our office to report the incident before I drove to Juárez. When I reached Villa's office, I explained to Rodríguez the reason for my visit and he took me to the general. We went through our usual handshake and introductory greetings, after which I proceeded (most respectfully) to tell him that one of his officers had opened fire on us on the Island, without provocation or warning—and an exchange of shots had followed. Villa was rough, but I was counting on the fact that he kept his soldiers fairly well restrained, and in some ways was strict with them. With a semimilitary force, which is what his army really was, discipline was an off-again, on-again proposition. Every once in a while a Villista with too much tequila in him would shoot off his gun at nothing in particular, but after the looting and drinking had run their course, Villa's men were surprisingly orderly. As a matter of fact, other than for a few killings, I don't remember hearing of any major crimes that took place while he held the town.

The general listened to my report with his usual frowning concentration. When I was through he remarked briefly, "I'll take care of him immediately."

"Thank you, *mi General*," I responded, "but you do not need to do that. We already have."

With that I indicated on the map hanging against the wall where the body could be found.

"*Está bueno*," was all he answered before shaking hands with me again and wishing me a good journey back to El Paso.

> "As for roads through this wilderness . . . there are none."
> —Hehn Hamilton Fyfe*

When the Revolution rendered trains inoperative, travel became exceedingly difficult. Hehn Hamilton Fyfe, an Englishman who decided to find out "firsthand" about conditions in Mexico, teamed up with other foreigners in making a frustrating trip to Monterrey, Nuevo Leon, in the fall of 1913. Prior to his arrival in Laredo, Texas, Fyfe had tried unsuccessfully to make his way to Mexico City via the state of Sonora. Perhaps his exasperation resulting from this initial failure explains in part Fyfe's racist and contemptuous comments about Mexicans he encountered on the trip.

At sunny, dusty Laredo, while I waited day after day for a train to run south, I began by treating the complete isolation of Mexico City, so far as railways from the United States border are concerned, as a joke. Before I left there I had ceased to see the funny side of it. There are some places in which I might be forced to spend a week without grumbling, but Laredo is not one of them. Dozens of us were cooped up in two arid, comfortless hotels, with nothing to do but ask each other, "Is there no chance of a train?"

Every morning a little party of us would cross the bridge from United

---

*Hehn Hamilton Fyfe, *The Real Mexico: A Study on the Spot* (London: William Heineman, 1914), pp. 29–42.

118

States Laredo to the Mexican town across the river (the Rio Grande) in order to ask the Mexican general if he had any comfort for us. He was invariably polite, although depressed. An oldish man with deeply furrowed forehead and lack-lustre eye, he looked at us wearily and mechanically repeated his formula, "Three or four days." At first he attributed the broken line to floods. But we knew there was fighting near at hand, for we saw troop trains going off, saw wounded brought in, and heard from rebel sympathizers of a plan to cut Laredo off from Monterrey. So after a while the old general dropped pretense and admitted that before he could repair the bridges blown up he had to clear the country of rebels.

That settled it. I gave up the railway as hopeless, and looked around for some other means of making my way south. With five others, who were very anxious to get either to their homes or their businesses in Mexico, I asked the general for a pass to go across country. He gave it on condition that we provided our own conveyance. We agreed cheerfully and he almost smiled. I wondered why at the moment. Afterwards I understood.

In high spirits we went to a motor garage on the American side. Could we have a car? Possibly. What would it cost? Fifty pounds. We gasped. Fifty pounds to go a hundred and fifty miles? Not a cent less, and in addition we must deposit £250, the value of the car, in case the Carrancistas seized it. "Ridiculous!" we said, and tramped off in a body to another garage. Here we had an amusing experience of the Mexican character. It was now nearing midday. In the shed which we entered half-a-dozen black-haired, olive-skinned chauffeurs and mechanics were lolling in attitudes of utter and unashamed laziness. Not one of them stirred. We asked for the proprietor. He was at home. Could he be telephoned to? A languid arm waved us to the instrument. Then the twelve eyes closed again, and we were left to do the best we could. We got no satisfaction. The same demand for a deposit was made. We went sadly away.

However, we soon cheered up again. We must have a wagon, then. It would take longer, but that we must put up with. So back we went to the Mexican side and set about finding someone who would take us in a wheeled vehicle with a good span of mules. We might as well have saved ourselves the trouble. If the Americans were afraid for their money, the Mexicans were afraid for their lives. Some of them said so frankly.

119

Others trumped up excuses. One man "could have started yesterday," but today did not feel well. Another pleaded that his wife would be nervous. A third was not sure of the way. We left the Mexican town to frizzle in its hot sunshine and tried carriage-owners on the American side. Some were ready to talk business if we would guarantee the value of their horses or mules. Most of them refused even to discuss terms. I explained that I had a pass through the Constitutionalist lines in addition to our federal safe-conduct. No, no they knew the danger too well!

Exasperated, we asked one man, an American Mexican, what he was afraid of. "They would kill me," he said. "Why? They are your own countrymen, aren't they?" "No, señor," he responded. "I am an American." (He could not speak a word of English.) "But why should they kill you?" "Because, señor," he said with magnificent simplicity, using a vulgar Spanish phrase, which I translate into words less terse than the original, "because they are all the offspring of abandoned women."

Our ill-luck scared two of the party off. Now we were four. One was a German, determined at all hazards to get back to his wife and children in Monterrey. The next, an Englishman, had important business there. The third was an American, a mining engineer bound for his mines near Saltillo. We talked over all possibilities. We asked the general if we could travel in a work-train. "Si," he said, "when the next one is able to run." "And when will that be, general?" He shrugged his tired shoulders. "We are at war, gentlemen. Who can say?" Next day we had further proof the bridge was closed. Our safe-conduct gained us passage, but no one without a permit was allowed through.

Another annoyance was the scarcity of silver. Mexican currency is largely in notes. One of our party tendered a five-peso note (a peso is in normal times worth two shillings) to the conductor of the rickety streetcar. He decined to give change, so four of us got our ride for nothing! At half a dozen places (including banks) he tried to get rid of it. Everywhere change was refused. No one would part with real money. Everyone distrusted notes. And they had some reason, for the silver peso contains very nearly two shillings-worth of silver, whereas the exchange value of paper money had dropped in some places to one-and-fourpence. That is one result of civil war.

At last we made out plans. We decided to take a train from Laredo to Brownsville, Texas, which is near the mouth of the Rio Grande.

120

Thence we would only take a suitcase each. But the prospect of escape was so heartening that I believe we would gladly have started without anything at all. The other people in the hotel wagged their heads at us. "You're running a great risk," they maundered. I quoted Kipling at them—

If there should follow a thousand swords to carry my bones away,
Belike the price of a jackal's meal were more than a thief could
pay!

Really there was no danger to speak of. But after a week of Laredo we would have taken any risk.

It took us eighteen hours to go by train from Laredo to Brownsville, and, when we arrived, we found that we had left the frying-pan for the fire. Laredo was hot but dry. The heat of Brownsville wrapped itself round us like steaming wet flannel. Thirst was incessant. The slightest movement brought on prickly heat. Meals were torture: exhausted though one felt, there was nothing in the multitude of saucers slammed down before one to spur the appetite and scarcely anything one could eat at all.

This barbarian method of serving meals all at once makes travelling in Texas a nightmare. The meat is like leather. The messes which the saucers contain are the production of Chinese cooks, and at their best untempting. How any stomach can long endure them, washed down by coffee or iced tea, the universal dinner and supper drinks, I cannot understand.

However, we had no idea of staying longer than was necessary to fit out our expedition and to get the good word of General Lucio Blanco, the Constitutionalist commander in Matamoros, a Mexican town a mile or two across the border. Almost everyone in these Texan frontier towns in on the side of the Constitutionalists, and many actively assist them, so we soon found a prominent man who was in their counsels and who agreed to be our friend. As the four of us jogged with him in a filthy streetcar drawn by one wretched mule, through the long street of Matamoros, the desolation of the once flourishing city lay upon our spirits like lead. It was cynically curious to hear the gentle young *insurrecto* officers talk about the benefits their party meant to heap upon the common folk, and to look out of window upon the deserted unkempt

121

plaza. The Constitutionalists may be the friends of the people, but the people do not seem to have realized it yet.

These young officers were clever fellows, one a doctor, one an engineer, another an accountant, and so on. They told us proudly how the division of land among the peasants had already begun. They were clearly in earnest about their radical pretence. One turned back his coat and showed me pinned over his heart a little button portrait of President Madero. "We most of us wear it," he said reverently. Then General Blanco came in, a big, dark, resolute-looking man of quite a different type. I doubt whether he had the Madero button on his shirt.

He was very civil to us, however, and issued through his chief of staff a permit to pass safely through the country held by the Carranza faction. This business settled, we did our shopping. First, we bought tin mugs and a tin can for boiling coffee in. For food we took baked beans, cracker biscuits and a few tins of jam. Then after a moving picture show, we went early to bed.

The journey next morning to a place called Sam Fordyce was tedious. We were to begin our two hundred-mile drive from there, and we were impatient of the long drag in a slow and fusty train. Yet when we saw the motor car which was to take us our first stage to a village called Roma, we heartily wished the train went further. I have never seen a car plastered so thickly with mud.

The driver said cheerfully he guessed there was a quarter of a ton of it. That showed us what the roads were like. I say "roads," but, to speak truly, there are no roads in this part of Texas, any more than there are in Mexico. There are "trails": we should call them cart-tracks, and bad cart-tracks at that.

If ever that driver wants a certificate of proficiency, I should be glad to give it to him. The way he took us through rivers and lakes and slush-ponds was marvellous. He covered forty miles in less than four hours and landed us in Roma just as dark fell with the suddenness of a switched-off electric light. We found we were in a queer place, an American village where there was only one American inhabitant (he was away) and scarcely anyone who could speak English.

At the inn we were served by a Mexican waiter (who seemed to me to have stepped out of *Don Quixote* or *Gil Blas*) with a Mexican meal of *tortillas* (thin flat maize cakes), goat's-flesh (uneatable), red sausage meat (very palatable), *"frijoles,"* the favorite Mexican bean, and coffee. When you get over the smell of tortillas (due, I believe, to the lime which is mixed with them), and the strong flavor of the meat, and the surprise of getting our mouth burnt by the red or green peppers with which every dish is seasoned, Mexican small-town cookery is pretty good—certainly better than American. On the other hand, I prefer the American small-town hotel. In five days—for a reason which I leave to be imagined—we only had our clothes off once: that was when we slept in a hospitable American house.

In Roma, having unanimously decided not to undress, we lay down disconsolate outside our dubious-looking cots. We were sad for this reason. After long negotiations with a pair of brothers, they had promised to find us a wagon and mules to carry us to a place called Alamo, nine miles up the river. Here we could cross the Rio Grande into Mexico, tramp to a town called Mier, and there try to hire a coach. One brother was to come and tell us as soon as the arrangement was made, but all the evening was wearily waited and he never came. Luckily about twenty minutes after we had dropped off, we were awakened. Everything was fixed for a start at four o'clock in the morning. We slept again, our hearts full of thankful joy.

It was not so joyful to rouse up in the darkness, but coffee put us right and we rumbled off in the moonlight quite content. By the time we got to Alamo it was day, and when, after ferrying across, we had walked the three miles into Mier (letting our bags follow in an ox-cart), the sun was already hot. Another deserted desolate place we found this, with scarcely anyone about but *insurrecto* soldiers. Our first visit was to the "jefe" or commander. He was a genial ruffian, who told us, though he had no English, that he had been one of Colonel Roosevelt's cowboys in Cuba. He grinned and shook his head at the notion of finding a coach in Mier. Happily one of his captains came to the rescue. He had one. Our hearts leapt. It was out on his ranch nine miles off. He would send for it and get it into town by noon.

That day we spent in Mier was like an unpleasant dream. We strolled round the abandoned houses, many of which had been used as stables for the troopers' horses. We played cards. We had a couple of meals, made hideous by millions of flies. We sat outside the guard-room with our captain, wondering miserably whether he had really sent for his coach at all. At last about five o'clock it rattled into the plaza behind a couple of the poorest mules we had ever seen. Down drooped our spirits once more. But the captain was a man of action.

"Go," he said to a couple of soldiers. "Say to Don Emilio that the 'jefe' would be glad if he would lend these gentlemen a pair of mules—and if he won't lend them, take them."

In a few minutes they came—we did not inquire whether lent or "taken"—and then we set to work to get our luggage strapped on. A small crowd hindered us with well-meant advice, but in spite of them we got everything stowed, and just as the last of the daylight went, our driver cried "Oola moola" to the animals, whipped them up briskly, and, swaying like a small boat in a choppy sea, we started off.

When you hear of "driving through a country," you think no doubt of a good road like the roads of Europe; of roadside inns; of villages at frequent intervals; of towns in which to pull up at nightfall. If the drive continues through the dark hours, you imagine a countryside dotted with friendly lights from dwellings, single or in groups. Driving through northern Mexico is not like that at all.

In the hundred and fifty miles which we had still to do when we left Mier in our mule-coach for Monterrey we only passed through three little towns; no villages. We drove one day from five o'clock in the morning until three in the afternoon without meeting a soul. The country is a desert, in autumn brightly green with low bush, and in places even made gay by grass and flowers after heavy rains, but usually grey and sullen. There is very little water, as we learned sadly. It is hard in a scorching noon to eat canned beans, with biscuits and jam to follow, and have nothing whatever to drink.

As for roads through this wilderness, well, to put it plainly, there are none. There are merely rough trails, sometimes quite difficult to find. They run through rivers, down steep "arroyos" (ravines) and up the other side, your coach-pole pointing to heaven. They set you ploughing through deep sand, or floundering in mud up to the axles of your wheels. They are so narrow that you have to be perpetually on guard against thorny switches tearing hands and face. As for their ruts, I shall not describe them, for no one would believe me. I will only say that for the first half-hour of our journey I expected every minute that our coach would turn over. I cannot even now understand why it did not.

Until that dark night (we started at sunset, and the moon did not rise until after nine) I had never known why some folks are fearful when ships rock at sea. After being pitched and tossed in that coach, I can enter into their feelings exactly. When you have got accustomed to this kind of driving, you take everything as it comes. Your vehicle may suddenly tilt to an angle of forty-five degrees, one wheel in a rut three feet deep, the other pursuing its course upon the level, without alarming you in the least. It may toss you violently by dropping into a hollow, and being jerked out again with a wrench that seems bound to burst it asunder; you pay no heed. But until the conviction is acquired that the coach, flimsy as it looks, will never turn over, the beginner has an anxious time.

We made slow progress. It was hard to pick out the track, and after we had passed a blazing campfire of Constitutionalists, the change from glare to blackness blinded us altogether; so we took it in turns to carry a lantern a little way ahead. We were challenged of course by the campers, *"Quien vive?"* (Who goes there?) was shouted as we came near. *"Gente buena"* (Honest folk) we cried in answer. Half-a-dozen kindly rough fellows, with rifles in hand, clustered round us, examined my pass, and gave us a hearty "God-speed-you," as we crawled on our way. After three hours' walking we saw the first light, and hoped it was the *"ranchito"* (little farm) where we were to beg shelter for a few hours' sleep. But that was still a mile or so ahead.

When we got there our driver had to wake the family up. Their dwelling consisted of two separate huts, each about ten feet square and seven feet high. In one was a fireplace; a few pots and cups and dishes on a shelf proclaimed it the living-room. The other contained a large bed: in and around it at least five people slept. From the living-room a man stretched in a cattle-trough was turned out sulkily yawning; and an unsuccessful attempt made to arouse a little boy. A calfskin was thrown upon the ground; a blanket over that made us imagine the uneven brick floor a shade softer; and we lay down to slumber brokenly for a few hours. At two I wished it were four. At four we rose up, glad to leave our hardcouch; made coffee in our pot over the fire; ate some beans; shook hands all round with our hosts (this must never be omitted); and drove off in the chilly darkness at a quarter to five.

We made up our minds we should reach our first stage, a place called Treviño, about midday. But we had not realized the laziness of our mules. They moved like slugs. The driver worked far harder than they did,

125

shouting at them, and cracking his whip, and tugging at the reins all the time.

We gave them a rest, sleeping ourselves the while in the shade of a thorntree, and taking care not to lie upon cactus plants. Still they went no better. At last one of us saw a long stout stick lying near the trail. He called to the driver, who stepped down and picked it up. Its effect was marvellous. The mules broke at once into a trot which they kept up, with an occasional reminder of the stick's persuasive quality, until we drove into Treviño between three and four o'clock.

Here at the insurrectos' headquarters we were received with enthusiasm after my pass had been read. The chiefs in this place were men of education and intelligence. They found time hung heavy, and were glad of any incident to while it away. We chatted; I took their photographs; they gave us sugarcane to eat, all the hospitality they could offer, they said ruefully. They got no letters or newspapers; in this part civil war was stopped the posts. In their wretched village there were no distractions. What a life for men of culture and active mind! One, who had been governor of a state, told me how he had luckily escaped being killed in the capital. "I was the man they meant to burn," he said calmly. A spectacled major had been before the revolution a bank manager. A captain told me he was formerly superintendent of a wax factory.

That night we slept at an American mine owner's house near Cerallvo, a town which he made by pouring out £10,000 a month in wages. Now his smelter is shut down, the population has dwindled, his enterprise is rewarded by insult and robbery. He had been obliged to provision his house against siege and famine, and was afraid of a visit from the rebels while we were there. They had threatened to search for dynamite, of which he had none; but he feared they would seize his flour and tinned foods.

After Cerallvo the road was worse, rock instead of sand, and loose stones. The jolting made one sore all over. We had better mules now: they kept up a steady trot. But there were times when I should have been glad for them to walk like our first pair. However, this was our last day but one, and in the evening at the "fonda" of a little town called Merín, we ate some excellent roast "cabrito" (young kid), our first fresh meat for several days. So we were cheerful in spite of our aching bones.

Off at half-past four the next morning, we soon met another enemy— mud. We had to get out and push the wheels out of deep thick mire.

126

We ruined our boots and trousers. We splashed through swamps, and clambered along barbed wire fences tearing hands and clothes. But so long as we got through, we minded nothing. Twelve miles out of Monterrey we met our first federals. They stopped us, but soon let us go. In a suburb we raided a baker's: after living on biscuits and tortillas, bread tastes really good. Just before noon we passed the federal post on the edge of the city. Three men slumbered outside the guard-room, a fourth was apparently walking in his sleep. A carriage from the enemy's country was allowed to drive in without being challenged. No effort made to get information from us! No questions asked as to how we had got through! We had not to wait twenty-four hours to mark the result of such slackness. At eight o'clock the next morning, the rebels were in the outskirts of the town.

Is there any pleasure equal to the joy of feeling clean and fresh after a long, fatiguing, dirty ride? If there is I do not know it. In our five days' journey across the wilderness from Matamoros to Monterrey we only had our clothes off once. Imagine the delight with which we bathed and shaved and put on our "other clothes." Picture the effect of a dainty luncheon-table upon men who had been eating canned beans and crackers off the lids of tins, and eating them three times a day! There was a wondrous contentment in our faces as we sat smoking after lunch in a sunny patio full of roses, with a glorious pink creeper smothering the walls.

Two of our party were at home now. The other two of us had no idea of letting Monterrey be our Capua, charming city though it is. Mountains on three sides of it cut jagged patterns on the hot blue sky. Its climate extolled by some of its inhabitants as almost perfect, denounced by others as "the meanest ever," is very hot in summer, but in autumn delicious—cold mornings and blue, cloudless days. The town is attractively perched on a gentle slope overlooking a wide plain. As yet it is in the growing stage, and like a girl who is not yet quite a woman it is rather red about the elbows. It will be a large and fine city. Now it is going through a transition period.

> "These were metropolitan days for
> Presidio, a straggling and indescrib-
> ably desolate village."
> —John Reed (1887–1920)*

At the end of November, 1913, General Salvador Mercado's battered Huertista forces decided to abandon Chihuahua City and make a stand at the border town of Ojinaga, Chihuahua, opposite Presidio, Texas. Mercado managed temporarily to hold Ojinaga with his rag-tag army, but eventually succumbed to the Villistas. John Reed, the famous international revolutionary and war correspondent, provides an eyewitness account of conditions at Ojinaga-Presidio during that period.

Mercado's Federal army, after its dramatic and terrible retreat four hundred miles across the desert when Chihuahua was abandoned, lay three months at Ojinaga on the Rio Grande.

At Presidio, on the American side of the river, one could climb to the flat mud roof of the post office and look across the mile or so of low scrub growing in the sand to the shallow, yellow stream; and beyond to the low mesa where the town was, sticking sharply up out of a scorched desert, ringed round with bare, savage mountains.

One could see the square, gray adobe houses of Ojinaga, with here and there the oriental cupola of an old Spanish church. It was a desolate land, without trees. You expected minarets. By day, federal soldiers in

*John Reed, *Insurgent Mexico* (New York: D. Appleton, 1914), pp. 1–9.

shabby white uniforms swarmed about the place desultorily digging trenches, for Villa and his victorious Constitutionalists were rumored to be on the way. You got sudden glints, where the sun flashed on field guns; strange, thick clouds of smoke rose straight in the still air.

Toward evening, when the sun went down with the flare of a blast furnace, patrols of cavalry rode sharply across the skyline to the night outposts. And after dark, mysterious fires burned in the town.

There were thirty-five hundred men in Ojinaga. This was all that remained of Mercado's army of ten thousand and the five thousand which Pascual Orozco had marched north from Mexico City to reinforce him. Of this thirty-five hundred, forty-five were majors, twenty-one colonels, and eleven generals.

I wanted to interview General Mercado; but one of the newspapers had printed something displeasing to General Salazar, and he had forbidden the reporters the town. I sent a polite request to General Mercado. The note was intercepted by General Orozco, who sent back the following reply:

Esteemed and Honored Sir: If you set foot inside of Ojinaga, I will stand you sideways against a wall, and with my own hand take great pleasure in shooting furrows in your back.

But after all I waded the river one day and went up into the town. Luckily, I did not meet General Orozco. No one seemed to object to my entrance. All the sentries I saw were taking a siesta on the shady side of adobe walls. But almost immediately I encountered a courteous officer named Hernández, to whom I explained that I wished to see General Mercado.

Without inquiring as to my identity, he scowled, folded his arms, and burst out:

"I am General Orozco's chief of staff, and I will not take you to see General Mercado!"

I said nothing. In a few minutes he explained:

"General Orozco hates General Mercado! He does not deign to go to General Mercado's cuartel, and General Mercado does not *dare* to come to General Orozco's cuartel! He is a coward. He ran away from Tierra Blanca, and then he ran away from Chihuahua!"

"What other generals don't you like?" I asked.

129

He caught himself and slanted an angry look at me, and then grinned:
"*¿Quién sabe. . . ?*"

I saw General Mercado, a fat, pathetic, worried, undecided little man,
who blubbered and blustered a long tale about how the United States
army had come acorss the river and helped Villa to win the battle of
Tierra Blanca.

The white, dusty streets of the town, piled high with filth and fodder,
the ancient windowless church with its three enormous Spanish bells
hanging on a rack outside and a cloud of blue incense crawling out of
the black doorway, where the women camp followers of the army prayed
for victory day and night, lay in hot, breathless sun. Five times had
Ojinaga been lost and taken. Hardly a house that had a roof, and all the
walls gaped with cannon shot. In these bare, gutted rooms lived the
soldiers, their women, their horses, their chickens and pigs, raided from
the surrounding country. Guns were stacked in the corners, saddles
piled in the dust. The soldiers were in rags; scarcely one possessed a
complete uniform. They squatted around little fires in their doorways,
boiling cornhusks and dried meat. They were almost starving.

These were metropolitan days for Presidio, a straggling and inde-
scribably desolate village of about fifteen adobe houses, scattered without much plan in the deep sand and cottonwood scrub along the river
bottom. Old Kleinmann, the German storekeeper, made a fortune a day
outfitting refugees and supplying the federal army across the river with
provisions. He had three beautiful adolescent daughters whom he kept
locked up in the attic of the store, because a flock of amorous Mexicans
and ardent cowpunchers prowled around like dogs, drawn from many
miles away by the fame of these damsels. Half the time he spent working
furiously in the store, stripped to the waist; and the remainder, rushing
around with a large gun strapped to his waist, warning off the suitors.

At all times of the day and night, throngs of unarmed federal soldiers
from across the river swarmed in the store and the pool hall. Among
them circulated dark, ominous persons with an important air, secret
agents of the rebels and the federals. Around in the brush camped
hundreds of destitute refugees, and you could not walk around a corner
at night without stumbling over a plot or a counterplot. There were
Texas Rangers, and United States troopers, and agents of American

corporations trying to get secret instructions to their employees in the interior.

One MacKenzie stamped about the post office in a high dudgeon. It appeared that he had important letters for the American Smelting and Refining Company mines in Santa Eulalia.

"Old Mercado insists on opening and reading all letters that pass through his lines," he shouted indignantly.

"But," I said, "he will let them pass, won't he?"

"Certainly," he answered. "But do you think the American Smelting and Refining Company will submit to having its letters opened and read by a damned greaser? It's an outrage when an American corporation can't send a private letter to its employees! If this don't bring intervention," he finished, darkly, "I don't know what will!"

There were all sorts of drummers for arms and ammunition companies, smugglers and *contrabandistas;* also a small, bantam man, the salesman for a portrait company which made crayon enlargements from photographs at five dollars apiece. He was scurrying around among the Mexicans getting thousands of orders for pictures which were to be paid for upon delivery, and which, of course, could never be delivered. It was his first experience among Mexicans, and he was highly gratified by the hundreds of orders he had received. You see, a Mexican would just as soon order a portrait, or a piano, or an automobile as not, so long as he does not have to pay for it. It gives him a sense of wealth.

The little agent for crayon enlargements made one comment on the Mexican revolution. He said that General Huerta must be a fine man because he understood he was distantly connected, on his mother's side, with the distinguished Carey family of Virginia!

The American bank of the river was patroled twice a day by details of cavalry, conscientiously paralleled on the Mexican side by companies of horsemen. Both parties watched each other narrowly across the border. Every once in a while a Mexican, unable to restrain his nervousness, took a potshot at the Americans, and a small battle ensued as both parties scattered into the brush. A little way above Presidio were stationed two troops of the Negro Ninth Cavalry. One colored trooper, watering his horse on the bank of the river, was accosted by an English-speaking Mexican squatting on the opposite shore:

"Hey coon!" he shouted, derisively, "when are you damned gringos going to cross that line?"

"Chile!" responded the Negro. "We ain't agoin' to cross that line at all. We're just goin' to pick up that line an' carry it right down to the Big Ditch!"

Upon these occasions the high sheriff of Presidio County would bluster into town on a small pinto horse—a figure true to the best tradition of *The Girl of the Golden West.* He had read all Owen Wister's novels, and knew what a western sheriff ought to look like: two revolvers on the hip, one slung under his arm, a large knife in his left boot, and an enormous shotgun over his saddle. His conversation was larded with the most fearful oaths, and he never caught any criminal. He spent all of his time enforcing the Presidio County law against carrying firearms and playing poker; and at night, after the day's work was done, you could always find him sitting in at a quiet game in the back of Kleinmann's store.

War and rumors of war kept Presidio at a fever heat. We all knew that sooner or later the Constitutionalist army would come overland from Chihuahua and attack Ojinaga. In fact, the major in command of the Border Patrol had already been approached by the federal generals in a body to make arrangements for the retreat of the federal army from Ojinaga under such circumstances. They said that when the rebels attacked they would want to resist for a respectable length of time—say two hours—and that then they would like permission to come across the river.

We knew that some twenty-five miles southward, at La Mula Pass, five hundred rebel volunteers guarded the only road from Ojinaga through the mountains. One day a courier sneaked through the federal lines and across the river with important news. He said that the military band of the federal army had been marching around the country practicing their music, and had been captured by the Constitutionalists, who stood them up in the marketplace with rifles pointed at their heads and made them play twelve hours at a stretch. "Thus," continued the message, "the hardships of life in the desert have been somewhat alleviated." We could never discover just how it was that the band happened to be practicing all alone twenty-two miles from Ojinaga in the desert.

For a month longer the federals remained at Ojinaga, and Presidio throve. Then Villa, at the head of his army, appeared over a rise in the desert. The federals resisted a respectable length of time—just two hours, or, to be exact, until Villa himself at the head of a battery galloped right up to the muzzles of the guns—and then poured across the river in wild rout, were herded in a vast corral by the American soldiers, and afterward imprisoned in a barbed-wire stockade at Fort Bliss, Texas.

But by that time I was already far down in Mexico, riding across the desert with a hundred ragged Constitutionalist troopers on my way to the front.

Part III

Border Crises:
Middle and Late 1910s

As disorders spawned by the Revolution escalated and spilled over the boundary, relations between Mexico and the United States deteriorated. Throughout the 1910s both revolutionary and counterrevolutionary elements used the U.S. borderlands to promote schemes for seizing power in Mexico.[1] Such activities prompted Washington to impose arms embargos and invoke neutrality laws. Another recurring difficulty involved Americans who suffered property loss or personal injury in Mexico and in U.S. territory along the border. A third source of friction was Washington's impatience with Mexico's chaotic political process. In 1913, President Woodrow Wilson stepped up the on-going diplomatic war, demanding that Mexico put its house in order and establish a democratic government. Victoriano Huerta, who had "usurped" the presidency, failed to comply with Wilson's desires, and for that the American chief executive withheld official recognition of Huerta's government. In 1914, relations reached a new low when American troops invaded Veracruz following a minor incident in Tampico. The loss of 300 Mexican lives (19 Americans were killed), along with the violation of national sovereignty, worsened already very hostile feelings toward Americans throughout Mexico.[2]

At the same time, anti-Mexican sentiment rose sharply in the United States, particularly along the border, with the increased frequency of hostile and intensifying revolutionary activity. At the Texas-Tamaulipas frontier, traditional illegal activities such as smuggling, gun-running, and cattle rustling were overshadowed by organized banditry, large-scale raiding, and irredentism. By 1915, a highly volatile climate pre-

137

vailed in South Texas. A series of violent, destructive raids were carried on by adherents of the Plan de San Diego, a Mexican document that called for an uprising against Anglo Americans. Ostensibly written in San Diego, Texas, the Plan provided for the reconquest of Texas, New Mexico, Arizona, Colorado, and California. This region would first become an independent republic, then be incorporated into Mexico. All Mexican Americans, blacks, and Indians would be liberated, but Anglo males over sixteen would be killed. Blacks would be assisted in seizing territory contiguous to the new republic, where they could establish their own nation.[3]

American authorities discovered the Plan in early 1915, when Basilio Ramos, one of the authors, was arrested in McAllen, Texas, while trying to organize the uprising. After spending some time behind bars, Ramos jumped bail and fled to Matamoros, but others pursued the Plan's objectives by carrying on raids against South Texas residents beginning in the summer of 1915. Yet because of the confusion, it is difficult to tell which attacks were perpetrated by adherents of the Plan and which were the work of independent bands with other motives.

Of the many disturbances that plagued South Texas for over a year, two will illustrate the level of violence then occurring. On October 18, 1915, about sixty Mexicans brought a St. Louis, Brownsville, and Mexico Railway train to a halt outside Brownsville by derailing the engine and two other cars. A few of the raiders boarded the train, and in the subsequent shooting several people died. The following morning Texas Rangers captured and executed four suspects for alleged complicity in the wreck.[4] Three days later, a party of Mexicans attacked some sixteen U.S. soldiers at the Ojo de Agua Ranch, a site very near the Rio Grande. The Americans put up some resistance until more troops arrived from nearby Mission. At the battle's end, eight men lay dead and seventeen wounded.[5]

Many Mexicans who participated in the raids wanted to undo the wrongs long perpetrated by Anglo Americans against Mexico and Mexican Americans alike. South Texas was notorious for its extreme anti-Mexican sentiment, and few local residents were surprised when the violence assumed the characteristics of a race war.[6] Of course, not everyone who took part in the violence had political or racial objectives; untold numbers were ordinary bandits who capitalized on the confusion to loot and plunder.

138

Whatever the motives and identities of the raiders, the people of South Texas paid a heavy price. Hundreds died, thousands had to flee their homes, and property damage reached millions of dollars. The raids reinforced existing hatreds, which led to severe repression against Mexican Americans. Many innocent people lost their lives in lynchings, hangings, shootings, and other forms of execution perpetrated by unscrupulous lawmen, soldiers, and vigilantes.

One controversial and emotionally charged subject is the role of Texas Rangers in the suppression of rebellion in South Texas. Many people protested bitterly that Rangers often exceeded their authority and treated suspected lawbreakers, particularly those of Mexican descent, with unrestrained brutality. To make matters worse, their behavior seemed to be sanctioned by Texas officialdom.[7] A contemporary journalist expressed incredulity at the atrocities committed against Mexicans and the apparent lack of legal justice:

Some Rangers have degenerated into common mankillers. There is no penalty for killing, no jury along the border would ever convict a white man for shooting a Mexican. Reading over Secret Service records makes you feel as though there was an open gun season on Mexicans along the border.[8]

Outraged by the behavior of the Rangers, J. T. Canales, an attorney and state legislator from Brownsville, led an exhaustive official investigation in 1919. Canales compiled nineteen charges against the lawmen, ranging from unprofessional conduct and drunkenness to torture and murder. Testimony filled over 1,600 pages and included statements from men and women of varied ethnic, occupational, and class backgrounds.[9] Canales's efforts resulted in the reduction of the force and other changes designed to improve the Rangers' internal organization.

While racial and economic injustices north of the border suffice to explain the rebelliousness of Mexican Americans, the driving force behind the raiding of 1915–16 came from Mexico, where the on-going Revolution affected the border area more strongly than ever. Domestic power struggles and political squabbles inevitably spread across the boundary, affecting diplomatic relations with the United States. Venustiano Carranza appears to have used the border troubles to advantage in his attempts to gain U.S. recognition for his foundering government. During the period of the raids Carranza controlled the Tamaulipas frontier, and he could have restrained his countrymen from terrorizing the Texas border. Yet the impasse with Washington gave him little reason to do so, and his followers in Tamaulipas encouraged and sometimes even joined the raids. When Carranza finally received de facto U.S. recognition in October 1915, the raids associated with the Plan de San Diego stopped. Whether Carranza actually instigated the 1915 raids or those that followed, is not certain, but there is no doubt he used them to his own advantage.[10]

Following the U.S. turnabout toward Carranza, the border enjoyed a short period of relative calm. Then a series of incidents involving Pancho Villa shattered the peace and brought the two countries to the brink of war. Villa was already enraged at the United States for recognizing Carranza and imposing an embargo on arms shipments for Carranza's rivals; the last straw came when the United States authorized Carranza to transport troops through the U.S. borderlands, enabling them to repel Villa at Agua Prieta, Sonora. By fall 1915, Villa's strength and status had declined drastically, thanks in no small part to the *norteamericanos*. In part out of a desire for revenge, Villistas then undertook two major actions against the hated *gringos*. On January 10, 1916, sixteen American engineers were taken off a train in Santa Ysabel, Chihuahua, and killed. On March 9, 1916, approximately 500 Villistas attacked the isolated hamlet of Columbus, New Mexico, inflicting injury and death on American civilians and soldiers alike.[11] Within a week, Gen. John J. Pershing led 6,000 U.S. troops into Mexico in pursuit of Villa, causing deep resentment among Mexicans who found themselves face to face with armed foreigners. Two skirmishes at Parral and Carrizal, Chihuahua, produced casualties on both sides. The crisis escalated; an invasion of Mexico by the United States seemed imminent. The two nations opted instead for diplomatic negotiations. After prolonged and acrimonious talks, the crisis was resolved. The U.S. troops withdrew in February 1917, having failed to capture Villa.

The events of 1916 created a very tense climate along the border, especially in El Paso–Juárez. Following the Santa Ysabel massacre in January 1916, many Americans called for military intervention, while a crowd of one thousand Anglos marched on the Mexican quarter in El Paso vowing to drive out its residents. Authorities averted a major riot by establishing a dividing line between the two groups and ordering a curfew. Some street fighting did break out, however, resulting in injuries to twenty-five Mexicans and an undetermined number of Anglos. Meanwhile, troops from the Juárez garrison were preparing to cross the border to aid their countrymen, while other enraged Mexicans readied themselves to repel any foreign invasion.[12] These incidents blew over without a serious confrontation, but relations were strained anew in March, when a fire broke out in the El Paso jail, injuring or killing approximately thirty-six persons, twelve of whom were Mexicans. Officials said the fire started accidentally, but rumors circulated widely that it had been deliberately set as an anti-Mexican act. Disorders followed in Juárez, during which an American streetcar operator was shot by a Mexican said to have been a uniformed soldier. According to the U.S. customs collector in El Paso, Juárez authorities "quickly quieted all rioting."[13]

In June 1916, the two nations teetered on the brink of war, with Juárez anticipating an invasion daily. Many Mexicans who had taken refuge in El Paso years before returned to Mexico. Some were motivated by a patriotic desire to defend Mexico's territory, others wished to avoid the anticipated fighting near the border. A large portion of Juárez's population reportedly deserted the town. Those civilians who chose to stay and confront the expected invaders armed themselves with shotguns, pistols, axes, and hatchets, while many received rifles distributed by the Juárez mayor. Fortunately, however, no major incident ensued.[14]

Following the international crisis precipitated by Villa in 1916, friction along the border persisted. Bandits continued to raid in Texas, New Mexico, and Arizona, making life hazardous for ranchers and farmers. In 1917, 1918, and 1919 various incursions led to skirmishes that produced casualties. U.S. troops and law enforcement officials repeatedly chased offenders into Mexico, which drew strong protests from the Carranza government.[15] One of the best known of these incidents is the March 1918 raid on E. W. Nevill's ranch, near Van Horn, Texas, which resulted in the deaths of Nevill's son and a Mexican housekeeper. After the attack, U.S. troops from the Eighth Cavalry pursued the raiders several miles into Mexico, where the Americans burned a ranch and killed thirty-three people. The local Carrancista commander notified the U.S. officer in charge that he was sending troops to resist the invaders, but no encounter took place.[16]

Besides bandit raids, two other disturbances had a significant effect on border relations during the late 1910s. At the twin cities of Nogales, Sonora, and Nogales, Arizona, an international battle broke out on August 27, 1918. The problem began when an unidentified person attempted to cross the border without stopping for the required inspection. Strong words quickly led to a shooting match between edgy American and Mexican guards, as each side attempted to exert its authority. Within minutes civilians and soldiers joined the fray, escalating the altercation to a full-scale battle that proved costly to all concerned. Evidently over one hundred Mexicans died, compared to half a dozen American casualties. Several companies of U.S. cavalry and infantry troops participated, including black soldiers from the Tenth Cavalry, who crossed into Mexico at one point in the fighting.[17]

Almost a year later, on June 14, 1919, Villa attacked Juárez in a last-ditch effort to reestablish himself as a military force. Using guerrilla tactics against the Carrancistas, Villa had won several engagements in Chihuahua, including the capture of Ojinaga twice in 1917. In the four-day battle for Juárez, however, his assault was foiled by American intervention. The motive for the Yankee intrusion was the killing of several soldiers and civilians in El Paso by shots from the Mexican side, presumably fired by Villistas. American artillery (situated in El Paso) pounded the Juárez racetrack, where many of Villa's men had camped, while black cavalry and infantrymen crossed the border in an attempt to engage the Villistas directly. The superior weaponry of the Americans prevailed, and Villa fled to the south. Carranza protested the Americans' entry into Mexico, saying that intervention had not been necessary since Villa was already beaten. Whether that was so or not, the Carrancistas certainly benefited from the American action, the government's wounded pride notwithstanding.[18]

The selections that follow include written and oral testimony, along with newspaper accounts, of the troubles in South Texas, the Columbus raid, the Nevill raid, and battles in Ojinaga, Nogales, and Juárez. These accounts vividly depict the tension, hatred, chaos, tragedy, sorrow, and confusion that marked the experience of borderlands people in this period.

NOTES

1. The literature on this subject includes the following works: Lowell L. Blaisdell, *The Desert Revolution: Baja California, 1911* (Madison: University of Wisconsin Press, 1962); James D. Cockcroft, *Intellectual Precursors of the Mexican Revolution* (Austin: University of Texas Press, 1968); Juan Gómez-Quiñones, *Sembradores: Ricardo Flores Magón y El Partido Liberal Mexicano: A Eulogy and Critique* (Los Angeles: Chicano Studies Center, UCLA, Monograph No. 5, 1973); Peter V. N. Henderson, *Mexican Exiles in the Borderlands* (El Paso: Texas Western Press, Southwestern Series, No. 58, 1979).

2. For a survey of U.S.-Mexican relations during the period, see Howard F. Cline, *The United States and Mexico,* 2nd edition (New York: Atheneum, 1963), part 2.

3. Most scholars see the Plan de San Diego as an extension of the Mexican Revolution, but there is disagreement over the responsibility for authorship. Some blame President Venustiano Carranza, who allegedly used the raids associated with the Plan to bring about U.S. recognition of his government. Others see deposed President Victoriano Huerta, who supposedly was trying to make a comeback, as the culprit. Another explanation holds that a Texas Ranger originated the Plan to cause problems for Carranza. See Charles C. Cumberland, "Border Raids in the Lower Rio Grande Valley, 1915," *Southwestern Historical Quarterly* 57:3 (January 1954): 286–311; Allen Gerlach, "Conditions along the Border—1915: The Plan de San Diego," *New Mexico Historical Review* 43:3 (July 1968): 195–212; Juan Gómez-Quinones, "Plan de San Diego Reviewed," *Aztlán* 1:1 (Spring 1970): 124–32; William Hager, "The Plan de San Diego: Unrest on the Texas Border in 1915," *Arizona and the West* 5:4 (Winter 1963): 327–36; Charles H. Harris and Louis R. Saddler, "The Plan de San Diego and the Mexican–United States Crisis of 1916: A Reexamination," *Hispanic American Historical Review* 58:3 (August 1978): 381–408; James A. Sandos, "The Plan de San Diego: War and Diplomacy on the Texas Border, 1915–1916," *Arizona and the West* 14:1 (Spring 1972): 5–24.

4. *Investigation of Mexican Affairs*, Senate Document 285, 66th Congress, 2nd Session (Washington, D.C., 1920), pp. 1243–1250.

5. Ibid.

6. Rodolfo Rocha, "The Influence of the Mexican Revolution on the Mexico-Texas Border, 1910–1916" (Ph.D. diss., Texas Tech University, 1981); Rodolfo Rocha, "Banditry in the Lower Rio Grande Valley of Texas, 1915," *Studies in History* 6 (1976): 55–73.

7. For a critical view of the Texas Rangers see Julian Samora, Joe Bernal, and Albert Peña, *Gunpowder Justice: A Reassessment of the Texas Rangers* (Notre Dame, Ind.: University of Notre Dame Press, 1979). The classic, fa-

vorable assessment of the Rangers is Walter Prescott Webb, *The Texas Rangers: A Century of Frontier Defense* (New York: Houghton Mifflin, 1935; Austin: University of Texas Press, 1965).

8. *World's Work* (January 1917); quoted in Rodolfo Acuña, *Occupied America: A History of Chicanos*, 2nd edition (New York: Harper and Row, 1981), p. 308.

9. *Proceedings of the Joint Committee of the Senate and House in the Investigation of the Texas State Ranger Force, 1919* (Texas State Archives).

10. Harris and Saddler, "The Plan de San Diego."

11. Seventeen Americans and over one hundred Mexicans perished at Columbus. Before the attack, rumors circulated for days that Villa was about to launch an offensive along the border; thus, the actual raid was not a total surprise. Available evidence indicates that Villa led the incursion, but his reasons for doing so are still a matter of debate. Among the major motives attributed to Villa are the following: (1) revenge against the United States for recognizing and supporting Venustiano Carranza; (2) revenge against dishonest American arms dealers; (3) desire to capture arms, supplies, and food; (4) desire to enlist German support in return for inflicting damage on the United States; and (5) desire to disrupt an alleged agreement between Presidents Carranza and Wilson that would turn Mexico into a virtual U.S. protectorate. The fifth explanation (which is also the most recently advanced) has been carefully documented and seems the most persuasive. In all likelihood, Villa's behavior was motivated by a combination of these factors. The Columbus Raid has led to a large body of literature. The best place to begin is Friedrich Katz, "Pancho Villa and the Attack on Columbus, New Mexico," *American Historical Review* 83:1 (February 1978): 101–30, which details the protectorate thesis; see also Katz, *The Secret War in Mexico: Europe, The United States, and the Mexican Revolution* (Chicago: University of Chicago Press, 1981), pp. 303–7.

12. *El Paso Herald*, January 14, 1916, p. 1. Portions of this and the next paragraph are reprinted from Oscar J. Martínez, *Border Boom Town: Ciudad Juárez since 1848* (Austin: University of Texas Press), pp. 39–40, by permission of the University of Texas Press.

13. *Records of the Department of State Relating to Internal Affairs of Mexico, 1910–1929* (U.S. National Archives, Microcopy No. M-274), 812.00/17095.

14. *El Paso Herald*, June, 1916.

15. Clarence C. Clendenen, *Blood on the Border* (London: Macmillan, 1969), p. 344.

16. Ibid., pp. 344–46.

17. Ibid., pp. 346–49.

18. Ibid., pp. 351–55.

144

"We will rise in arms against . . . the United States."

—Plan of San Diego
(January 6, 1915)*

Historians disagree on the origin, authorship, and base of support for the Plan of San Diego, but it is clear that conditions prevailed in South Texas that would prompt Mexicans and Mexican Americans to rebel against the dominant Anglo Americans. The extreme measures called for in some of the articles yield insights into the level of racial hatred that existed at the time. A modification of the Plan in February 1915, emphasized the elimination of exploitation of minorities and the promotion of socialist objectives; an undated manifesto enlarged the territory targeted for conquest.** In view of the Third World ideology embraced by U.S. ethnic minorities in the late 1960s, the Plan's declaration of support for Indians, blacks, and Asians is especially significant.

We, who in turn sign our names, assembled in the revolutionary plot of San Diego, Texas, solemnly promise each other on our word of honor that we will fulfill and cause to be fulfilled and complied with, all the clauses and provisions stipulated in this document and execute the or-

*Translated copy, *Records of the Department of State Relating to the Internal Affairs of Mexico, 1910–1929,* 812.00/1583.

**See James A. Sandos, "The Plan of San Diego: War and Diplomacy on the Texas Border, 1915–1916," *Arizona and the West* 14:1 (Spring 1972): 9–10.

ders and the wishes emanating from the provisional directorate of this movement and recognize as military chief of the same Mr. ————, guaranteeing with our lives the faithful accomplishment what is here agreed upon.

1. On the 20th day of February, 1915, at 2 o'clock in the morning, we will rise in arms against the Government and country of the United States and North America, one as all and all as one, proclaiming the liberty of the individuals of the black race and its independence of Yankee tyranny, which has held us in iniquitous slavery since remote times; and at the same time and in the same manner we will proclaim the independence and segregation of the States bordering on the Mexican nation, which are: Texas, New Mexico, Arizona, Colorado, and Upper California, of which States the Republic of Mexico was robbed in a most perfidious manner by North American imperialism.

2. In order to render the foregoing clause effective, the necessary army corps will be formed under the immediate command of military leaders named by the supreme revolutionary congress of San Diego, Texas, which shall have full power to designate a supreme chief who shall be at the head of said army. The banner which shall guide us in this enterprise shall be red, with a white diagonal fringe, and bearing the following inscription: "Equality and Independence"; and none of the subordinate leaders or subalterns shall use any other flag (except only the white for signals). The aforesaid army shall be known by the name of "Liberating Army for Races and Peoples."

3. Each one of the chiefs will do his utmost by whatever means possible, to get possession of the arms and funds of the cities which he has beforehand been designated to capture in order that our cause may be provided with resources to continue the fight with better success, the said leaders each being required to render an account of everything to his superiors, in order that the latter may dispose of it in the proper manner.

4. The leader who may take a city must immediately name and appoint municipal authorities, in order that they may preserve order and assist in every way possible the revolutionary movement. In case the capital of any State which we are endeavoring to liberate be captured, there will be named in the same manner superior municipal authorities for the same purpose.

146

5. It is strictly forbidden to hold prisoners, either special prisoners (civilians) or soldiers; and the only time that should be spent in dealing with them is that which is absolutely necessary to demand funds (loans) of them; and whether these demands be successful or not, they shall be shot immediately, without any pretext.

6. Every stranger who shall be found armed and who can not prove his right to carry arms, shall be summarily executed, regardless of race or nationality.

7. Every North American over 16 years of age shall be put to death, and only the aged men, the women and children shall be respected. And on no account shall the traitors to our race be respected or spared.

8. The Apaches of Arizona, as well as the Indians (red skins) of the territory shall be given every guarantee, and their lands which have been taken from them shall be returned to them, to the end that they may assist us in the cause which we defend.

9. All appointments and grades in our army which are exercised by subordinate officers (subalterns) shall be examined (recognized) by the superior officers. There shall likewise be recognized the grades of leaders of other complots which may not be connected with this, and who may wish to co-operate with us; also those who may affiliate with us later.

10. The movement having gathered force, and once having possessed ourselves of the States above alluded to, we shall proclaim them an independent republic, later requesting, if it be thought expedient, annexation to Mexico without concerning ourselves at that time about the form of government which may control the destinies of the common mother country.

11. When we shall have obtained independence for the negroes we shall grant them a banner which they themselves shall be permitted to select, and we shall aid them in obtaining six States of the American Union, which States border upon those already mentioned, and they may from these six States form a republic and they may therefore be independent.

12. None of the leaders shall have power to make terms with the enemy without first communicating with the superior officers of the army, bearing in mind that this is a war without quarter, nor shall any leader enroll in his ranks any stranger unless said stranger belongs to the Latin, the negro or the Japanese race.

13. It is understood that none of the members of this complot (or any

147

one who may come in later) shall upon the definite triumph of the cause which we defend, fail to recognize their superiors, nor shall they aid others who with bastard designs may endeavor to destroy what has been accomplished with such great work.

14. As soon as possible each local society (junta) shall nominate delegates, who shall meet at a time and place beforehand designated, for the purpose of nominating a permanent directorate of the revolutionary movement. At this meeting shall be determined and worked out in detail the powers and duties of the permanent directorate and this revolutionary plan may be revised or amended.

15. It is understood among those who may follow this movement that we will carry as a singing voice the independence of the negroes, placing obligations upon both races, and that on no account shall we accept aid, either moral or pecuniary, from the government of Mexico, and it need not consider itself under any obligations in this, our movement.

EQUALITY AND INDEPENDENCE.

> "Marauder bands have crossed from Mexico."
>
> —Weekly Report*

During the years of crisis, the U.S. State Department assembled comprehensive weekly reports concerning disturbances, military movements, and other troublesome activity along the border. The information derived from various sources, including local military commanders. Below are abstracts from the report prepared for one week in July 1915.

BROWNSVILLE, TEXAS:

Telegram dated July 8 from Judge H. L. Yates, Cameron County, Texas:

Marauder bands have crossed from Mexico into Cameron County, penetrating as far as fifteen or twenty miles from the Rio Grande. They have stolen horses and other equipment and terrorized American citizens. The people of Brownsville and other towns of the Rio Grande Valley are practically helpless against an attack by a strong armed force. We have less than three hundred American soldiers in Brownsville and no other town has half as many. There are strong armed forces of Mexicans across the river and within striking distance of any of the better towns on the American side. We regard the danger very real and unless we can interpose the moral effect of a large American force the danger will certainly materialize. On behalf of

*Records of the Department of State Relating to the Internal Affairs of Mexico, 1910–1929, 812.00/15517.

citizens of Cameron County and Lower Rio Grande Valley, I ask that you and as many as one thousand or fifteen hundred troops be sent to Brownsville.

Radiogram dated July 9 from Colonel Blocksom at Brownsville:

I went to Santa Rosa ranch about twelve miles north and east of Harlingen. Mexicans there said a mounted party of from four to six came to the ranch about eleven o'clock the night before. Thought they were armed though it was dark. Left in a few minutes without any disturbance; they took nothing; they went north. I went to several other ranches between Santa Rosa and Harlingen but nothing had been seen of the marauders. County officials are scouring the country in that vicinity. I saw two autos filled with them yesterday afternoon. So far as I can learn they have seen nothing of the marauders. I cannot help believing people's alarm largely created by the stir that has been made in the matter by officials and the more influential citizens.

DEL RIO, TEXAS:

Report dated July 10 from the commanding officer at Del Rio:

All Carrancista soldiers have left their camp opposite Langtry, and have moved in the direction of Las Vacas. About 500 of Villa's troops arrived in and near Las Vacas on the evening of July 9th. Carranza force commanded by Col. Ramón Muzquiz appeared at the San Miguel Ranch, 60 miles southwest of Las Vacas. This ranch is operated by the American firm of Meier and Rose. The Carrancistas killed three ranch employees, captured the others, and seized all saddle horses on the place. The number of horses seized was between 60 and 70. This force is the one previously mentioned as having left the vicinity opposite Langtry, Texas.

Report dated July 12 from the commanding officer at Del Rio:

At about 12:30 P.M. today a force of approximately 200 Carrancistas commanded by Col. Ramón Muzquiz, attacked and captured Las Vacas. The Villista force consisted of twenty-seven men. Eight of these escaped to the U.S. side and were arrested by men of the Las Vacas ferry detachment. They are now being held under guard by U.S. troops in Del Rio. One horse and one saddle were taken at the same time.

The Carrancistas requested that their one wounded be brought to the

150

U.S. side for treatment. In view of existing orders and the fact that they made no attempt to care for wounded of the opposite side this was refused until instructions could be had from higher authority. As there was great likelihood that the Villistas would get together a sufficient force to attempt to retake Las Vacas, steps were taken to prevent the crowd of Americans who desired to go into Las Vacas from [going there, thus preventing them from] endangering their lives and causing international complications. No one was injured on this side of the border, all civilians being required to remain outside any possible danger zone. A few shots struck on the American side; these were fired at the Villistas as they swam the river. Patrols are being made in the vicinity of the ferry. It is thought that by tomorrow conditions will be normal.

Report dated July 13 from the commanding officer at Del Rio:

In compliance with telegraphic instructions, the eight Villista soldiers who crossed from Las Vacas have been turned over to the immigration authorities. The officer in charge of the immigration service is taking them to Eagle Pass, for deportation to Piedras Negras.

The horse and saddle mentioned in my report dated yesterday have been turned over to the collector of customs as no duty has been paid, and no one has claimed the property.

The Carrancista force has left Las Vacas and withdrawn a short distance into the interior. They are expecting an attack from the Villistas any time. Information has been received since report of yesterday that their losses were five killed and one wounded. The Villistas lost eighteen killed.

Conditions normal today.

NOGALES, ARIZONA:

Report dated July 10 from the commanding officer at Nogales:

The subject of possible intervention by the United States is said to be a matter of daily discussion at Maytorona's headquarters. The officials there voice the opinion that the American government contemplates no intervention else why permit the exportation to Mexico of the large quantities of arms and ammunition which in case of intervention would be used against the American forces crossing the boundary. They claim that Americans do not understand Mexican patriotism and honor, and that any attempt at intervention would call for the utmost resistance in their power, and while they would ultimately be defeated by the overwhelming forces

America could send against them the cost to America would be far greater than is contemplated, for the warring factions would unite against the foreign invader and offer a resistance far beyond American conception of the power of Mexican patriotism. This, however, is the viewpoint of men holding the reins of government. The land and property owners, commercial interests, and the great mass of the population are weary of the strife, the insecure and unsettled conditions, and will welcome a change. In Sonora this is particularly true for the country is overrun with two or three bands of Callesistas from Agua Prieta and small bands of Yaqui Indians, who are robbing and killing whenever they appear. Americans who have been traveling in Sonora mingling with the people the past two weeks claim the sentiment among these Mexicans toward American intervention has undergone material change and that in personal, confidential conversation they openly recognize it as the only hope of peace and security for life and property.

> "I noticed that the train began to
> bump and slow up."
>
> —John I. Kleiber*

*On October 18, 1915, a band of Mexicans derailed and
attacked a passenger train outside of Brownsville, Texas, in
one of the most violent raids in the Lower Rio Grande Valley.
The murder of several Anglo Americans enraged the Texas
Rangers, who quickly executed four Mexican suspects the very
next day. John I. Kleiber, a local district attorney, provides
an inside view of the attack. He also reflects on racial relations
along the border, offering somewhat paternalistic but interesting views toward Mexicans.*

I was returning to Brownsville from Corpus Christi, where I had been
attending court for a month or so. We were within a very few miles of
Brownsville, due about 11 P.M., and we were a few minutes late. Besides
the engine and tender and express car, the train consisted of two passenger coaches. The forward coach was divided into compartments, the
forward compartment being the negro compartment, and the rear compartment the smoker; the second coach we called the day coach, or
ladies coach. I was seated in the smoker on the right-hand side going
south. Just ahead of me were two drummers, and across from them
were two soldiers and an ex-soldier. The two soldiers in uniform were

*Testimony given in San Antonio in 1920. *Investigation of Mexican Affairs*, Senate
Document 285, 66th Congress, 2nd Session (Washington, D.C.: 1920), pp. 1269–82.

153

Corpl. Laymon and Corpl. McBee, both of the Sixth Cavalry, and with them was a man who I learned was John W. Sword, who had either been discharged from the service in the same regiment or was on furlough, or sick. He was in citizens clothes. Immediately back of them, across the aisle from me, was Pvt. Brashear, likewise of the Sixth Cavalry, in uniform. Back of them on a double seat was a Mexican family, an elderly man and wife and another woman, and a young boy perhaps sixteen or eighteen years of age. Almost across from the corner was seated H. J. Wallace, an ex-ranger and Dr. Edgar S. McCain, the state quarantine officer stationed at Brownsville.

I noticed that the train began to bump and slow up. I felt it slacken speed and began to bump quite violently, and listed—to use the nautical term—to my side. That will explain something that I shall state later on in my testimony, in a way very relevant. At that moment the train stopped. Scattering shots and then irregular volleys broke out and increased in volume. They shouted, *"Viva Carranza!" "Viva Luis de la Rosa!" "Viva Aniceto Pizaña!"* I remember that distinctly, and shortly afterward I spoke of it to others who were on the train and they heard exactly the same cry. They repeated again the *"Viva Carranza"* a number of times.*

It was a warm night and the windows were up, as well as the curtains, and everyone went to the floor in between the seats. You could hear bullets whistling through the car. I afterward learned Dr. McCain and Mr. Wallace, and I think, the boy, took refuge in the toilet. I could hear them getting aboard the train and passing to and fro. I had only been lying there a few minutes when I saw Brashear, the man across from me, stick his head out into the aisle, and a look of intense terror came into his face. I was only a short distance from him. He threw his hands up and his eyes became set and he gasped. Just then I saw the mouth of a rifle go by, and I saw the flash. I saw the blood spurt, and he fell. I laid there, and the firing continued. The blood from Brashear had come down in a pool and I was covered with blood. I had on a blue serge coat and a pair of summer linen trousers. The next thing I knew a large man with a common Mexican bandana handkerchief, made into

*President Venustiano Carranza sympathized with the Mexican insurrection in South Texas; Luis de la Rosa and Aniceto Pizaña were two Mexican Americans who became leaders among the raiders.

a mask—there were holes in it for his eyes and it covered the upper part of his face down to his mouth—came to where I was lying and stuck his gun a number of times into my upper arm, punched me with the gun and said, "Give me money, give me money." He doubtless thought I was grievously wounded, else I am satisfied that he would have shot me. I reached and gave him my purse from my pocket, and he saw a fob and he said, "Give me watch," and I handed him my watch. By that time the leader was evidently standing at the rear door of the coach and he kept calling to them, "*Venganse*," "*Venganse*." He cursed them in Spanish. He used a number of Mexican obscene terms. By that time this fellow had observed my shoes. I had on a pair of tan shoes much the style of the service shoe worn by the military, practically a new pair. He said, "Give me shoes." Whenever he spoke to me I would reply in Spanish. My experience in Mexico was that whenever they found you spoke Spanish—it is but natural in any country— you are always accepted with a little more degree of frankness. I answered him in Spanish, "*Tome, tome*." "Take it." He laid his rifle to one side and started to unlace my shoes. Then the leader became a little more urgent, and cursed him in Spanish, and I kicked off the shoe. I unlaced the other one and kicked it off and he picked up the shoes and picked up his rifle. By that time I could hear them retreating, hollering for one another to come on, that relief might arrive. They were badly rattled, and they then left the train. I glanced over to this man Brashear. Up to that moment I had thought he was dead. He saw that I was alive and began to move his finger, pointed to his mouth, and I could hear moans.

Dr. McCain was in intense agony, and so was Wallace and the others, and the Mexican woman was excited. I pulled out my drinking cup. I told one of the men to pull down the shades. The car was a perfect shambles, blood from one end to the other. I got to the water cooler and I saw Dr. McCain right in the aisle on his back. He recognized me and said, "Mr Kleiber, they have got me." I said, "Where?" He said, "They have got me in the abdomen." He called for water, and I got him water, and Mr. Wallace also. By that time they had quieted down, and the conductor came back. The brakeman had jumped off the train and was going north to Alamita for relief; he got in touch with someone and sent word into town. Just ahead of Brashear in the car was Corpl. McBee. He was murdered. They shot him through the head. They took his shoes, and took the shoes of Brashear. In other words, they seemed to

155

have a weakness for these military tan shoes, and those were the three whose shoes they took, the two soldiers and myself. Wallace was wounded in the shoulder, and one of his fingers was shot off.

Wallace stated that he and Dr. McCain were seated in the last seat across from the toilet. When the train bumped and the shots rang out, Dr. McCain got out of the seat, looked around, and went into the toilet. They fired and Wallace went into the toilet and the young Mexican boy got into the toilet as well, and closed the door. Dr. McCain stood on the toilet seat. They came to the door and battered on. Either the Mexican boy or Wallace opened the door and as they did so they dragged the Mexican boy out. He told them that he was a Mexican and that there were two *gringos* in there. The minute he said there were two *gringos*— I will say *gringos* is a term for Americans that the Mexican uses in contempt just as many Americans do "greasers"—they immediately fired into the toilet. As I understand it, Wallace was standing on the lavatory, and he was shot in the shoulder. The shot that struck Dr. McCain went through the door. He evidently must have been standing, because it was quite high in the door. They killed McBee; they wounded Brashear; they thought I was mortally wounded. They killed the engineer; that is, he was caught in the engine as it turned over in the ditch. They took everything out of these two cars that was portable, baggage, luggage, etc., from everyone on that train, except the Mexicans. I heard the Mexican woman and man pleading with them telling them that they were Mexicans, and their reply was, "*Mexicanos no, gringos nomas.*" As they came into the car they saw the soldiers in uniform and it evidently enraged them because they began to cry, "*Maten los soldados, Americanos cabrones,*" that is, "Kill the soldiers," using this obscene term. In the rear coach they robbed a gentleman from Chicago of his watch, his chain, his ring, and what jewelry he had on him and money. They were about to shoot him when Mr. Edelstein, a Jewish merchant from Brownsville, said to them that this man was a German. They did not touch Edelstein, they didn't take anything from him. There was an American lady returning from San Antonio in an invalid condition at the time. They robbed her of a diamond ring or two and money and what jewelry she had. There was a Mexican lady whose husband is a merchant in Brownsville. I noticed when I went into the car afterward that she had on considerable jewelry. They did not take a thing from her at all, and in fact stated to her that she need have no fear, they were only going to rob Americans. She told me that and expressed indignation. I will say that for the lady.

I was born and raised [on the border] and my people were pioneers in that country. My paternal grandfather came there in 1848 and my father came there in his youth; my wife's father came there after that time, and our people have lived there ever since. My father and my grandfather and all of his people did business with those Mexicans. I was raised amongst them, and have lived amongst them, and I can say without boasting that no one knows the Mexican any better than I do, and few know them as well. Without boasting, but an actual fact, I also know them, I think, to a great extent better than they do themselves. The Mexican, the ordinary Mexican, if treated properly by those who know how to treat him, know how to handle him, is a law-respecting and a law-fearing man. It is only when he is misled by those in whom he unfortunately has confidence and he should not have confidence, and also by his own patriotism. They are an intensely patriotic people. If any of the Mexicans that reside on this [U.S.] side, that were born and raised here, were misled in this thing or went astray, it was because they were deceived by people of their own kind that had what I call a superficial education, whose head was educated and not his heart. That is the trouble today in Mexico, of the 15,000,000 people down there, 13,500,000 are absolutuely illiterate, and the other 1,500,000, the ruling class, they are educated in their brains and not in their heart. When these raids started, these poor Mexicans were as much astounded and were as much against it in heart as I or any law-abiding citizen.

I will say this for them, that where they could aid us or were in a position to help us without putting themselves or their wife and little children in fear of life, that they did so. If the average Mexican in Cameron County or in Willacy County failed to do what we considered he should have done affirmatively to aid the officers of the law throughout that awful period, I am satisfied it was for fear of his own life and those that he had around his little house. I have known of instances and instances, and I am satisfied that other officers will say the same thing, that Mexicans helped us perhaps not a great deal, but helped us all that they could, because it was in their heart.

I say these people, Mexicans of the lower class especially, were very much frightened and wrought up. Due to fear they may have had because of their nationality and race that they might suffer at the hands of the Americans for what other fellow citizens of theirs had done, they listened to propaganda and advice to get out, and there was an exodus. There is no other word for it. They left Cameron County by the thousands. I saw them and everyone in Brownsville saw them come through in their wagons with their little belongings. They sold what they had, that is, what they could not carry with them, for a mere nothing, to get out of the country.

That is one of the things that men like myself who were born and raised right there among these people have had to contend with. Our every effort had been and will continue to be to bring back the not only harmonious but almost affectionate relations that existed between the two races in that lower country. I traveled that country for years when it was sparsely settled by every mode of conveyance known. You would travel miles before you met anyone at all, and when you did strike a place it was some little Mexican *jacal*. No matter where you went, when you went, or how you went, armed or unarmed, whether you carried food with you or whether you did not, whether you had money with you or whether you had not, those people would take you in and share the last tortilla with you, or a cup of coffee if they had it. And if you offered them money they would almost with dignity but with the grace that is peculiar to that race decline it. I have traveled all over that country without even a copper.

"The reasonable conclusion seems to be that these men have been sent to keep up the trouble along the Texas border."

—J. B. Rogers*

A lull in the border raids during late 1915 and early 1916 brought temporary peace to the Lower Rio Grande Valley, but rumors persisted that a Mexican invasion of South Texas was imminent. Seeking information on alleged preparations for the attack, U.S. Department of Justice Special Agent J. B. Rogers went to Tamaulipas on an undercover mission. That he was able to move about without restriction and talk with a great variety of people about sensitive matters suggests that anti-Americanism in Mexico at the time was less than what Americans perceived. Rogers wrote the following report about his trip across the border.

On December 23rd, I went into México, under authority of the Department of Justice for the purpose of making certain investigations *under cover*. It was necessary, of course, to make it appear that my mission was purely on personal business. I did not consider it prudent to make notes, and therefore depended solely on memory, which is not very satisfactory when exact details as to names, dates, etc. are desired.

*Department of State. Records of the American and Mexican Joint Commission, 1916. RG 43, Box 1, Memorandum No. 11. National Archives, Washington, D.C.

159

My first stop was at Monterrey, México, where I arrived Christmas Eve. The next morning I set out to pay my respects to the U.S. consul general. The streets were full of beggars; hungry children almost mobbed you. When I came within a block of the consulate, I could go no further, the crowd of poor people completely blocking the streets about the building. The consul afterward told me the crowd was larger than ever before and that they were nearly as insistent as they were the time they stormed the house to kill him when the U.S. troops landed at Vera Cruz. And he admitted that he supposed many of them were the same. One of the purposes of my visit to México was to study the Plan of San Diego from the inside. Colonel J. C. Flores, an officer of the Carranza army, whom I met at the Continental Hotel talked quite freely with me about this revolutionary movement. Colonel Peña, a friend of Colonel Flores was present. They both impressed me as being entirely unconscious of giving any information that was new. They talked as though it were well known the Carrancistas were actively prompting it. Colonel Flores said that many of these leaders did not know anything about the United States. They thought it was all like the part they had seen along the Rio Grande. Colonel Flores said, however, that since the recognition of Carranza, the activity had gradually diminished and that he thought it had ceased altogether. But he added that the ignorant and more desperate subordinates, having once been encouraged by their superiors, would undertake to plunder the border if an opportunity were given them. Colonel Flores says that Carranza took away with him some of the leading spirits of his movement, and he named especially as one of those Colonel Rodríguez.

From the common soldiers, who spend much of their time sitting on the plaza, I could get no information about the proposed invasion. The most impressive fact gotten from them is their indifference to the progress of events and their hopelessness of the early return of peace. Among those with whom I talked were a Negro and an Indian who called themselves *citizen soldiers*. The Indian, whose name is Salazar surprised me by saying "Democracy! Democracy! What the Devil do we know about Democracy." Many of these soldiers now on garrison duty are former Villistas and it is easy to see that their hearts are not very firmly converted to Carranza. They contrast the treatment they received as Villistas with what they get now. With Villa they say they had three suits of clothes, a sufficient allowance of food, and two pesos a day "*pura*

160

plata," while now they get only one suit of clothes, no allowance of food, and only fourteen bits a day *"billum billetas."* This is the name used to express the worthlessness of the provisional money. This incident is mentioned to show how weak is the hold Carranza has on his soldiers and how easy a division against him would be. All the way down to Tampico, I found many former Villa men and I failed to find one whose conversion was very genuine.

On December 26th I called on Consul General Hanna and learned from him that there was at one time considerable activity in regard to the proposed invasion of the United States and that the German consul at Monterrey was evidently interested in the matter. The consul general said that parties had come to him and offered to collect the evidence for him but that he had not had them do so because he knew that it would get the consular service in bad and ruin its efficiency with the Carranza government. Therefore he could not give me definite information; but he told me that Vice Consul Robertson could give me a few leads, which he had collected before the consul general had stopped him, because he did not think it good policy to make the investigation through the consular office.

Mr. Robertson referred me to the Spanish consul and the Italian consul. I learned from these officers that members of their colonies had been approached by Carrancista officers soliciting funds for this expedition. These men had been told by these officers that the German consul was assisting them with money and munitions. The Spanish consul and the Italian consul were convinced that those things were true but they would not give the names of their colonists who had been approached, because, as they said, it might subject them to great danger. These consuls both said they had positive evidence of the activity of the German consul in the connection but that they could not with prudence give the evidence first hand. Both say that there has not been so much activity during the past month. The German consul Mr. Bouchard has been away visiting in California.

Mr. J. J. Gallaher, an American business man, living in Monterrey, says the Germans do not treat him like they used to. Mr. Gallaher speaks the German language, his wife is of German descent, and the Germans have always been very friendly to him. Recently, he decided to join the German Club. When he made known his wish to a German friend who had once solicited his membership, he was advised not to

161

put in his application as he would be rejected because the Germans now have some secrets of a peculiar nature and did not want anyone but pure Germans about their gatherings. I met also Dr. Ferguson of Linares, in Monterrey. He told me that his town had been visited by a member of the firm of C. Holck & Co., of Monterrey, who had approached certain Carrancista officers there in reference to the invasion of Texas. In a subsequent visit to Linares, I was told by Colonel Ruís that he had been offered money to assist in the invasion.

On December 28th, I went to Victoria. One of the first men who attracted my attention there was Alberto Cabrera, who assassinated Judge Stanley Welch at Rio Grande City. He was tried, convicted, and sentenced to a life term in the Texas Penitentiary. He escaped from a convict camp and came to México. He is now a captain in the Carranza army. I think Judge Edwards, county judge of Hidalgo County, also knows Cabrera and that he knows him well.

From my friends in Victoria I learned that there is no activity in the Plan of San Diego, but that a few months ago there was and that the purpose then was to force the United States to recognize Carranza. Having accomplished that purpose as they think, activity has ceased. Among those to whom I talked, are Don Jesus Cardenas, presidente of Victoria, Eng. Martíanamo Villareal, Juan Salazar, Guerinimo Rodriguez, and Don Zeferino Romero. The impression is that when the First Chief was recognized he pulled off his generals who had been assigned to this particular work.

I learned at Victoria that Luis de la Rosa* had been there with General Nafarrate and that they had gone to Tampico. I also heard that Aniceto Pizano* had been at Ximenes, and that he was recruiting men to make an invasion of Texas. Captain Saldivar told me this and also that Pizano and de la Rosa had a list of the names of the rangers, sheriffs, and all the citizens who had taken part in the border troubles. I went to Ximenes, which is thirty miles from the railroad, but arrived after Pizano had left there. Through confidential information I ascertained that Pizano left San Fernando about the 8th of January to go to the Texas border. There can be no reasonable doubt that Pizano was recruiting in this section. This is the home of Governor Luis Caballero. He lived here

---

*De la Rosa was the chief of operations and Pizano (correct spelling Pizaña) was the chief of the general staff of the Plan of San Diego revolutionary forces.

162

before he became great and rich. It would be easy for the governor to apprehend anyone here.

Going on to Tampico I stayed at the same hotel as Luis de la Rosa and General Nafarrate, the Hotel Imperial. I frequently saw these two men together. Some say that de la Rosa is a member of Nafarrate's staff. The facts here recited should throw a strong light on the professed friendship and co-operation of the *de facto* government. General Carranza is reported to have told the governor of Texas that he would deliver de la Rosa and Pizano to the American authorities if he could find them. That he can find them is certain. That he has not delivered them is equally certain. Equally certain is the duplicity of the First Chief. I followed de la Rosa from Tampico to Victoria and saw him there in company with the *jefe los armas*, with his buckskin suit on, the hero of the day. From Victoria, I followed him to Monterrey, from which place he went to Camargo on the Texas border. The indications were that he was expecting to make a meeting with Pizano and his men who left San Fernando on horseback about the 8th of January, this being the 11th. San Fernando is about ninety miles from Brownsville. The reasonable conclusion seems to be that these men have been sent to keep up the trouble along the Texas border. Carranza took with him into the interior of México General Murguia, General Madero and Colonel Rodríguez. In order to pull Nafarrate off he had to promote him to a brigadier general, and give him a more lucrative field around Tampico.

It is not a pleasure to me to point out these dangers because I am not hopeful of the solution of this Mexican problem by the Mexicans themselves. I have been called an interventionist. This is not true. I am opposed to intervention; but I cannot close my eyes to facts that seem to me to make the salvation of México by México hopeless, and I will not misrepresent the situation to my government.

J. B. Rogers
February 5, 1916

"The Rangers have adopted a policy that is a shame and disgrace to my native state and to my American citizenship."

—J. T. Canales (1877–?)*

Mexican Americans in the Texas Lower Rio Grande Valley lived in constant fear during the latter 1910s when the Texas Rangers used gestapo tactics in their pursuit of raiders and bandits. The Rangers killed, wounded, or violated the civil rights of countless innocent people unfortunate enough to cross the path of this notorious law-enforcement group. In a statement given during the 1919 state investigation of the Rangers, representative J. T. Canales explained the circumstances that started the police repression against people of Mexican origin.

I have lived in Brownsville and its vicinity since 1904 and am well acquainted with conditions there. I have known the Rangers since I was born; in fact, my home, La Cabra Ranch, has been a haven for the Rangers. They stayed there, were stationed there, came there at all hours, got our horses, got our meals there, and they got our services. I have known among the Ranger forces some of the noblest and best men that I know. Captain Hughes, Captain Rogers, Captain Wright,

*Testimony given in 1919. *Proceedings of the Joint Committee of the Senate and the House in the Investigation of the Texas State Ranger Force* (Austin, Texas, 1919), pp. 856–74. Texas State Archives.

and various other individuals. At that time they gave us protection. They were a capable set of men, and did not need any restriction because their own conscience was a self-restraint and law. In 1915, so far as my recollection goes, is when the first general outrages perpetrated by Rangers began. The service began to degenerate since that time. I will describe the condition of my town and my country about that time.

Unquestionably what we call the bandit troubles had their origin in German propaganda. I have in my home in Brownsville letters written to clients of mine threatening their lives if they did not join in the band [of raiders] and stating that they [the raiders] were financed by the Germans, that they [the clients] need not be afraid because there were 70,000 German soldiers in Texas who would take up arms with them. This condition existed just immediately prior to the bandit trouble. I handed those letters to my sheriff, Captain Vann, and consulted with him. At that time they [the law officials] never believed there was any truth in the German propaganda. Since that time we have established beyond question that German propaganda was initiated for the purpose of forcing either an intervention or a war between the United States and Mexico, so as to prevent the United States from entering the European war.*

There was a great deal of dissatisfaction in wages. Some Mexicans were not paid by men who employed them. Some of those Mexicans were beaten and mistreated by what I supposed, or who were reputed to be good men in my country, who took advantage of the conditions so as not to pay them, and in that manner agitated the friction between the two races. There was nothing but general stealing—they [Mexicans] stole saddles, arms and ammunition, and horses, but no life of an American in any way was threatened. It was about the latter part of June 1915, or the first part of July, that the first trouble commenced. [On July 28,] Daniel Hinojosa, who is now in the Ranger Service, and Frank Carr, a deputy sheriff of Captain Vann, arrested a man by the name of Rodolfo Muñoz nineteen or twenty miles from Brownsville, at eleven o'clock at night. They could have taken Muñoz to Brownsville in the morning. They could have taken him on the noon train, or on the

*German revolutionary intrigue in the borderlands is the subject of Michael C. Meyer's article, "The Mexican-German Conspiracy of 1915," *The Americas* 23:1 (July 1966): 76–89.

afternoon train; they could have taken him safely in an automobile in the afternoon, but they started with him about eleven o'clock. It was generally known that Muñoz was in concert with certain citizens, among them some leading citizens not only of San Benito but of Harlingen. [On the way they were met by a band who] took the prisoner from them and after torturing him, they hung him. That incident immediately had this effect: every person who was charged with a crime refused to be arrested, because they did not believe that the officers of the law would give them the protection guaranteed to them by the Constitution and the laws of this State. The immediate effect, then, was that all men who were charged with crime would refuse to submit to arrest.

The next incident took place about a week later. It was called the Las Teulitas fight. Jeff Scribner led a party of United States soldiers and deputies to the Pizaña Ranch, near Las Teulitas Ranch. They arrived there early in the morning. Scribner had it in for one of the Pizaña boys, and Aniceto Pizaña afterward became one of the leading bandits, but at that time he resided at his own ranch. The purpose the soldiers had in being there was not to follow bandits but with regard to some private matter, some private animosity between Jeff Scribner on the one hand and Pizaña on the other. They were there with a company of soldiers and surrounded the house. The Pizaña boys were there, some eating breakfast, others were in the corral getting their horses ready to go out and gather cattle. The fight immediately started. McGuire, a soldier, was killed, and Aniceto Pizaña, afterward bandit leader, was shot through the thigh. Ramón Pizaña, the leader, was arrested, tried, and given fifteen years. I represented him. That was the first reason leading to the bandit trouble and this undesirable conduct of the Rangers. In that particular instance I stated that the man was absolutely acting in self-defense. The Rangers arrived almost immediately after this incident.

The incident that followed happened at Paso Real, where people were killed in their own house.* Then there was the killing of the Austins at Sebastian, for which two Mexicans were convicted and hung.** Then there was the Norias fight [on August 8], in which no Ranger partici-

*On August 3, 1915, Rangers and deputy sheriffs attacked the Desiderio Flores ranch, north of Brownsville, killing Mr. Flores and his two sons, who were alleged to be bandits.

**On August 6, 1915, a band of fourteen Mexicans killed Charles Austin and his son after robbing them.

pated. They were there, but they were out on a scout. Five Mexicans were killed, and not a single American was killed at that time, one was slightly wounded. The Rangers arrived about an hour after the incident. Captain Ransom was sent there, and they began to kill Mexicans without giving them absolutely no chance. On the mere *dicta* or information given by any man the Rangers would go over there and unceremoniously kill him.

The effect was that immediately every relative of that Mexican would go to Mexico with his tale of woe, and it aroused a strong feeling between them and the bandits. That feeling increased to the extent that practically the Mexican border on the other side was at war with us, sympathizing with the relatives of these men that had been wrongfully killed, taken out of their homes at night after the Rangers had said, "If you surrender your arms we can protect you." Yet after they surrendered their arms the Rangers would go into their homes afterward and shoot them at night. Ten men were killed right near San Benito, right near the house of the father of Miss Janes, my stenographer.

Now, matters got very bad, until it culminated in the wreck of the train October 18, 1915. I was in constant touch with the situation and I co-operated with the military authorities there and furnished evidence to them. Sheriff Vann, who had been only elected shortly before and didn't know the Mexican character very well, was adverse to putting in Mexican deputies. I insisted to Captain Vann to put in Mexican deputies, because they could get in touch with those other Mexican bandits and thereby trap them easily. After that wreck, he realized that the condition was serious. General Nafarrate* was openly co-operating with the bandits and helped them with money and ammunition. We knew that. I then suggested the means of establishing Mexican scouts to co-operate with the military authorities that had camps every five miles. I told him it was necessary to get the Mexicans that lived in there and had been farmers and tenants along that border to give out information and to act as guides. The suggestion was taken up by Captain Vann and endorsed by him.

I then went to Colonel E. P. Blockson, gave him my plan, and he endorsed it. He gave me a short letter, giving orders to every commanding officer along the border to admit into full confidence any Mex-

---

*The Carrancista commander at Matamoros.

ican that I would recommend to him. Those scouts were unarmed; they were not to arrest anybody; they were merely to give information and serve as guides for the soldiers in order to trap those bandits. They were organized about three days after the railroad wreck. I spent three months organizing, guiding, and supervising this system of scouts. They were especially to watch at night while the soldiers were in camp, and they were instructed how to come at night into the camp without any risk to their lives. The first bandits connected with the wreck of the train were arrested at San Pedro Ranch on information given by my scouts. Major M. C. Butler, who was afterward murdered at Alpine, was in command at that time. I have his own letter stating that since the organization of the Mexican scouts, not a single band of Mexican bandits crossed through his line through the efficient information given by these scouts. I also had on the other side of the border men whom I had represented and who were in close touch and would give me information. I would furnish that immediately to the authorities on this side.

In December 1915, by the time the raids had been minimized, General Carranza came to Matamoros, and I was a member of the committee who called upon him. We requested of him the removal of General Nafarrate because we had information and evidence that he was assisting the bandits. He soon gave us his word he would relieve him, and he sent his own nephew, General Ricant, who was stationed there, and from that time we had no further trouble with the bandits.

But the Rangers had estabished a precedent, that is, whenever a suspect was arrested they would unceremoniously execute him on the road to Brownsville or to the jail, without giving him any opportunity. Frequently we would find dead bodies, and the ranches burned. Relatives were intimidated to the extent that they would not even bury their own relatives. That condition existed until it was nauseating, nauseating. It was terrible. I wrote to Governor Ferguson and told him what Captain Ransom and his men were doing. I received no information or reply from him.

I went to Austin in 1917 and the special Ranger bill was passed in the first called session in May. I was openly against it, because I knew that the Rangers had not reformed, that they were living up to the reputation they had acquired of killing their prisoners without giving them a chance to be heard or to prove themselves innocent. I was called to see Governor Ferguson. By that time we had declared war against

Germany. In his office he asked me, "Are you going to oppose this Ranger bill?" I says, "Yes, I am going to oppose the Ranger bill and I am going to oppose the appropriation." He says, "I understand Jim Wells is also here against it." I says, "I don't know, I think Judge Wells is a very strong friend of the Rangers but I don't care about Judge Wells. He does not control my conscience. I am going to fight this bill because these Rangers have adopted a policy that is a shame and disgrace to my native state and to my American citizenship." I related to him these incidents and the number of men that have been killed without any justification and without any opportunity to be heard. Then he said,

Canales, I realize that that is true, but we have just entered into war. I have reliable information that the Germans are making propaganda on the other side among Mexicans. You are an American citizen and I appeal to you as an American citizen not to make that fight, because it will imperil the property and the liberties of American citizens. I will give you my word of honor, I will remove whatever undesirable men. I will remove any man you will tell me that does not demean [deport] himself as a humane and good officer.

With tears in my eyes I shook his hand, and I said,

Governor, on that appeal, to show you I am a loyal American, I am going to take you on that. Although the crimes that have been committed are terrible and I know these have disgraced my state and my American citizenship, yet on that appeal, Governor, I am going to show you. I am going over there and champion that bill.

And I went there and helped to champion that bill and it became a law.

It was soon after the governor vetoed the University Bill. We called him in that matter, and we impeached him. Whatever good intention he had to comply with his promise to me, he had no opportunity. A new governor was elected and a new adjutant general was placed in there, and I thought the new administration would correct the faults of the old, so the matter remained that way. While there were occasional misdeeds committed by the Rangers, the wholesale slaughter had stopped.

After my services in the House in May 1917, I went to Brownsville, and there was a great exodus of Mexicans into Mexico. The charge was made that it was on account of the Rangers and also on account of the registration [for the draft]. General Morton asked me to make speeches with him in my county to explain to the Mexicans the registration law and to show them that Governor Ferguson had promised to put a stop to all this mistreatment of the Mexicans, and I did. It was printed and circulated; it was translated into Spanish and my name was signed to it. The exodus stopped.

In 1918 Captain Stephens was sent to my county, and so far as I know, he is a good and conscientious man, but I believe he was under the influence of men who had private reasons for disturbing conditions in my county. I mentioned names to General Harley, and I mentioned them to Captain Stephens when he came to my office. I told him not to be misled by those gentlemen, but to do his duty. He began to disarm our men. He would even take double-barreled shotguns along the river. I said then that that should not be permitted. They were disarming Mexican deputies who had done loyal service to the government of the United States and had acted as spies at the risk of their own lives. They disarmed Pedro Lerma, who was the deputy sheriff, and they disarmed by own brother, who had made a trip with his family from my father's ranch in Jim Wells County to Brownsville and had a Winchester rifle .22. They took his rifle from him. He had to travel one hundred and twenty or thirty miles across open country. They took his rifle away from him and quite a number of other Mexicans who had only shotguns for the purpose of killing rabid dogs and coyotes. Those persons could not even have chickens because they had nothing to kill the coyotes who came stealing their chickens and the wildcats who would prey on them.

At that time the river was very dry and you could cross it anywhere. The various regulations and provisions were such that people across the river could not get anything to eat and they were hungry. They would come at night and would steal corn and cows, would steal everything from our tenants. My own tenants were left without absolutely a beast of burden to protect them. We could hear those people come from across the river. They would take our beasts of burden from our own yards, and we were afraid to go out because we didn't even have a shotgun. They disarmed us. That was the condition of affairs. The Rangers were not living there. They would go in the daytime and disarm the people, and at night sleep in good beds of ease at the hotels in Brownsville and Harlingen and San Benito. And there were our people disarmed and at the mercy of their countrymen on the other side who would come and steal everything they had. That was the condition in August 1918.

170

"The *'rinches'* killed him without
asking any questions."
                    —Cecilia Almaguer Rendón
                                    (1900–)*

*In pursuing Mexican bandits and raiders, Texas Rangers
frequently terrorized people suspected of being sympathetic
to the law breakers. Cecilia Almaguer Rendón, a native of
Brownsville, recalls how the hated "rinches" (derisive term
meaning Rangers) invaded her family's home and then executed her cousin without bothering to conduct an investigation.*

They sent many "rinches" to the area where we lived because they
thought we were helping the Mexican bandits, that we were feeding
them. At that time we were quite scared. The bandits would come
around and ask for food, and if you didn't give them any they would
take what was already prepared. But the bandits never came to our
home because the "rinches" were nearby.

On one occasion the "rinches" apprehended my cousin in Encarnación
Garza right in our farm because they thought he was a bandit. He had
come from Kingsville to visit my mother, because she had raised him.
He would spend time with his mother and then come and stay with us
for awhile. He arrived one night at about nine. Shortly thereafter when
it was time to go to bed he said he would sleep outside because it was
too hot indoors. It was summertime. We didn't want him to sleep outside

*Interviewed in Brownsville in 1978 by Virgilio Sánchez. On file at the Institute of
Oral History, University of Texas at El Paso.

because we had heard talk the "rinches" were coming around, and didn't know when they would arrive. At about 2:30 A.M. the "rinches" came and the first thing they found was my cousin. They got him up just the way he was, in his underclothes. They didn't let him put on his shoes or anything. They put on handcuffs and made him stand in front of the car lights. One guarded him and the others searched the place.

Three of them entered our home, yanked us out of bed and threw us on the floor. We all bunched together. I was small and got very frightened. They wanted to know how many other men were in the house. At that time my father was not there. My uncle had taken him to Brownsville. The "rinches" didn't ask permission of anyone to enter homes. They didn't conduct any investigation. If you didn't open the door they would break it with their carbines. They would then shine their lights all over the house. They asked us where the kitchen was, and we had to tell them because we were scared; they had their guns drawn. Then they looked everywhere for food. We had lots of corn tortillas and sweet bread. They took almost everything because they assumed it would be given to the bandits.

The "rinches" then put my cousin in the car and left. They took him to a cemetery about a block away, placed him in front of a cross and shot him dead. We heard the noise. They left him laying there. The following morning instead of going to work in the fields as usual, we went to the cemetery. Poor cousin, there he was, just laying there. It happened that he had fallen right on my grandfather's grave, although the "rinches" didn't know that. He was about twenty-one years of age. We didn't put him in a box. We just wrapped him in a sheet and a blanket, dug a deep grave, and put him in it. Then we covered him up. The "rinches" killed him without asking him any questions. They just apprehended people and took them. We were afraid to challenge them because they were like big animals and they had guns. We had heard from others that the "rinches" had hurt some families previously by poking them with their carbines, trying to get them to tell where the men in the family were. They just looked for the men. There was no remedy but to pray to God that the "rinches" go away, that matters calmed down. That was all.

After that we went to Brownsville. Many families abandoned their farms and lost their belongings. We had lots of cows, chickens, and pigs. Everything was left behind.

"Never heard of such a thing."

—John Edds*

When Texas Rangers went after a suspect, they frequently trespassed into private property without regard for the constitutional rights of citizens. This practice led to numerous abuses and sometimes tragedy. In the following testimony, Ranger John Edds explains how he mistakenly killed the wrong person in 1918 when looking for a deserter at the Jesús Sánchez ranch near Roma, Texas. J. T. Canales accused Edds of murder, but since there were no witnesses to the shooting, legal action was not brought against the Ranger. (Questions asked by several members of the 1919 Texas investigation committee).

Question: You said you killed Lisandro Muñoz on or about October sixth, 1918. Please tell the committee about that fact.

Answer: Myself and a couple of other Rangers went up to a Mexican house to arrest a deserter. It was early in the morning, just about daylight. I got into a difficulty there with a man and was forced to kill him.

Q: Who was that man?

A: Lisandro Muñoz.

Q: Was that the man you wanted to arrest?

*Testimony given in 1919. *Proceedings of the Joint Committee of the Senate and the House in the Investigation of the Texas State Ranger Force* (Austin, Texas, 1919), pp. 483–91. Texas State Archives.

A: No, sir.

Q: Who was the man you wanted to arrest?

A: Alonso Sánchez.

Q: Did you have a warrant to arrest him?

A: He was a deserter from the army.

Q: Answer whether you had it or not: Did you have a warrant or not?

A: Why, no, sir.

Q: This man Muñoz, whom you killed, seeking for Alonzo Sánchez, was sleeping in whose house?

A: They were sleeping in the yard just back of Jesús Sánchez', who was the father of Alonzo Sánchez.

Q: What reason did you have to believe that the deserter was there?

A: I had learned that he had come across the river or was coming across the river that night, about dark. . . .

The house was on the corner of the block facing east and north and there were trees leading out of the house, opening out right into the street on each side. I stationed one of the Rangers right at the corner of the house so in the event this man was in the house and tried to get out through the front door this man stationed at the corner would have a chance to apprehend him. Myself and Ranger Wells went up a string of yard fence, trying to find a gate to get into the back part of the yard. When we got to the north side we could not find any gate but we could get a good view of the yard from there. It seemed there was one or two little outhouses and a wood patch and wagon or two. I didn't know where the deserter was sleeping. Those men on the dodge, you can't tell where you will find them. Sometimes they sleep at home and sometimes they sleep out in the lot. I told Wells to stay there while I went down the corner and to the other string of fence. I thought there surely would be a gate on the other string of fence. I went around and got into the yard that led into the back part of the house.

I noticed two men sleeping on cots there. The cots were close together—about two or three feet apart. I didn't know this man Sánchez [the deserter]. They had given me a description of him and said that he was a man that wore a black mustache and also described his brother being a clean shaven man. They told me that there was no one in the habit of sleeping at the house but the old man and the other boy, and if I found another man there in all probability one of those would be the deserter. So I went into this little yard and eased up to the cots and they were both asleep. I looked at it a good while the best I could. They were covered up but I could see their faces; they were covered up to the neck with a sheet or something. I saw one that was clean shaven and the other had a black mustache, so I naturally thought it was Sánchez, this deserter we were looking for. So I eased up to his cot and began to call him, "Alonso," softly, trying to wake him up. He woke up after I called him two or three times, he woke up and straightened up in his cot and said, "What is it?" I said, "The Ranger, John Edds, that is my name." And he said, "What do you want?" I said, "I want to talk to you. What is your name?" He could not answer me. I guess he seen the rifle cocked. I don't know what struck him, he got to where he could not talk to me. He got up from his cot. I said, "Sit down, I want to talk to you." Suddenly he reached and grabbed my rifle by the barrel and I said, "Turn it loose, I ain't going to hurt you." He never paid any attention to me, and around and around we went, scuffling in the yard. He was trying to take my rifle away from me. He was a little bigger man that I was and I called to Ranger Wells, "Come here quick, Munroe." But there was a high fence and he was stationed outside of it. He had trouble getting over the fence and before he could get to me I shot this man. The gun was right up against him when I shot him. It burned a big hole in his drawers and powder burned his flesh; it shot him right in the groin.

Q: Did that man die?

A: Yes, sir.

Q: At that time did you still think it was the deserter?

A: I thought it was him.

Q: Instead of talking to you he made the attack?

A: He made the attack.

Q: And in the scuffle he was shot?

A: Yes, sir.

Q: Was that reported to the authorities?

A: Oh, immediately. I stayed there and sent one of the boys to phone, to see the county judge first, but the county judge wasn't there. They said he lived at this little ranch, but I heard afterward he didn't want to come down, and I told them to phone and notify Captain Wright, who was in Rio Grande City at the time, and notify the sheriff and justice of the peace. We stayed right there. That was just after daylight. We stayed right there and didn't let anyone come near the body so they would not put out the tracks, because there were the signs where we had scuffled plainly visible, and I wanted the justice of the peace to come there and hold an inquest. We stayed there until about ten-thirty, when Captain Wright and the local authorities got there.

Q: Your information was that this boy was coming across and being harbored there?

A: Yes, and my information was perfectly reliable. The people themselves, this boy's father, and his brother, both admitted to us and to all the Mexicans that were there that he had been there and that he had left shortly after midnight that same night.

Q: That he had been down there that same night?

A: Yes, sir.

Q: Now, after you were advised, did you have time to get a warrant?

A: Get a warrant for what?

Q: For his arrest?

A: Why, for this deserter?

Q: The deserter.

A: I never heard of a warrant for a deserter. President Wilson in his proclamation gave us that authority.

Q: No warrant under the law, as you understand it, was required at all?

A: Never heard of such a thing.

"The United States had been invaded!"

—Mary Means Scott*

Villa's 1916 raid on Columbus, New Mexico, shocked Americans everywhere, but particularly border residents. Gunfire, thundering hoofbeats, and cries of "Viva Villa!" and "Muerte a los gringos!" rudely awakened the tiny desert hamlet in the early morning hours of March 9. What followed would be the most important historical event the townspeople ever witnessed. Their stories reveal fright, horror, tragedy, narrow escapes, and all manner of adventures. Mary Means Scott wrote about her family's experience many years after the attack, bringing to life the recollection of a child caught in frightening but at the same time exciting circumstances.

Many mothers, fathers, and loved ones over the country were anxiously awaiting just such a message as this. There were no ham operators feverishly relaying distressed or calming news. The one telephone line was busy. In fact, the heroic operator had continued at her post amidst chaos and fear, but telephones then were few and seldom used for long distance. The telegram was the accepted bearer of urgent messages, and our short message to El Paso was urgent.

Pancho Villa had raided Columbus! The United States had been in-

*Written memoir; first place winner in the 1974 Historical Memories Contest of the El Paso County Historical Society. *Password* 20:4 (Winter 1975): 163–67. Reprinted by permission of *Password*.

vaded! The town was a holocaust, and many were said to have been murdered in their beds—military and civilian alike.

It has been many, many years, and I was a very small child, but there are countless, disjointed impressions indelibly imprinted on my mind.

Villa's skirmishes and short-lived battles were a familiar sound to the people of Columbus. Palomas, Mexico, was but one mile away, and often I had heard my mother say as the sound of firing came through the night stillness, "Well, Villa is certainly shooting up Palomas tonight."

Sometime in the chilly, early morning darkness the shooting began. There was no doubt it was nearby and in earnest. Our house, "the little brown house," was only a block from the town's main street and we were next door to the "White House" where Colonel Slocum lived. Of course, my father's first thought was of his family's well being. He discarded the thought of our escaping to safety. Where was safety? Who knew what was lurking outside in the street? Shouts and running footsteps were easily heard.

There were four of us besides my father, Elliott Means, in our family my six-months pregnant mother, Grace, and my twelve- and three-year-old brothers, Elliott and Billy. My father was afraid that even though our house was not entered, we would be hit by stray bullets, for it was only a frame house. He put the three of us children on the floor of the living room, the room with the most walls between it and town, and covered us with the big single-batting Sealy mattress. He knew that cotton would do most to stop a bullet. He and mother kept watch at the windows, and I heard them whisper instructions and encouragement.

Small Billy was not impressed with the battle and thought only of his uncomfortable, confining situation.

"Daddy, I'm hot!" brought silent immediate attention. Daddy solicitously knelt down and turned the pillow over, providing him a little cool air as well as a cooler side of the pillow case. Never had Billy's complaints received such quick, ungrumbling results, and he repeated the routine several times.

By daylight, the shooting became sporadic and finally ceased. Daddy and mother began to speak in normal tones. Elliott and I, they decided, should get up and see Columbus in flames! We stood at a window facing the center of town, aghast at the spectacular and horrifying sight. The golden red flames rose high into the still air, furiously crackling and roaring as it consumed the dry, lumber-constructed store and hotel

178

buildings of a two-block area. Other smaller fires dotted the horizon. The towering flames were topped with bursts and rolls of black smoke that billowed to heaven and blotted out the sky. We could feel the heat on our faces and Daddy worried whether or not the heat might catch on fire the houses of our block. At least there were only fitful flames and boiling smoke.

My father left the house to see what was to be done. There were still running men, shouting, and swearing. In a short while he returned.

"I think Elliott is old enough to see this and I think he should. This is history," he said after giving mother a description of the devastation and a summary of the rampant rumors and chilling stories of death. There were excited accounts of soldier heroism and the frustrations of unpreparedness and conflicting orders. I heard the names of townspeople—some families singled out for revenge and others sacked and murdered because they were in the path of destruction. Our men were now chasing the brigands and outlaws deep into Mexico.

Elliott and Daddy went to town and what Elliott saw there was seared on his memory the whole of his life. Main Street was in chaos. Men were frantically digging in the smoldering ruins for bodies. Others looked distractedly at yesterday's places of business, now blackened junk. Everyone was trying to piece together a picture of what truly had happened.

The real horror lay in the streets and on the sidewalks. Villa's men who had fallen lay dead and dying. Some twitched, some mumbled, most were sprawled in the abandoned posture of death. Except for an occasional curse, they were ignored. Later in the day, they were gathered, stacked, and burned.

Elliott caught the glint of yellow metal in the black ashes. After picking it up and blowing to cool it, he realized he had a small golden blob, no doubt a ring or a gold piece melted in the heat of the hotel fire. It became a life-long talisman in memory of perhaps his most unusual and unforgettable day. It was the day before his birthday.

A near state of hysteria continued throughout the day. Rumors were rampant that Villa's bandits planned to return that night. So, during the day, it was decided that everyone would gather and sleep in the school house, a sturdy two-story, square building with a big bronze bell on one corner. Families consulted one another and planned what to carry and what to leave behind. Excitement was high and the children listened wide-eyed and scared. Billy and I, consumed with haste and urgency, decided we should go on to the school house and wait. No one saw us go or knew where we were. This injected a new crisis into the already charged atmosphere; however, Juan, the same Juan Favela, in a stroke of intuition, went to the school and found us—a little more wide-eyed and a little more scared.

Our family and many others slept in the big classrooms that night. The mothers quieted children and kept them comfortable while the men stood at the windows fingering their guns. They watched, tense, whispering, and alert at every real or imagined movement in the mesquite bushes outside. It was a long night, but a quiet one. Villa did not return.

The remainder of the United States read blaring and garbled headlines. More military protection for Columbus was assured and the army set about it at once. The town had been caught with only a small part of the 13th Cavalry on hand; other segments had been diverted to other settlements strung along the border. Nevertheless, within a week, almost the entire United States army had arrived in Columbus and was taking over the situation. General Pershing was in command and soon became very popular with the townspeople.

I saw it as great excitement. The town ballooned and there was commotion and confusion. From a quiet, backward, out-of-the-way border town, Columbus became a bustling small city. Each train that arrived from east or west was filled with soldiers. They overflowed onto the freight trains and I was fascinated with the flat cars that arrived bristling with uniformed men. Stores filled with milling bodies were unable to serve all their wants and needs. At the grocery store, I retreated behind the show case to save being trampled upon, but peeped out admiringly at the sea of uniforms. To me it was a mammoth circus with only the big tent missing.

But—there were tents. A city of tents grew up south of the railroad tracks and south of town. It was a dry, dusty, rock strewn area supporting only unfriendly prickly pear cactus and thorn-armoured mesquites.

Some of the men, perhaps officers, rented rooms in town where they made lasting friendships. One young man, a fine photographer, made pictures of our family. Four-year-old Billy was dressed in the familiar cavalry campaign hat with crossed hatband and holding a bugle. In fact, Billy was a favorite. One day, in his independence, he decided to visit the "claim" (homestead) two miles from town. There was a great stir when mother discovered his absence. After her own shouts and searching brought no results, the soldiers were asked for help. The town was scoured but there was no Bill. At dusk, tired and dusty, he wandered in and was picked up by two of the soldiers who delivered him to mother. With exasperation, she scolded, "Billy, why did you run off and get lost?" In wounded seriousness, he answered, "I wasn't lost. I went to the claim to play." (Curiously, forty years later, Billy ran into a man in Salt Lake City who helped in the search.)

"Grown-up" talk centered around catching and punishing Pancho Villa. In our childish minds, he became villain, ogre, and arch enemy. Our games changed to "Soldiers Chasing Bandits," and we galloped through the brush and peered stealthily around adobe corners.

The town continued to overflow with the military. Streets were filled with cavalrymen on sleek, prancing horses and with lumbering horse-drawn artillery pieces, as they continued to arrive. Huge supply trucks, new and awesomely powerful in our horse-and-buggy town added to the dust and noise. And airplanes! There was often a choking sputter, followed by a roar from the edge of town, we caught a glimpse of helmet and goggle—and that proved to us there was a man inside.

And then the day arrived when General Pershing planned to enter Mexico! Men, horses, field artillery, trucks, supplies, repair units, all poised for the start. As usual, the townspeople were caught up in the great moment—at last—retribution was at hand. It would be the cul-minting show.

Early, at the border, marked by a barbed-wire fence, families began to gather. Mother and Daddy drove out in our rubber-tired buggy with the children, Elliott, Billy and me standing in front holding onto the dashboard. We watched for hours, it seemed, as the horses and riders passed in a giant parade: flags and guidons flying; pistols at the waist, sabres at the saddle, all enveloped in a canopy of dust. There was applause, whistles, waves, and shouts of "goodbye" as friends came into view. The men and boys volunteered much advice on what to do with Pancho Villa when caught.

It was a great exodus—an historic hour. The might of the United States army departing on a punitive mission to right a wrong visited upon an unsuspecting border town—the cavalry to the rescue! It was a thrilling sight to us, but we did not and could not have known that we were witnessing and cheering the last real cavalry action.

General Pershing passed, smiling and waving. He was a handsome figure, an epitome of "spit and polish" and we were proud of him and our army.

The crowd waved wildly and shouted encouragement. Excitedly, we children jumped up and down. . . . Dexter, our horse, stood at ease, calmly flicking his tail. . . .

U.S. Army camp during troop buildup of mid-1910s. (Courtesy, El Paso
Public Library, Photograph Collection)

Troops from Pershing's Punitive Expedition take a break, Chihuahua, in 1916. (Courtesy, El Paso Public Library, Photograph Collection)

U.S. soldiers captured by Mexicans during the skirmish at Carrizal, Chihuahua, in 1916. (Courtesy, El Paso Public Library, Photograph Collection)

American and Mexican sentries patrol the border at Nogales, Arizona, and Nogales, Sonora. (*Collier's Weekly*, August 19, 1916)

Villistas captured after the raid on Columbus, New Mexico, 1916. (Courtesy, U.T. El Paso Library, Aultman Collection)

U.S. Army moves equipment through El Paso's streets during the crisis created by Villa's assault on Juárez, 1919. (Courtesy, U.T. El Paso Library, Aultman Collection)

American soldiers cross the Rio Grande into Juárez to help thwart Villa's attempted capture of the town, 1919. (Courtesy, U.T. El Paso Library, Aultman Collection)

U.S. Army parade in El Paso, late 1910s. (Courtesy, U.T. El Paso Library, Aultman Collection)

> "Well, my time has come."
> —Susan A. Moore*

During the Columbus raid, survival became the first prior- ity of the townspeople, and to accomplish that, many had to find good hiding places or a way to leave town undetected. Susan A. Moore lived through the ordeal, but her husband did not. It is possible that Mrs. Moore has exaggerated her attackers' cruelty as well as her own valor, but in her mind this is the way things happened that unforgettable day.

Sometime previous to the raid there had been a number of reports to the effect that Villa was going to raid Columbus, and there were also a number of strange Mexicans in town, say, for about a week before hand. On the day before the raid, after I had had my Spanish lesson, the young lady said to me: "Mrs. Moore, you are not afraid of Villa?" I said, "No, and you?" She said, "No, I have no fear, but my mother and brother have very much fear." There were two Mexican women in the store the same afternoon, and one of them said to the other, "Do you think there is any truth in the report that Villa will raid Columbus?" and one of them shrugged her shoulders and said, "No." After they went out I said to Mr. Moore [her husband], "Do you think there is any danger?" and he just smiled.

A little later I was sitting in the back of the store doing some lace

*Interviewed in El Paso in 1919. *Investigation of Mexican Affairs*, Senate Document 285, 66th Congress, 2nd Session (Washington, D.C., 1920), pp. 956–67.

work, and a customer entered. I got up to wait on him; as I got within about twelve feet a cold chill swept over me. I looked up at him; I saw he was a small man with dark eyes, black mustache. He had on one of these high-class Mexican hats, and I thought to myself, "He must be a lieutenant in the Mexican Army," and I asked him what he wished in Spanish, and he said, "Pantaloons." I was a little bit uncomfortable all the time I was waiting on him because I felt he was looking at me continually. I did not look at him any more until I handed him the change, and I took a good look at him again because I thought if it was ever necessary to know him again I would recognize him, and he smiled and took his change, and I could feel his eyes on me all the time. As he passed out he gave Mr. Moore a very earnest look. I asked Mr. Moore if he noticed him, and he said, "Yes." I said, "He must be a Mexican officer."

Between that time, which was about 4 o'clock, and 6, I was debating in my mind whether it would be better to stay in town that night or go out to our country home a mile and a half southwest of Columbus. I decided it would be better to go out there because if they did come in they would raid the stores and hotels, and I thought they would hardly come out of their way for just one family. We went home between 6 and 7 P.M. About 10 o'clock I stepped out on the porch and listened a while, and I did not hear anything. I stepped out into the yard, and it was a beautiful moonlight night as I ever saw, clear as crystal. I could not see or hear anything, and I went back in the house rather reassured. Before retiring I laid out a heavy, long coat, just in case I should need it. We retired about 11. I studied the situation for an hour and went to sleep. About 4:30 in the morning I was awakened by some shots, and I laid still and listened; then directly I heard a number of shots, and I thought, "That is a machine gun." In a little while I heard some more shots from this machine gun. I did not hear any noise around the house, so I hurriedly awoke Mr. Moore. I said to him: "Look, Villa has come in, and he is burning the town." He looked out. We were on the sleeping porch facing town. He said, "You are right, we had better get dressed." We hurriedly dressed in the dark so as not to attract any attention by making a light; then we went to the front of the house and listened and looked. Not seeing or hearing anything, we drew the blinds within 6 inches of the bottom of the window, so we could see out without being seen. Then we went to the back of the house. Mr. Moore stood at the

184

pantry window screening his body and just put his head over so he could see. I got up in front of the window, and he said to me, "If I were you I would not stand directly in front of the window; you might be hit by a stray shot, or someone might see you." I then went to the kitchen and sat down opposite the table and watched the burning of the town through the window.

From time to time I would go in where he was, and on one of those occasions I saw a dark object coming down the road. We watched it come to the front, and we decided it was a man on horseback. He was coming just as fast as he could and did not even look toward the house. We watched him until he was well by, and in a little while there were two more Mexicans on horseback come down, and they rode past. Then there were five and seven and nine, and as we watched these all pass I said to Mr. Moore, "Maybe we had better go to the mesquite bushes and hide. Some of these fellows may take a notion to come in." He says, "No, I don't think so, we have always been good to them, have harmed none of them, and carried them on our books; we have nothing to fear." We went to the back of the house, looked up the road, and I saw a large number coming down. I counted seventeen. These stopped right in front of the house; a number of them got off their horses. There was a group that stopped beside the well and was looking at the top of the water. I again said to Mr. Moore, "I wonder if any of them will come in." He said, "No, I just think they want some water." I then looked out of the north window at Mrs. Walker's gate, at the beginning of our land. There was a man on a white horse with a cape coat. He looked down the road to these men and motioned to them and a number of them, about ten I suppose, went over and began rapping on the door and looked in the windows. I glanced up toward town, and I saw that the road was thick with them, and they were breaking from town just like a sandstorm; I guess the entire army was coming that way. It seemed to me like a quarter of a mile on either side of the house the road was filled with men.

This man on the white horse, I looked back at him. Then he motioned toward our house, and there were forty or fifty all around the gate, opened the gate and began pouring into the yard. Mr. Moore said to me, "We had better get in the dining room; we will have better protection." I hurriedly stepped to the dining room and then heard these men come up on the porch. They tried the door, which was locked, and

185

then one of the leaders, who had been leaning on the fence previously looking at the water and house, took the butt end of his gun and smashed in the west bedroom window. When I heard the crash I stepped where I could see, and I saw him just in the act of entering. Mr. Moore then opened the door. This leader came in, followed by a number of men, just as many as could come into the house, and he said something to Mr. Moore, which I did not hear, and Mr. Moore said no. Then this man looked across Mr. Moore's right shoulder at me and said something else, which I did not hear. Mr. Moore again said no. Then this leader raised his gun and shot, and others raised their sabers, and a few began shooting and stabbing him. He made one rush for his gun, which stood right at the corner of the door, and they blocked his way, preventing him from getting it, and closed right around him.

Just then I heard a number of steps on the back porch. The kitchen and dining room opened and the same Mexican who had been in the store the day before purchasing a pair of 32 overalls came in, with his gun just about on a level with my heart. He said to me, "Gold, money." I told him in Spanish there was no money here; the money was in the bank in Columbus. I told him to take anything that he wanted, only to leave us. He then saw a ring on my finger, my wedding ring. I started to show him my hands. He came around in front of me, grabbed hold of my hand, and started to take off this ring. The house was filled with Mexicans then from all sides, and one of his men stepped up and grabbed me by the right wrist and another one by the left. I knew the ring was very tight. I had my doubts whether they could get it off. I had tried it the day before with a silk string. I thought they could cut my finger off, so I tried to help them get off my ring. As I did, he noticed two rings on my right hand, so he started to take these off. They were quite tight; I started to help him.

I looked out to see how Mr. Moore was getting along. He was about halfway across the porch and there was blood all over him. I knew he was either dying or just at the point of dying, staggering. They got the two rings off then, and they started in on the other hand. I looked out again and I saw Mr. Moore on the front steps. I knew then that he was absolutely killed. One man was taking off his rings, another man had his watch in his hand, and they were taking his clothes. I thought at that time that to save myself I would either have to outwit them or startle them. The thought came to me to scream. Just as the wedding

186

ring was leaving the last joint of my finger I screamed twice, and at the same time I looked toward Mr. Moore to attract their attention away from me to him, and their hold loosened on my wrist just a little. I gave one big jerk and jerked away from them. I pushed the dining room door open, and I was shot at in the kitchen. I ran across the porch, and as I stepped down I looked out, and there were a number of Mexicans around the garage. When they saw me they shouted, "*Señora, señora, mira,*" and began laughing. The camp was about a mile from home, and I started to see if I could run there. I ran just as fast as I could; the bullets were flying very fast all the time. When I got within 100 yards I felt a sensation in my right leg. I knew I had been struck. I went ahead. In about 50 yards from there I fell. I knew I must not lay still, because it would mean certain death, so I got up again and went a little ways farther, and my right leg buckled up on me and I fell again. I got up again and went as well as I could, rather slowly. I had to kind of hop on one leg and carried my wounded leg.

I got up to the fence, and then went to get on the other side. I thought that would be impossible, because it was a rabbit-proof fence, buried about a foot in the ground. On the top was three barbed wires. I did not see how I could climb it. I knew I did not have strength to dig in with just my hands, but I tried, and I got over the fence without even catching any of my clothes. I fell right down the side of the fence. I laid still a little while; the shots were coming just as fast as they could come. I looked back and saw that the house was almost surrounded by Mexicans in great numbers. There were, I guess, fifty or more guns pointed in my direction, all shooting. There was a cluster of mesquite bushes about twenty-five feet from me. I thought if I could get over there and crawl under and cover myself up with the dark coat they might think I was dead and stop shooting. I was unable to get up at all, so I dragged myself on my left side over to these bushes and got in around them as well as I could. I covered myself up so nobody would see that I was a woman, and turned my face in the other direction. My clothes were all saturated with blood; it kind of sickened me. I thought, "Well, my time has come." I closed by eyes, and prayed, and was unconscious for the first time in my life. Later I was aroused by the sound of horses' hoofs, and I looked up and I saw the United States cavalry. I looked down at the house and saw there was no one down there at all.

I then took out my handkerchief and reached as high as I could and

187

hung it on a mesquite bush and called and waved. Directly I saw three horsemen turn out in my direction. As they came up I recognized Captain Smyzer, with a private on either side. As they came up he said, "Why, it is a woman. My God, Mrs. Moore." He asked me if I was hurt, and I said, "Yes, Captain, I am shot, but I can wait if you will go down to the house and see what you can do for Mr. Moore. They have killed him, and you will find him on the front porch." He said, "But we must do something for you first." I said, "I am only shot in the leg. I can wait. I would rather you go take care of him." He then said to the private on the right, "Get the ambulance." This man almost turned his horse over in his haste, and he said, "All right, Mrs. Moore, we will go down and take care of Mr. Moore. We are chasing the bandits into Old Mexico, and we will have to hurry." I said, "All right." I watched them until they got down to the house. I thought the ambulance would soon be there. My leg was paining me terribly and bleeding very freely, so I tore my petticoat ruffle and bound myself both above and below the wound. I closed my eyes again, and was unconscious. I was very cold, too. It was early morning and very cold. I closed my eyes, thinking the ambulance would soon be there and I would be all right. A little later on I was aroused by pain in my leg. I looked out and saw a number of the United States boys scouting, with their guns drawn. I raised up and motioned to them. One of the boys came over to me and said, "Mrs. Moore, you raised your face just in time. I thought you were a Mexican, and was going to finish him. I never dreamed of you being way out here."

A number of them rushed up then, and two pulled off their coats and made a bed for me. Sergeant Johnson cut my clothes and gave me first aid. When this was finished, Lieutenant Castleman, who was officer of the day, asked if the ambulance had not arrived yet. Someone said, "No." He said, "See that it gets here at once." He said to me, "Have patience, Mrs. Moore. We are very busy this morning; you will be taken care of just as soon as we can." I said, "All right." At this point a woman, Mrs. Maud Hawks Wright, came up. She was dressed in a coarse linen dress with a little Dutch bonnet, and was very, very dirty. However, I was glad to see a woman, especially an American. She came up to me and she said she had been a prisoner of Villa for nine days. She looked like she was hungry. I asked her if she had had any breakfast. She said, "No." I told her when we got to town to go to any of these restaurants and get whatever she wanted and have it charged to me. I asked her

188

to stay with me and go to town with me in the ambulance, which she did. When they started to put me in the ambulance they thought my leg was broken, so they dug up a fence post and bound it to the right side of my body, so as to lift me easier. I had them bring a mattress from my home and put in the ambulance. I was taken to headquarters, where Dr. Cummings, an Army doctor, began dressing my wound. I was then taken up to the Hoover Hotel. As we passed through town I raised up sufficiently to see the hotel, Lemon & Rumney's store, Juan Sevilla's home, and some other buildings in ruins. I also saw a large number of dead and wounded Mexicans. As we passed our store I noticed the windows were all smashed in. The store was raided. I arrived at the Hoover Hotel about 10:15.

All that night the town was heavily patroled. The guard outside of my window told me if I could sleep to do so; he would see that no one got there. The Hoover Hotel was just covered with men that night, and women came there for protection and to spend the night. The next day there was a great deal of excitement, as someone reported that the Mexicans were coming back. I was carried from the front room back to Mrs. Hoover's room, covered with a mattress, and my nurse covered herself as well as she could. I was at the Hoover Hotel Thursday and Friday.

Saturday I was put aboard a train, the same train on which the dead bodies were taken to El Paso. I decided to have Mr. Moore's body taken back to his home at Bucyrus, Ohio. I wanted to accompany him. They told me that was impossible, but I told them to get me a ticket and make preparations. I had decided to go. I was taken to the big hospital in El Paso, Hotel Dieu, where I was again treated. I was there the rest of Saturday and Sunday, and Monday I was taken to the train and put aboard on a stretcher for Ohio. I had just one change to make at Chicago. That was made with difficulty, because I had to be taken in and out of the window. At the latter part of the journey I had to be turned about every five minutes; I was in such pain. When we got within about two blocks of the depot at Bucyrus I looked out of the window, and I saw a funeral procession. This was Mr. Moore. My train cut the procession right in two. This was as near as I got to attend the funeral.

> "Why, kid, there is not a Villista
> within a thousand miles of Ojinaga."
> —Norman Walker*

Like other border towns, Ojinaga had its share of excitement from disturbances and battles which often involved prominent leaders of the Revolution. In 1917, after he had been reduced to a guerrilla fighter in Chihuahua, Pancho Villa twice took this town from the Carrancistas, each time forcing them to flee to the United States. Newsman Norman Walker witnessed one of those battles, and more than two decades later he recalled some colorful details. It is possible that Norman has exaggerated the role of the two American soldiers in Villa's initial setback, but the fact that they were involved is of interest, as is their derisive reference to the Mexican soldiers.

Pancho Villa took Ojinaga, Mexico back in 1917 like Grant took Richmond.

He had confiscated $500,000 worth of silver bullion from the Alvarado Mining Company in the Parral District, and had loaded it on pack mules in saddle bags, which he brought to the Rio Grande at Ojinaga to smuggle across to exchange it for ammunition on the American side of the border.

I got the tip on the expected battle from Señor Gómez Morentín, Villa's secret service chief, who is now postmaster general in the Mexican

*Associated Press Correspondent. El Paso Times, April 3, 1939, p. 3:2. Published by permission of the El Paso Times.

190

government. He had Mrs. Theodore Kyricopulos telephone me. I went to the Kyricopulos residence where Gómez Morentín had come from Villa's camp in the field. He told me that Villa was going to take Ojinaga Wednesday night and that he wanted me to be present to give him the benefit of A. P. press agent material. I went to Marfa that night, eighty miles over the then roughest roads in the Big Bend and arrived promptly at dinner time at Colonel George Langhorne's military quarters.

"Hello, Boy Scout," the colonel greeted me. "What are you doing down here?"

I told him.

"Why, kid, there is not a Villista within a thousand miles of Ojinaga," the colonel chuckled. "Don't take my word for it, ask General Espinosa y Cordova, who is having dinner with me right in the next room."

I asked the Carranza commander and he confirmed Colonel Langhorne's statement.

I decided to stay there for a day or two. After 285 miles to see the battle I told the colonel I would stay a few days and visit with him in his quarters. The colonel made me at home, gave me a bed and an old plug cavalry horse to ride about camp, where the officers took their cue from Colonel Langhorne and called me the "Boy Scout."

But, on Wednesday night, I had the laugh on the shavetails. I went to bed early, taking off only my boots and leaving my clothes on. I had tied old "Rosanatie," my horse, to the hitch rack and was prepared for battle.

In the midst of a dream of being at home in Indiana, before an old Franklin stove popping corn, I was awakened and I realized that the pop-pop continued. It was Villa attacking promptly at midnight as he had promised. I was dressed, down at the Ojinaga ford and telephoning my lead on the battle into headquarters before Colonel Langhorne had had his cold bath, without which he never went into battle. Villa's failure to take the town on the first try was accounted for by the presence of American machine gunners. Villa made good his threat against the border town, however, by taking it with hand-to-hand fighting the next night at sunset.

After the smoke and smell of battle died away, I started an investigation which revealed the reason [why Villa was repelled the first night]. Two buck privates from the glorious Eighth Cavalry had deserted from the command in Presidio and had started to Chihuahua City in pursuit of excitement which they had been unable to get in Presidio. Before they were well started on their way to Chihuahua City overland, they were arrested by the Carranza outposts at Ojinaga, taken before General Espinosa y Cordova and impressed in the federal forces defending the Big Bend Mexican border town.

They were compelled to tear down four old machine guns in the federal garrison, and from them make one good machine gun which would spit bullets and destruction from its muzzle. This they did, and set the revamped gun on the cuartel at Ojinaga.

Villa led his staff up the hill. As they started to ride up the winding trail to the town after the main body of the Villa force had attacked from the south, the American machine gunfire cut loose on them and, as Private Doolittle said afterward: "Old Calamity Jane (the machine gun) was cuttin' grass that night." He added, in his army parlance, that "I gets Jacks and better when I opened up with the old grass cutter." The Villa hospital in Presidio, Texas, was crowded with Villa officers next morning after the attack.

The two deserters fled the Mexican federals, came across the river and surrendered themselves to American army officers. They gave a thrilling account of their experiences among the Mexican federals, and I was delegated to take down their report as I, as Associated Press correspondent in the field, wore the uniform of a second lieutenant and for all the deserters knew, they were talking to a second "louie." They told me how they deserted, started for Chihuahua City to join the army "and see the world," had been impressed and forced to run a machine gun against Villla's attackers. Private Doolittle told of his experience at the crank of the machine gun, which he was operating. "I looked around finally to tell my 'Spik' helper to fill another machine gun belt with cartridges. When I looked back the poor little 'Spik' had his head blown off. We beat it then, hid in the stocks and came to the Presidio side, where it was some safer after that awful larripin' we took."

The two deserters were sent to Fort Bliss under arrest. Later they escaped from the bull pen and went overseas on their own to fight the Boches without waiting to accompany the American army.

Don Pancho had an instinctive sense of the spectacular. He lined up on the south mesa mules loaded with silver in their leather packets, his staff and his cavalry leading.

Gosh, how he took the town. Women were screaming, men swore, and the din of battle in the air was deafening. The first one across the Rio Grande was General Espinosa y Cordova.

The entire federal army followed and was promptly interned on the American side and brought to Fort Bliss for later deportation to Mexico with their camp followers, pots, pans, and children.

"I saw an exchange of shots between the guards which started the difficulty."

—Consul E. M. Lawton*

The unfortunate 1918 battle at Nogales arose out of a confusing incident which triggered gunfire at the border crossing. E. M. Lawton, the U.S. Consul at Nogales, Sonora, places the blame on Mexico in his report to the State Department. Lawton also tells of his involvement in the peace negotiations, and of his concern for the Alvaro Obregón family, whose house was damaged by American bullets.

[August 28]. The trouble was started by an individual, presumably a Mexican who tried to cross the line at the American customhouse, whom the guard stopped just at the international line because he evidently had packages concealed on his person. The Mexican custom guard at that point demanded that he be released, although on American soil and threatened with his pistol. Two Mexican guards then came from another post one block distant and fired on and killed the American corporal on duty at the customhouse. An American sentry returned the fire and the first Mexican guard, above cited, fired several shots and immediately Mexican armed custom guards and civilians appeared in numbers and a general engagement began which lasted for nearly three hours, though our soldiers were recalled and ceased firing about one hour after the start.

*Records of the Department of State Relating to the Internal Affairs of Mexico, 1910–1929, 812.00/22207.

194

I endeavored to arrange a parley, but the telephone service was very poor and I could not leave the office where I was until a white flag appeared on the Mexican customhouse. I then went on the street, having previously communicated with the Mexican commander, and took Colonel Fred J. Herman of the Tenth Cavalry and a lieutenant to the line and then crossed to the Mexican side, and succeeded in bringing three Mexican officials to the consulate and our officers crossed for a parley. It was then agreed that three-quarters of an hour would be allowed for the Mexican officials to stop the firing from the top of the hills, and in the meantime no shooting would pass from the Arizona side.

I returned to the Arizona side and assisted to withdraw the negro troopers and the wounded who had crossed into Mexico and to prevent our civilians from firing on the snipers who continued to fire from the hill tops. At 6:30 P.M. I again returned to the consulate bringing with me the American collector of customs and the two army officers above named. We met the commander of the town, the federal judge and a prominent civilian and it was agreed that the American forces would not fire on snipers or in any way unless attacked in force, until 8:00 A.M. today, when a conference would be held at the American customhouse. Firing finally ceased from the Mexican side about 7:00 P.M.

One of the most serious incidents was the violation of the consulate. I had phoned Vice Consul Maguire to keep the consulate closed and stay under cover. At the first sign of trouble, the Chinese janitor took the girl clerks across the line and Mrs. Lawton was at the Mexican market and went to a Mexican home for protection and concealment. Mr. Maguire endeavored to obey instructions but an armed guard came to the consulate and at the point of a rifle compelled Maguire and Elmer E. Cooley (a man who was on trial here for possible appointment as clerk), to go out into the zone of fire. Cooley was shot through the fleshy part of the thigh and lay for two hours unattended, and Maguire escaped the rain of bullets by a miracle and was hid in the home of a friendly Mexican. Cooley believes he was shot from behind by the said guard.

The consular premises is riddled with bullets, mostly from the American side, because the front yard and stone wall was evidently used to fire from, as evidenced by the large number of shells found in the yard. No special damage was done to the consulate however, except broken glass. The municipal president, Sr. Peñaloza, was killed early in the fight, when he tried to stop the shooting by his own people, shot of course from the Arizona side. The latest reports of casualties is an officer and a corporal dead on the American side and eighteen wounded and fourteen dead and forty wounded on the Mexican side. I believe that the feeling among the best people on the Mexican side is that the blame for it all lays with the Mexican people. The commander of the soldiers here states that the soldiers were in quarters all the time and took no part in the fighting.

[September 13]. The residence of General Alvaro Obregón, like the American Consulate at Nogales, Sonora, is right on the international line. The Obregón residence, however, is one block nearer to the railroad station and practically opposite thereto. During the shooting at Nogales on August 27th, people in the American customhouse saw shooting come from the Obregón's residence. As a consequence, a very heavy fire was directed against it and the house was absolutely riddled with bullets. One window had eleven shots through the glass. Mrs. Obregón was at home at the time of the shooting with her small children and other children and some poor women whom she had brought in from the outside. General Obregón was absent in California.

As soon as possible after the shooting I went to see Mrs. Obregón to offer my services and to see that she was all right. She told me that at the time of the shooting she was alone in the house and that two men came into her yard, early in the shooting, so that they could shoot protected by the stone wall at the rear of the house; that she went to them and compelled them to leave the grounds in order to prevent just what did occur, viz, that the shooting attracted the fire from the American side. I believe that this is absolutely the truth and that there was no shooting from the Obregón residence but that of unattached civilians, who came into her yard without any authority. I know that General Obregón feels very keenly about the shooting up of his house and the incident is to be regretted. It has occurred to me that it might not be improper for the State Department to express suitable regret at that feature of the occurrence.

On the night of the 28th of August, when fire began again I went across the line and conducted Mrs. Obregón and her two small children to the home of her father on the American side. Since his return from San Francisco, General Obregón has called upon me to express his thanks and appreciation for my attention to his family.

196

"There were many bullets from the
U.S. side."

—Miguel Noriega (1899–   )*

Memories of 1918 battle at Nogales:

On the 27th of August of 1918, I was working as a carpenter at Nogales,
Arizona in the Catholic Church, and the priest sent me to the pharmacy
to get some patches that he used on his back. It must have been about
two in the afternoon. Upon arriving where the railroad station was, I
heard some shooting on both sides, and I took refuge to see what was
happening. I couldn't get to where I was going. I was hearing shots in
both cities but without knowing what it was about. In about thirty
minutes, I went to the post office.

I had the opportunity to see the armed black soldiers from the infantry
who were coming from the camp to the dividing line. In front of city
hall, a store was being built, and they climbed up there. I watched a
sergeant aim at a big clock. He threw himself, chest to the ground, and
fired three shots at it.

From there I waited a little longer, and I heard shots here and there.
I saw some ambulances go by. I still didn't know why there was shooting.
From there I headed to another street after an hour and a half, more
or less. Things were peaceful by then. I wanted to go to Nogales, Sonora,
because my parents were over there. Several of us tried to cross, but

*Interviewed in Nogales, Sonora in 1979 by Oscar J. Martínez. On file at the Institute
of Oral History, University of Texas at El Paso.

197

the American soldiers would not let us through the international crossing. At that time there was no fence at the dividing line. Another young man and I gained courage little by little, and we succeeded in passing through. Once on the Mexican side we didn't care if they shot at us, but we weren't shot at. We went toward the customs office. There I saw some of the injured and some of the dead, including one with a bullet in his head.

In front of the customs office, there was a plaza, and people started gathering. There were many dead there also. Toward the edge of Cortines Street, the municipal president lay dead. He was killed when he came out of a pharmacy with a handkerchief trying to stop the fire.

Later I heard that the trouble started when a carpenter crossed with a package where the railroad was. An American soldier told him to halt, but the carpenter did not hear him or I don't know what. The fact is that the soldier shot at him, but did not hit him, and the carpenter fled. Then the Mexican watchmen who were very close to the dividing line started to shoot toward the other side. The Mexicans and Americans shot at each other and that's how this thing began.

There were many bullets from the U.S. side, and there were no soldiers in Nogales, Sonora. The Mexican soldiers had left a day before, I think for Agua Prieta or Naco. Here the only ones who fought were the townspeople. If the soldiers had been in Nogales it would have been worse. There were only five or ten soldiers but the captain would not let them out, because it was an international thing. He didn't know what it was about; he could not order them to go fight. The people got arms wherever they could and started shooting. The townspeople felt bad. They wanted arms to fight. Some understood why and others didn't, but they were moved when they saw what was going on. All those who died were buried together. That's how it was.

The next day General Calles arrived from Hermosillo with his special guard. He had conversations with Nogales, Arizona, and they reached an agreement. The next night there was some shooting, but it was a small thing. General Calles tried to find out who had shot from the Mexican side, because he wanted to punish them. Then things calmed down.

"I could not see my son."

—E. W. Nevill*

Among the border raids that took place between 1917 and 1919, perhaps the most important was the attack on Nevill's ranch on March 25, 1918. E. W. Nevill gives his account of the incident.

John Wyatt and I owned a ranch about thirty-five miles south of Van Horn, Texas, bordering right along the Rio Grande. I was in charge of the outfit and had my son there also, and a Mexican family. I had been in Van Horn three or four days. There was a patrol of soldiers out there on what I call the upper ranch, and they told me that they understood there was a bunch of Mexicans in the country somewhere, that they had heard they were going to raid somebody. I was separating calves from cows at that time, feeding them, and trying to get some weans; that was the only place we had where I could fence off in that place. I had gone uptown to pay bills, as I did about once a month. When I talked to these soldiers and told them that they had better come on down to the ranch, that I would be there that evening late. They said they would. I still had a little business to do that morning before I could leave. I never thought anything more about it. I left town, as near as I can remember, about 10:30 A.M., and I rode on down.

I gets to the ranch just about sundown, and this Mexican woman who

*Interviewed in 1920. *Investigation of Mexican Affairs,* Senate Document 285, 66th Congress, 2nd Session (Washington, D.C., 1920), pp. 1510–15.

was staying on the ranch, she had supper ready. I unsaddled my horse, put him in a little pasture, where I had a number of other horses that were fed, went on in the house, and we ate supper. After we had finished, my son Glenn and I went into our room and sat down. I asked him if he had seen any Mexicans, and he said he had not. I then asked him what the report was that the patrol of soldiers had. He said they reported a bunch of bandits, that they were going up or down the river, they did not know which. So we sat there possibly fifteen minutes, and we heard the tramp of feet outside, and I supposed that it was this patrol that was coming down from the upper ranch. I got up and went out in the hall and looked through the screen, I saw that it was Mexicans. There was something like fifty of them. They all came in with the exception of five. They all ran right into the hen house and immediately came out. As soon as they came out, they started shooting at the house.

I walked across the room to this hall and saw five more standing over there on the other side of the house with guns in their hands waiting, I suppose, for us to come out; the others were shooting this way. They were waiting for us to come out the door so they could kill us. Instead of going out I just walked back to this partition door that is in our room.

I went outside and looked around the corner as well as I could to see if there was any of them in sight. They were not, so I called to my son to come on. There was a ditch down there, I guess 250 or 300 yards. I was trying to get to that ditch. We could not stay in the house, because those bullets came in through the walls just like paper. As I started off I glanced around and saw my son turn to the right; he did exactly what I wanted him to do. I went straight off. I never thought but what I was going to be killed, but by him turning to the right I knew I was drawing all the fire, giving him an opportunity to get away. I had not gone far until they saw me, and they all began shooting. They shot my hat off, and shot my rifle out of my hand three times. The last time I left it laying there. I got down in this ditch and stopped and looked back. I could not see my son. I then crawled back and got plumb back on top of the hill. I was at the ditch on top of the hill, and looked back up that way. I did not see him. I supposed he got away and ran down in the hills, so I got in the ditch and ran down to this open place. I did not see him, and I did not hardly know what to do. I thought possibly he had gone off through the country and gotten in some bushes, and ran around the other way. So I ran straight across this level place. When I got over there I hunted around there and could not find him, so I supposed then he had hid himself, and as soon as everything was over he would come out, and we would get together. I did the same thing, I hid. After they ransacked the house, three of them took my trail, followed me up and prowled around there. I don't know how long it was, something like a couple of hours.

I saw one of them once; I heard them three different times coming back. They trailed me so far, then could not trail me any further because I mussed up my trail before I hid. I went in many different directions, and crossed back so many times they did not know where I had gone, but I could see them and hear them three different times. I could not get out of there to go back to the house until 3:30A.M., when G Troop of the 8th Cavalry came up. When I got back I found that my son had been shot all to pieces. There was a hole in his forehead. You could drop a hen egg through this hole in his forehead; in fact, like it had been shot out. He had been beat with rifles and a stick, and he was black and blue all over his face and head. His body was within four feet of the house and about twelve feet from the door. The Mexican woman was dead in the kitchen. Everything in the house was torn upside down, scattered all over, and everything gone. Nothing was there except some empty boxes, empty trunks, old bedsteads; everything else was carried away.

The band was made up of people that hang out along this border. They were not Carrancistas, they were not Villistas, they were not anything.

> "It was ticklish work, this march
> through a hostile town in the dead
> of night."
>
> —J. R. Montgomery*

Following long estabished practice, U.S. troops intervened in the Juárez battle of 1919 when it was determined that American lives and property were in jeopardy. This incursion into foreign soil made the difference in the fighting, resulting in the Villistas retreating from the town. Some of the experiences of the American soldiers are told by J. R. Montgomery, an El Paso reporter.

History was made when the 24th Infantry marched across the Santa Fe bridge at 11:15 o'clock Sunday night and took possession of Juárez and environs.

Juárez has been "taken" many times, particularly in recent years, and almost everybody along the border has anticipated that sooner or later Yankee soldiers would have their inning in the game of capturing the notorious little border town, but it will be admitted that Sunday night's adventure of the colored troops came as a distinct surprise.

It is soldiering de luxe to march down a paved street under electric lights to the prospective battlefield with signal corps men going along stringing wires so that the commanding officer may talk at any moment to the general in the rear.

*El Paso Times, June 17, 1919, pp. 1, 3.

It is the last word in military modernity to carry along couriers in side cars, motor-driven ambulances, machine guns, one-pounders and Very pistols.

A Very pistol is not a weapon, but a signalling device—a single-barrelled pistol which throws flares high in the air. A flare is a combustible which resembles a roman candle ball. Sunday night green flares were used to designate the position of the front lines.

General Erwin could sit in his office in the Mills building and locate the position of the front line troops in Juárez by these green flares. In France the Very lights were used to call for barrages, mark out front lines, and other purposes.

Also, in France, the doughboys used to sell Very pistols to the members of the Q.M.C. for souvenirs—telling the unsophisticated S.O.S. boys they were German anti-aircraft guns and getting beaucoup francs for them.

Preceded by two heavily armored automobiles the march of the dusky doughboys of the 24th through the streets of Juárez to the racetrack was a model of efficiency. The commanding officer took no chances.

It was ticklish work, this march through a hostile town in the dead of night. It was known that the place was full of Villistas, and for some reason no one seemed to trust fully the Carrancistas. Ambushes might easily be attempted. Therefore, flank patrols darted through all cross and paralleling streets. Thus maximum protection was given by a minimum use of men.

The head of the column turned toward the east at the customhouse and followed the street car line to the racetrack. Bullets whistled constantly overhead, strange bugle calls from the Carrancista troops filled the air, and the shells from the American field pieces shrieked and burst just beyond the colored soldiers, but still they marched steadily to their objective.

Once the advance party was fired on. Quickly the men deployed and poured a rain of bullets in the direction from whence came the insectivorous-sounding hostile bullets.

Occasionally bandoliered and white-hatted Carrancistas clattered up on little ponies and gave advice and information to the Americans. The Carrancistas were sure the Americans would meet with hot resistance from the Villistas. These assurances of a forthcoming fight seemed to cheer the invading force.

203

Onward they pressed toward the Villista lines, frequently coming across and relieving hard-pressed Carrancista detachments. After these passages of lines the Carrancistas wended their way back to Fort Hidalgo, the haven of safety of the federals.

Finally the Americans reached their objective—the Villista trenches. They were empty. There would be no fighting, and the colored soldiers seemed greatly disappointed. So there was nothing to do but settle down in comfort until daylight. The terrain in front was thoroughly reconnoitered, but contact with the enemy was never established. He seemed to have flown far away, but the colored soldiers took a good look at Juárez before they returned to El Paso yesterday and seemed to regard the adventure as a wonderfully invigorating relief from the stagnation of several years they have endured on the Mexican border.

"We were gonna race that day, when
they started this goddam revolution!"
—Pete Leyva (1894–   )*

Memories of 1919 battle of Juárez:

During Pancho's last attack on Juárez in 1919, the racetrack was
destroyed, one of the most beautiful tracks in the world. The American
troops shot the hell out of it. Before the battle I went over to see my
father, who was with Villa in the outskirts of Juárez, and found out when
the attack would begin. At that time I used to go to the track all the
time to sell the owner papers on which appeared the lineups for the
day. A lot of Americans worked there, but some got scared and wouldn't
go to work, afraid the revolutionaries would take the town at any time.
The day before the attack I told all the horsemen, "They're gonna attack."
They said, "Aw, you're full of shit." I said, "You better get your horses
and your ass across the river." They said, "Nah," and I said, "All right."

The next day the owner told me, "Come here, boy. Get up on this
window. I want you to sell tickets." And we were gonna race that day,
when they started this goddam revolution! All the gringos left on the
streetcar! A few of us stayed because I knew that I wouldn't get hurt,
because all I had to do was to hide behind them cement walls, and my
father's troops and Pancho's troops wouldn't hurt me because some of
them knew me. That's why I agreed to sell tickets.

*Interviewed in El Paso in 1976 by Oscar J. Martínez. On file at the Institute of Oral
History, University of Texas at El Paso.

205

When the fighting started they started telling me, "Hey, Pete, take my horses!" I answered, "You take them, not me! I'm not gonna get out there and get shot!" Finally a good friend of mine came up to me with three horses. He said, "Pete, I'll give you a horse if you take my horses across." I agreed to do that and I was given a race horse.

"Whenever American officials have deemed it necessary or convenient to invade our territory, they have done so."

—Venustiano Carranza*

Recurring border incidents and tragedies involving citizens of both countries figured prominently in U.S.-Mexican relations. About the time New Mexico Senator Albert B. Fall was compiling his catalog of atrocities committed against Americans (see Part IV), President Venustiano Carranza included in his annual report to his countrymen a long list of U.S. violations of Mexico's territorial integrity as well as deaths or woundings of Mexicans at the hands of Americans. A brief extract from the lengthy report follows; the incidents described occurred in 1919.

In April, at a spot known as Vado de Piedra near Ojinaga, Chihuahua, some American soldier twice penetrated about twelve kilometers into our territory while they pursued some bandits. They attacked the outlaws, inflicting five casualties, including the accidental wounding of a young woman and a man. We protested through our embassy, but to date the guilty parties hae not been punished.

In May, Jesús Aguirre, a Mexican shipyard worker in Bockport, Texas,

*Venustiano Carranza's Presidential Report to the Nation, September 1, 1919. Report of the Secretaría de Relaciones Exteriores. *Excelsior*, September 2, 1919.

was unjustly beaten-up by three American citizens, and local authorities did nothing to bring them to justice. Our consul in Corpus Christi reported that in Bockport there is marked enmity toward Mexicans. They are not admitted in the hotels, boarding houses, restaurants, barber shops, and other public places; their children are confined to a special school that has many deficiencies.

In June, the California Department of Education excluded Mexican children from the public schools of Santa Paula, El Centro, and other places, sending them to the schools for negroes.

In June, Villa and his followers attacked Ciudad Juárez. Having failed in three successive assaults, Villa tried to provoke an international conflict by shooting into U.S. territory, where he caused personal tragedies. U.S. troops crossed the border with the intention of dispersing the Villistas, returning the next day to their country. General Francisco González [the Carrancista commander in Juárez] demanded the immediate departure of those troops. Our government protested the invasion and Washington explained that the troops crossed only for protection, having as their only objective to repel the Villistas.

In July, Mexican paymaster M. Palma was assaulted at Marfa, Texas, by three individuals and dispossessed of the money he was carrying for our soldiers in Ojinaga, Chihuahua. The foreman of the grand jury of Presidio, Texas, told our consul that after a detailed investigation they were unable to fix responsibility for the robbery. They also concluded that the paymaster's decision to travel so early in the morning was reprehensible. The guilty ones have not yet been apprehended.

In July, a patrol of U.S. troops from Los Adobes, Texas, fired at some Mexican workers thinking that they were deserters. Julio Carrasco was killed. Our embassy presented the case to the American government; it was recommended that the U.S. Congress approve a law to indemnify Carrasco's family.

In August, three American soldiers crossed the border into San Juan, Chihuahua. Our troops tried to capture the invaders, who shot back and fled after killing one Mexican soldier. Our embassy has presented the case to the U.S. government, but it is not known if the guilty ones have been punished.

Many Mexicans have tried to cross the Rio Bravo [Rio Grande] without abiding with established [U.S.] laws and regulations. This has resulted in tragedies, since U.S. guards shoot at such travelers. Feliciano Hernández and Reyes Payanes are among those killed at San Antonio, Chihuahua. The Mexican government has taken appropriate action.

On various occasions U.S. army airplanes have flown in our territory. In all cases our embassy has been instructed by the Secretaría de Relaciones Exteriores to submit the necessary protestations, but the incursions have continued. Last August one airplane landed in Chihuahua 112 kilometers from the border. Before it was known where that plane was, U.S. officials asked us for permission to have another plane look for the lost aviators. We granted that permission but it was never utilized. A band of Villistas captured the aviators and demanded a ransom. Seeking to liberate their compatriots, some U.S. forces invaded our territory. The Mexican government protested and asked that the invaders leave immediately. By August 27 the invading forces had returned to the United States. That grave and unprovoked act constitutes a violation of our rights. It has profoundly hurt the patriotic feeling of Mexicans. Unfortunately, in the history of our relations with the United States this is not the only example of such an abuse. Whenever American officials have deemed it necessary or convenient to invade our territory, they have done so, thus violating the rights of a friendly country.

Part IV

Victims of War

Tragedy and suffering mark any armed conflict, and the Revolution spread plenty of both throughout Mexico. In the countryside, the scant protection afforded by established authority quickly collapsed, leaving the people in constant fear. *Federales* and *revolucionarios* victimized rich and poor alike, seizing whatever they needed or felt like having, inflicting personal harm on those who resisted. Armies desperate for manpower raided villages of their young men, creating a dilemma for their families: whether they hid the young men or allowed them to join the army, the villagers lost their services as protectors. Young women were especially vulnerable to that lawless climate; many became kidnap victims, destined to serve their kidnappers' sexual and other personal needs. Legends abound about Pancho Villa's insatiable appetite for women, and his ruthless methods of fulfilling it. Whatever the degree of truth behind the legend, it is a fact that thousands of families reacted with terror to word that Villa was headed their way. A common precaution was to hide all young women or to send them to stay with far-off relatives. At the border, women repeatedly crossed into the United States seeking temporary refuge whenever attacks from Villa or similarly feared insurgents were expected.[1]

The execution of prisoners by firing squad or hanging party organized on the spot was commonplace, as was the unceremonious burning and mass burial of corpses in large, common graves. Dignified burial became a luxury. We do not know exactly how many Mexicans, including civilians, died during the period, but knowledgeable sources place the number at approximately two million.[2] Violence was, of course, only one

213

cause of mass deaths; malnutrition, disease, lack of medical care, and other hardships also took their toll.

The horror of war was perhaps most dramatic in the fighting in urban centers. In the city of Zacatecas, an especially grisly battle in 1914 between Villistas and federales left several thousand dead. Because epidemics were a constant threat, the triumphant Villistas had to rapidly dispose of the corpses. Thousands of bodies were doused with gasoline and burned; others were thrown into trenches or abandoned mine shafts; and still others were loaded on flatcars and dumped unburied in the countryside. The misery of Zacatecas's residents was exacerbated by the persecution of suspected government collaborators and widespread looting.[3] Other cities and towns throughout the northern states and along the border endured comparable trials, though on a lesser scale.

To live a normal life under such conditions became impossible. Surrounded by violence and its attendant chaos, hundreds of thousands faced poverty and destitution. Recurring food shortages prompted many Mexicans to abandon villages and towns for the bigger cities, where their problems were compounded by overcrowding. At some point, almost everyone had the experience of waiting in line for provisions that never arrived; predictably, this situation triggered food riots throughout Mexico.[4]

For many emigration became the only alternative to the dangers and uncertainties unleashed by the Revolution. Thus an estimated one million Mexicans, most of them from the lower classes, fled to the United States during the 1910s. Migrants from middle- and upper-class backgrounds frequently had to abandon property and personal possessions in their flight; such was the case with affluent supporters of the Porfirio Díaz regime. Hardships did not end at the border, however. Many refugees encountered serious economic problems and most had some difficulty adjusting to a strange country. An undetermined number of these people eventually returned to Mexico, but circumstances caused most of them to settle permanently north of the Rio Grande.

A majority of these refugees settled in such southwestern cities as San Antonio, El Paso, Tucson, San Diego, and Los Angeles, but some made their way deeper into the United States. The influx of Mexican immigrants had a profound impact on the population of the U.S. borderlands. Mexican culture was more in evidence, and in some urban centers persons of Mexican descent came to outnumber Anglos. In El

214

Paso, for example, by 1916 Mexicans made up 53 percent of the city's 70,000 residents.[5]

Emigration from Mexico also involved foreigners traumatized by the Revolution. In 1910, 60,000 Americans resided south of the border, but ten years later their number had shrunk to 12,000.[6] Throughout the period many Americans were terrorized, forced to pay tribute, dispossessed, and looted; in extreme cases, they witnessed the deaths of relatives or friends. The constant recurrence of such disturbances prompted a subcommittee of the U.S. Senate's Committee on Foreign Relations to investigate conditions in Mexico, focusing on personal and property damages suffered by Americans. Headed by New Mexico Senator Albert B. Fall, the subcommittee in 1919–1920 held hearings in New York City, Washington, D.C., San Antonio, Brownsville, Laredo, El Paso, Tucson, Nogales, San Diego, and Los Angeles. A parade of nearly 300 witnesses related many horror stories, which Senator Fall promptly used (unsuccessfully) to promote U.S. intervention in Mexico. When completed, the subcommittee's 5,000-page report included countless descriptions of rapes, murders, and many other outrages. In sum, 587 Americans were said to have died as a result of the Revolution, with over a fourth of those deaths taking place along the border. The subcommittee placed personal and property damages in excess of $50 million. To indemnify the families of the departed, the report demanded that Mexico pay almost $15 million.[7]

With the recitation of tragedy after tragedy that befell Americans in Mexico, the subcommittee aroused U.S. public opinion against its neighbor. The report is a clear example of selective investigation, exaggeration, and slander. Yet there is much truth in the individual testimonies gathered by Senator Fall, and extracts from the report have been included in this section to illustrate the harrowing experiences of many U.S. citizens.

One group of Americans particularly affected by the Revolution were the Mormons, who had made western Chihuahua their home since the 1880s. In the early 1910s, these colonists tried to follow a policy of neutrality, seeking friendship and guaranties of safety from the various chieftains who controlled the region. A complicating factor in relations between the Anglo Mormons and the Mexicans was the relative affluence of the former. Naturally this contrast caused resentment among the impoverished local population. By the summer of 1912, the leaders of

215

the Mormon colonies concluded that their lives were in jeopardy, and they decided to evacuate the area. About 2,000 people fled to El Paso. They hoped that once peace returned to Mexico they would be able to return to their farms. Eventually a bold minority in the exiled group returned to their adopted homeland, but most of the Mormon refugees remained in the United States.[8]

To understand the treatment accorded foreigners in Mexico, one must recall the deep resentment Mexicans felt toward the United States. Americans had invaded Mexico and taken half her territory only two generations earlier. In what then became the U.S. Southwest, Mexicans had been subjected to racism and exploitation since the signing of the Treaty of Guadalupe Hidalgo in 1848. In Mexico proper, U.S. interests had exercised considerable economic control. Repeatedly Washington had interfered in Mexico's internal affairs, and on occasion U.S. troops had violated Mexican territorial sovereignty, as was done in the 1914 invasion of Veracruz. The ideology of the Revolution called for liberation not only from native oppressors, but from foreign exploiters and manipulators as well. Washington was distant, but anger against the United States could be directed at Americans then residing in Mexico. Of course, many atrocities committed against U.S. citizens had little to do with politics; lawless elements repeatedly victimized the vulnerable regardless of nationality.

The selections that follow are divided into two parts. The first part includes the stories of Mexicans, most of whom eventually migrated to the United States, who experienced various types of difficulties associated with the Revolution. Interestingly, some of these emigrants were of mixed ancestry, with one Mexican and one foreign parent, but their culture was predominantly or at least half Mexican. The second part deals with the memories of Anglo Americans and other foreigners who found themselves in such difficult circumstances in Mexico that they were forced to seek refuge north of the Rio Grande.

NOTES

1. When John Reed sought Villa's comment on stories that he had violated many women, Villa reportedly asked Reed if he had ever met any male relative of females such abused. "Or even," Villa continued, "a witness?" John Reed,

Insurgent Mexico, Albert L. Michaels and James W. Wilkie, eds. (New York: Simon & Schuster, 1969), p. 124. Several oral history interviews at the Institute of Oral History at the University of Texas at El Paso deal with this theme.

2. Charles C. Cumberland, Mexico: *The Struggle for Modernity* (New York: Oxford University Press, 1968), p. 241.

3. William Weber Johnson, *Heroic Mexico: The Narrative History of a Twentieth Century Revolution* (New York: Doubleday, 1968), pp. 204–15.

4. *El Paso Herald*, 1914: January 20, p. 3; June 26, p. 1; October 7, p. 3. *El Paso Herald*, 1915: May 19, p. 1; June 19, p. 2A; June 21, p. 2.

5. U.S. Bureau of the Census, Department of Commerce, *Special Census of the Population of El Paso, Texas, January 15, 1916* (Washington, D.C., 1916), p. 4.

6. *Investigation of Mexican Affairs*, Senate Document 285, 66th Congress, 2nd Session (Washington, D.C., 1920), pp. 3311–13.

7. Ibid., pp. 3318, 3325, 3382.

8. Florence C. Lister and Robert H. Lister, *Chihuahua: Storehouse of Storms* (Albuquerque: University of New Mexico Press, 1966), pp. 220–25.

Mexicans Who Took Refuge in the United States

"We had the luck of being able to get out of the house."
—Enrique Acevedo (1898–   )*

Memories of the Juárez battles of 1911 and 1913:

When Madero attacked Juárez, my family had already taken refuge in El Paso, but I had gone that day to school in Juárez. In those moments I was in our house in the high part of Juárez, and I was able to see the revolutionaries who came protecting themselves with the bank of the river so that the federalists wouldn't shoot at them, because the bullets would go over into the United States. Then my father found me and we returned to El Paso. It was certainly luck that we didn't get hit by a bullet because on Juárez Avenue we protected ourselves in some adobe walls so that the bullets wouldn't hit us. We got across the bridge fine on foot and a few days later we returned to Juárez because order was reestablished right away. Everything returned to normal. A municipal president was named and the revolutionary forces were very much in control of things.

When we *didn't* return for a long time was when Villa attacked Juárez in November of 1913. My father was the owner of a customs agency, and since things weren't being imported or anything because of the Revolution and the customs agencies were useless, then in order to support us my father had to get politically involved as secretary of the

*Interviewed in El Paso in 1974 by Robert H. Novak. On file at the Institute of Oral History, University of Texas at El Paso.

219

municipal government of Juárez. Villa had attacked Chihuahua and had been turned back. Then Huerta ordered that propaganda be disseminated on every corner in Juárez, telling the public by means of a public speaker, that Villa had been annihilated and that that was proof that the government was strong and that they should have confidence. My father had to speak in public on every street corner some five days before Villa entered Juárez. Naturally he dwelt upon the bad points about Villa, that he was a bandit, etc.

Villa captured Juárez the 15th of November. On that occasion various officers, volunteers, and some police passed in front of our house twenty minutes before being shot by the firing squad. That's what would have happened to my father if Villa had caught him! He would have been executed immediately. But we had the luck of being able to get out of the house. Villa took Juárez around 2 or 3 in the morning, and my father and I left the house for El Paso around 2 in the afternoon, both of us on bicycles. We were able to cross the river and we arrived safe and sound. My mother and my brother went to El Paso a little later because they were afraid that they would be captured and my father would have to return to Juárez. We didn't return to Juárez for several months.

The fall of Juárez was famous because Villa was a very sly man. Somehow he got the train into the center of the city, got the troops out, and they began to attack the public buildings which weren't prepared for an attack. In some 3 or 4 hours they took over the federal barracks and the municipal building where there were several volunteers. There were some who were already dead, and the next day Villa executed several federal officers and several people in the barracks. We heard the shots of the firing squad because we lived relatively close to there. We went to El Paso without absolutely any money because my father hadn't been paid for two weeks. There wasn't any money in Juárez; the federal government as well as the state and city governments was in bankruptcy. The first weeks in El Paso were very hard. We were living with some relatives of ours. As soon as he could, my father began to work on some hard jobs although he wasn't accustomed to that because he had always been an office worker, bank employee, customs employee, and secretary of the municipal government. But he had to work at whatever he could in order to support us. I, recommended by a family here, began to work as a youngster delivering packages for the White House Department Store, where I still am sixty-one years later.

In my opinion El Paso began to grow after 1910, '11, '12, when there was a great immigration of Mexicans, many with a lot of money, who came to live in this city. Many millionaires from Torreón, México, Guadalajara, and Chihuahua established themselves in El Paso for many years. They bought property everywhere. Many families stayed here and others, the majority, returned to México. At present there are still families living here that came during that time; for example, my family is one of those. Afterward the children, the grandchildren now, are American citizens, born here. Others are naturalized like myself, and others are Americans by birth.

"I put my finger in his wound."
—María Trinidad Jaso de
Barrionuevo (1904–   )*

Many children became exposed to the danger and violence of the Revolution at an early age. A native of Zacatecas, María Trinidad Jaso de Barrionuevo recalls how she aided her father on two occasions, and how she managed to see the light side of otherwise grisly situations.

When I was eight years old and living in Zacatecas, there were bands of bandits who hid in the mountains and periodically attacked the villages down below. One night they attacked my father, who owned some cattle. My mother had gone to the city, and I had stayed with my father. The leader of the bandits was named Ramón Díaz and they called him "El Loco Ramón." When my father heard shots and then found out that they were trying to break down the door with axes, he took me by the hand and we ran out the back door.

As we walked in the darkness we could hear firing back at our house. We were very scared. We couldn't see very well where we were going and that area was full of holes. I grabbed him from behind and warned him he was going to fall in! He said, "Daughter, you have saved my life! Thank God!" We then took another road toward the cemetery. He covered me with a blanket that we had and, feeling that my heart was

*Interviewed in El Paso in 1979 by Virgilio Sánchez and Mario Galdos. On file at the Institute of Oral History, University of Texas at El Paso.

beating fast, told me not to be afraid. We could still hear the commotion back at our house. We spent the night at an abandoned house nearby and in the morning we could hear dogs barking. The bandits were going back to the mountains.

We headed toward a nearby town named San Francisco and went to the plaza, where several people had gathered. My father asked them what was going on. One of them told him that "El Loco Ramón" and his band had killed German Gemá and his wife, and that their bodies were laying in a nearby street. The same bullet had gone through both of them. They died trying to prevent the bandits from carrying off their two daughters. The girls were taken to be abused by the men.

Later the bandits came to our house again and this time they did capture my father. There was nothing we could do. They tied a rope around his neck and they would pull him until he would fall. My mother and the rest of us were locked in one of the bedrooms. When we would hear father's outcries and supplications we yelled, "Dear God!" Finally I opened a window and jumped out, injuring myself slightly. My mother then became concerned about me and said, "They are going to kill her!" I reached the spot where they had my father at the moment they pulled on the rope. He seemed half dead. I grabbed at the bandit and said, "You will not kill my father, because we are all small! Leave us our father!" Either that man felt sorry for me or lacked courage to throw me off because he then commanded his men to leave. My father was all beaten up. After that my father would tell everyone that I had saved his life twice. My father was quite scared and he sold everything and we moved to Guadalupe. That town organized a *defensa social* (self-protective association) and the group would search the mountains for the bad men. Each week they would return with several of them, sometimes even half a dozen. One time they brought in "El Loco Ramón." We felt sorry for him when the firing squad shot him.

On another occasion they captured two young men whom my father knew. Their parents tried very hard to save them, but there was nothing they could do. The father did request that his sons not be shot in the face. He didn't want to see them disfigured. That day I was on my way home from school with two of my girl friends, and we found out about the execution; we decided to go see it. I stood behind the man who shot Alfonso, the older of the two brothers. They shot six bandits at the same time, and each one was killed by an individual rifleman. Alfonso was a big man with blue eyes. He was the only one who didn't want a blindfold. He just tightened his belt, put his hands by his pockets and said, "Go ahead!" He got shot in the heart.

After he went down I got near him and said, "It's good that they didn't hit your face, but what a shot they gave you." Then I put my finger in his wound and decided to show the blood to his father. I said, "Don Poncho, they didn't hit Alfonso in the face. They hit him right in the heart, and very deeply. Look, I stuck my finger in his wound." My father was standing there and hit me with his hand, telling me, "What is the matter with you? How could you show a father his son's blood?" I felt very ashamed and hurt.

After things quieted down, the town learned of a note that Alfonso had left with his wife, where he had written, "You know, my darling . . . in the oven." I managed to read that part of the paper myself, and I went around telling everybody what it said. When my father found out, he ordered me to keep quiet, to stop talking about that. Shortly thereafter the *defensa social* found that oven. A lot of riches were found there, including ornaments and gold from the church. They had stuffed the oven with things they had been stealing.

After the battle of Zacatecas my older brother Nicolás and I decided to go see the dead soldiers. We walked several kilometers and saw many bodies. Some were being buried in big trenches and others were being burned. And there we were, just prying. Nicolás liked to gather bullet shells, and he filled his pockets with them. We noticed a yellow dog sitting by a dead sergeant. Nicolás warned me not to go near the dog because he might bite me. But as we walked away the dog followed us. We tried to shake him off by frightening him, but he stuck with us.

When we got home father was upset at seeing us with the dog. He said, "Dear God, why have you brought this animal here? Someone is going to recognize him and they might think we are part of that dead sergeant's family. They will come here and it's possible. . . . Go ahead, shoot him." I answered, "No, poor dog." We convinced father to let us keep the dog. After all, it had not been our fault that he had followed us. He was well mannered and we loved him very much.

One day I went to where my father did the banding of the cows. They had just branded some and the fire was still hot. The branding iron was off to the side and I decided to put it in the fire. When it got hot I looked around for some animal to brand, and I branded the dog. Poor animal, he ran and hid under the bed! When Nicolás got home he asked about the dog because he was not around. Nicolás thought the dog was lost. Then we heard dog cries. Nicolás took him from under the bed and saw that he was burned. He really got angry at me. "You are wicked," he said. "You have an evil soul. I don't know what kind of a woman you are." Later [when the wound healed] the brand I put on the dog looked really good.

"It may be a girl, or it may be a boy."
—John Reed (1887–1920)*

Refugees who had straggled through the desert for days in November 1913 following the evacuation of Chihuahua City by the federal forces encountered further troubles as they crossed the border. John Reed, who was at Ojinaga-Presidio as a war correspondent, describes some of the difficulties faced by the exiles.

Along the main street passed an unbroken procession of sick, exhausted, starving people, driven from the interior by fear of the approaching rebels, a journey of eight days over the most terrible desert in the world. They were stopped by a hundred soldiers along the street and robbed of every possession that took the federals' fancy. Then they passed on to the river, and on the American side they had to run the gantlet of the United States customs and immigration officials and the Army Border Patrol who searched them for arms.

Hundreds of refugees poured across the river, some on horseback driving cattle before them, some in wagons, and others on foot. The inspectors were not very gentle.

"Come down off that wagon!" one would shout to a Mexican woman with a bundle in her arm.

"But, señor, for what reason? . . ." she would begin.

"Come down there or I'll pull you down!" he would yell.

*John Reed, *Insurgent Mexico* (New York: D. Appleton, 1914), pp. 4–5, 7.

226

They made an unnecessarily careful and brutal search of the men and of the women, too.

As I stood there, a woman waded across the ford, her skirts lifted unconcernedly to her thighs. She wore a voluminous shawl, which was humped up in front as if she were carrying something in it.

"Hi, there!" shouted a customs man. "What have you got under your shawl?" She slowly opened the front of her dress, and answered placidly: "I don't know, señor. It may be a girl, or it may be a boy."

Sometimes a rich refugee, with a good deal of gold sewed in his saddle blankets, would get across the river without the federals discovering it. There were six big, high-power automobiles in Presidio waiting for just such a victim. They would soak him one hundred dollars gold to make a trip to the railroad; and on the way, somewhere in the desolate wastes south of Marfa, he was almost sure to he held up by masked men and everything taken away from him.

"Huertistas would run their horses through the orchards."
—Juseta Sumaya (1901–   )*

Born in Cabo San Lucas, Baja California, Juseta Sumaya comments on the disturbances that drove her family to San Diego and on the impossibility of returning to the life she had left behind.

My grandfather and all of his sons had their own ranches and other businesses all around. My father was on the side of Madero. Hundreds of Huertistas would come to our ranch and run their horses through the orchards, destroying the fruit and other things we had planted. They were dressed very badly; only the chiefs wore uniforms. One day the soldiers came from Cabo San Lucas and killed chickens, turkeys, and other animals that my grandfather had. They cooked underneath the trees. The soldiers stayed one day.

We had a friend who had a large ranch named La Laguna. The soldiers arrived one night and burned his house, just because he supported Madero. All the families slept in the fields because they were scared of Huerta's soldiers. They would take away the girls and abuse them.

We left Baja California by boat to San Diego in 1917, where we rented a house. In 1918 it was terrible during the Spanish flu [swine flu epi-

*Interviewed in Chula Vista, California, in 1978 by Oscar J. Martínez. On file at the Institute of Oral History, University of Texas at El Paso.

demic]. Our whole family got it. We would wear a mask on the street, and at work we would spray ourselves with a disinfectant. Everyone wore masks. A godchild of my father's died. He worked in the fields and during weekends he would come home. One day he came home very sick and he was sent to the hospital. The authorities would check the homes, because many did not want to go to the hospital. Many who went to the hospital died there. It may have been because the doctors were not familiar with the disease. My mother would cure the sick ones at home with remedies she knew about, with herbs and pills. The symptoms were headache and a very high fever. My mother would hide us so the health authorities would not find out, because those who went to the hospital would not return.

We went back to Baja California in 1919. My father had left our home, our cattle, everything, in the custody of a nephew. When we got there our home was in ruins; there were no animals. The nephew had sold them; he did not care. I returned to San Diego in 1923.

"What do you think this is, a horse
stable?"
—Millie Gossett (1902–1976)*

*In recalling confrontations with insurgents, people often
stress how they rose to the occasion, maintaining dignity and
respect by verbally challenging the intruders. Mollie Gossett,
a native of Monterrey of Mexican–North American parentage,
relates with a light touch how her family handled such situations.*

In 1913, my daddy was working as assistant superintendent for the
American Smelting and Refining Company plant in Torreón. He had a
wonderful job, and it was great living there. We had everything we
needed, including private tutors because the schools were closed on
account of the Revolution. We had an English teacher in the morning
and a Spanish teacher in the afternoon. We had a fourteen room house
with beautiful furniture. My dad was a fanatic about furniture, and my
mother had the most beautiful bedroom imported from Germany, with
a red velvet canopy. We had two living rooms; the first one had long
drapes and beautiful love seat suites.

My mother had a rule that the children were not supposed to go into
that first living room, and I remember one day walking in there when
she had company. I was about ten or eleven. My mother made signs
with her eyes for me to get out. I got so scared I fell off the chair because

*Interviewed in El Paso in 1975 by Sarah John. On file at the Institute of Oral History,
University of Texas at El Paso.

230

I knew I was going to get a whipping! "You're going to get it!" she said. So I had to get out by walking backwards.

It wasn't too long after that that we had to leave Mexico. One day my dad called and said to get all the kids inside, that Villa's men were coming to kill the *federales* who were stationed in Torreón. My brother Willie and I thought the whole thing was a lot of fun and we were up on the roof. Bullets were just "psst-psst" shooting over our heads! Mother finally sent one of the men who worked for us, a *mozo* [man servant], and he got us down. By that time, there were three or four men at our door on horses. Well, they walked right in, horses and all, into our patio! We had a garden in the middle with a little fountain, Mexican style. They let their horses drink water right inside our garden. They said, "Get moving! We want to eat!"

The *cabecilla*, or head of the troop, was a famous leader named Díaz. There were four or five men with him. My mother came out of her room and told them, "What do you think this is, a horse stable or a barracks? Get out this instant!" My *mother*, imagine! And they all had big rifles! She said, "I will not feed *anybody* unless you take your horses out to the backyard. You can eat here, but get your horses to the back where they belong." So Díaz said, "Ah! Get going! Out!" because mother was so brave. Imagine, they could have killed her and the rest of us! But he respected mother since she was not afraid.

We had a few refugees in our home because there had been a flood and the *peones* had had their homes washed away, so they came to stay with us. Díaz thought that my father was getting men together for a revolution or something because there were about ten or twenty extra men at the house. So, he took my father out, and they were going to execute him across the street. They marched him out there. My sister Maggie, who was fourteen at the time, went with them. Díaz said to my father, "We're going to shoot you, *gringo*, because you are recruiting men." Maggie stood in front of him and said, "All right. If you're going to kill my daddy, you have to kill me, too!" Finally Díaz said, "Well, this family is something else! We can't do *anything*. Leave, then. But get out in two hours!" Boy, were we crawling!

The company sent a car to take us to Torreón to a special train sent from the United States. Mother only had time to get sheets to put our clothes in. There were eleven children; the baby was five months old. After waiting inside the train in Torreón for two days (I don't know why), we left for San Pedro. But there a bridge had been burned, and we couldn't go any farther. All the men on the train then proceeded to build the bridge with lumber the train was carrying in the flat cars. Halfway from Torreón to Monterrey we had three *asaltos* (holdups). The bandits would steal some of our food. We had a whole load of canned goods; the government had furnished everything. So they stole what we had. We'd been on the train two weeks when somebody saw a cow or a bull out on the prairie. They all got out and killed it. They had big tubs and made soup and cooked that meat to feed us. Of course, mother would nurse the baby, but she needed food.

You can imagine mother with eleven kids without a bath! She saw a ditch out in the prairie, I think where the cattle would drink water. Right away, they stopped the train and said, "Everybody get out and take a bath if you want to." It was muddy water. We hadn't been there very long when someone began shooting at us. We had to get on the train, full of soap! That's the way we stayed till we got to Monterrey!

On the train, my brother Willie and I would sneak away and go to another car. He'd look out one window on one side of the train, and I'd look out the other, to see how many corpses we could see hanging on the posts. We counted them. Some of them were bloated; some of them had their tongues out. It scared the heck out of me. I couldn't sleep at night!

In the Monterrey area, Villa and his men came along and got on the train. They were killing the *federales*. Some of them were cutting the bottom of their feet, and they'd throw them on our train. Mother hid one of the *federales*. He was kind of *güerito* [blond] and she said that he was one of her sons. Since the *villistas* were also stealing girls, my mother had to tie my sisters' heads with some rags so they wouldn't see them. We were especially worried that they might take the two older girls, who were very beautiful. My daddy, who had a gun, told the girls to get on one end of the coach. "If some of those bandits get on this train, I'm going to have to shoot you both." He'd rather shoot them than let the bandits take them. You can imagine how hard it was for both dad and mom.

In Monterrey we were told we could not proceed to El Paso. We had to go back to Tampico and take a boat from there to Galveston. We were at sea for five days, had a terrible storm, and I nearly died. They told mama they'd have to bury me at sea, because I was vomiting all over

232

the place! But I got by. When we got to Galveston they kept us in quarantine for ten days before they let us out of the boat. Daddy then took us to a hotel so we could all get cleaned up. Then we got a train to El Paso.

We went to El Paso because of the ASARCO plant there, where daddy could work. We arrived on November 1, 1913, and he reported to the plant right away. After he found a house for us he started working. The superintendent of the plant came to our home and gave us a lot of first aid and got the doctor to see us. But on the third day after we arrived daddy came home with his lunch and went to bed. He never got up again. He died a week later. So there we were. The whole family was sick with influenza, except me. I took care of my baby brother, feeding him rice water because there was no milk.

My brothers Hugh and Willie went to work in Juárez as chauffeurs driving a car that my mother bought with the money she had brought from Torreón. My cousin Luis was also working in Juárez, importing leather from the United States and selling it in Mexico. He was arrested and taken to jail. Somehow we heard that they were going to shoot him behind the Juárez jail, so mother got dressed, and there we went. She took me along to Villa's headquarters. Finally they let us in. Villa said, "What do you want?" "We came to see my nephew. He is detained." "That's nothing," said Villa. "Tomorrow we will shoot him along with his whole generation." "Why?" asked Mama. "Because he is a smuggler." "No!" said Mama. "That's been his business for years, to buy and sell leather. He pays taxes." "It doesn't matter. Tomorrow he'll be shot." But Villa saw that Mama was so brave that he finally said, "Take him, but I don't ever want to see him around here." So we took him on the streetcar from Juárez to El Paso.

Villa was dark and ugly, with a mustache. They say he was doing a lot of charity work, but he was killing people, anybody who got in his way. We brought our cousin over, but Hugh and Willie kept working in Juárez. Both used to drive Villa around in Juárez, imagine! My mother didn't know. One day, Willie was standing on the corner of 16th of September and Avenida Juárez, right by Villa. Some man came up to Villa, and of course he was nervous, the poor old guy. He put his hand in his pocket to get his handkerchief and Villa shot him two times right in the stomach. Villa thought the man was going to kill him. Willie came home and told us, and Mama said, "You can't go back." And Willie answered, "Oh, no! He's my friend." Villa kind of liked him; he used to give him good tips.

On one occasion Hugh went to take one of our cousins, Eloisa, to Torreón. Halfway between Juárez and Chihuahua bandits stopped the train. They were robbing everyone, taking jewelry and clothes. My brother had a ring that belonged to my daddy and one of the bandits asked him to hand it over. My brother said it wouldn't come off, so the guy took out a *machete* and told Hugh to stretch out his finger so he could cut if off. Hugh just shook his hand and the ring fell off! Just from fright! They took their clothes, leaving both Hugh and Eloisa in their underwear. They took Eloisa's skirt to give to a *soldada* [woman revolutionary soldier]. These women would go everywhere with the revolutionaries. They'd have a baby down in the prairie, pick it up, and be on their way. I saw that myself when we were traveling on the train. We were stopped. A woman went off to a little place and had her baby. Mama helped her out by throwing cloth and bread from the train window.

"The people took with them what
they could hide."
—Angel Oaxaca (1889–1980)*

*Fearing for their lives, many families fled Chihuahua City
for the border whenever Villa attacked the town. Such trips
were often undertaken hastily, as Chihuahuense Angel Oaxaca
relates in the following memoir. Oaxaca also offers interesting
comments about his own initial economic adjustment to life
in the United States.*

In 1913 when Villa attacked Chihuahua City I was working in a bank.
It was a beautiful stone building with hand-carved decorations; it had
a basement and three more floors. The managers were all Spanish. The
revolutionaries came to the bank and took 750 sacks of thousand silver
pesos. Each sack weighed twenty-seven kilos. They used two-wheeled
carts with mules or horses to carry the sacks. They took everything; they
didn't leave anything but a few fifty-cent pieces. Afterward President
Victoriano Huerta took care of the debt and the bank didn't lose even
one cent.

Among the people of Chihuahua who left for El Paso, those who had
money in our bank took it out. That is, they took their money in paper
bills because it was difficult to carry two or three kilos of silver in their
pocket. Because of this, for a time it wasn't possible to obtain any bills

*Interviewed in El Paso in 1977 by Oscar J. Martínez. On file at the Institute of Oral
History, University of Texas at El Paso.

235

in Chihuahua. Everyone who had money in the bank asked for letters of credit that said that the person was "good for" a certain amount. For example, if a person was "good for" 20,000 pesos, he asked for a letter of credit for 20,000 pesos. With that letter he could withdraw money from any of the places that were mentioned in the letter, whether it be an American, French, German or Spanish bank. The people took with them what they could hide and sometimes the rich people would make arrangements with the poor people to carry money on the train.

Some of the prominent families went to live in Alamogordo, others to Las Cruces, but the majority went to El Paso. Chihuahua was left empty; the only people who stayed were those who didn't have anything that would be worth stealing. Some left their houses unattended; others left maids to stay in them.

Villa considered everyone who was identified as a supporter of the government as an enemy, and he executed many. We saw a prominent man who was called *Coronel Botitas* ["Colonel Little Boots"] hanging from a water tank beside the railroad in Villa Ahumada. Villa caught him and had a falling out with him. They called him *Coronel Botitas* because he was always well-dressed; he always wore German style boots. The only ones whom Villa respected were the doctors because he needed them.

When my family left Chihuahua that year, we had to leave the house in the care of one of the bank janitors whose name was Pancho García. I didn't return to Chihuahua until fifteen years later, and Pancho was still in the house. Some furniture was missing, and he informed me that he had the piano in his saloon. He said, "Since you didn't come back for so long, I took that furniture out of the house. But don't worry; I'm going to pay you for everything. I'm very glad to see that you're alive and that you want to come back here. You know that it's your house." The next day he moved out, but I told him that he could stay because I had only gone to see how things were going. He was very honest; he paid me in coins made of pure gold for everything that was missing in the house.

When we were going toward Juárez in the train, the *villistas* stopped us to ask us some questions. Luckily I had a letter from a *villista* general whose name was José Prieto. He was a big bully, but we had become friends before the Revolution when he used to come to the bank on Saturdays very broke and each one of the employees gave him a peso.

He got 10 or 15 pesos. So when he found out that I was leaving Chihuahua, he told me, "Oaxaquita, I'm going to give you a letter so that they won't bother you on the way." Then when the *villistas* boarded the train and they saw that I had a letter from Prieto, they didn't say anything to me. Because of that I'll never forget Prieto.

There were several rich families that were already in Juárez or in El Paso. They were all bankers, lawyers, or doctors. They didn't lose their prestige when they left Chihuahua; when they came to the border they still had it. Some of them didn't work at anything at first; they took pleasure trips, thinking that the Revolution would be over in two or three months. Later they realized that the Revolution was continuing and that they had lost their property in Chihuahua. Some returned to Chihuahua years later, and others set up stores in El Paso or bought property. I believe that 50 percent of them returned to Chihuahua and the rest of them permanently settled in El Paso and in other parts of the United States. Some went to Chicago, New York, Los Angeles, St. Louis, and Boston.

We stayed with one of my mother's sisters in Juárez. Then when we were going to go to El Paso, a lady came to the house to ask us to do her the favor of taking 5,000 pesos to the American side for her because she didn't dare do it herself. My aunt had told her that my mother could take the money, and that's what we did. At the bridge, when the Americans saw that we had 5,000 pesos in coins of pure gold they said, "Go ahead." I think that they thought that we were some of the rich Mexicans. We were middle class, not rich or poor, but more poor than rich! I think that the quantity of money that we had with us had a lot to do with our being able to cross the river so easily. If the Americans knew that you weren't going to be a public burden, they'd let you cross without any difficulty. We didn't have any problems; the Americans treated us well.

I began to work for the Galveston, Harrisburg, and San Antonio Railroad taking care of the payroll on payday because all the employees were Mexican. We were at a station not very far from El Paso, close to Sierra Blanca. There were sixty workers who used to sleep in the freight trains. At first I began as an ordinary worker also, releveling and throwing dirt on the track during the rainy season. I wasn't afraid of the work; I felt capable of doing anything. After three days I saw an American typing the payroll with just one finger and I said to him, "Listen, if you want, I'll do that for you in a few minutes and in triplicate like it should

237

be done. Buy some carbon paper and I'll do everything." He told me, "Oh, you dumbbell. What do you know?" I told him that I wasn't a dumbbell, that I had an education. He told me, "If you know how to do this, tomorrow we're going to pay you more and you can sleep in the passenger car where we sleep." Well, they promoted me right away. How was that *gringo* going to spell surnames like Hernández or Jiménez? Not even if his life depended on it!

I stayed with that job for three months and then I decided to go back to El Paso to be with my family, but the railroad people didn't want me to go. In El Paso a person whom I knew gave me a letter of recommendation and told me to go to a furniture store that was owned by a German, and I got a job there. They accepted me as a salesman on commission. I told the German, "I know everyone in Chihuahua and I'm going to bring just rich people here. Don't think I'm going to bring you clients who pay in installments of a peso a week. Nothing like that— pure cash." The first client whom I took to him was a rich man from Parral who had some pool halls in El Paso. I sold him one of those wardrobes that have three doors with mirros—$250 cash. The *gringo* was really surprised. A few days later I made a really big sale. I sold the complete furnishings for a house to a very rich old man from Juárez who was living in El Paso. Then the German told me, "I'm going to pay you $35 a week, and at the end of the year you'll get a commission on everything that was sold during the year." Well, I was delighted because back then a *big* salary was $18 a week and the average salary of the ordinary people was about $9 a week. Well, $35 seemed like a lot to me. *Then* money was worth something; a family of three or four could eat on a dollar a day, a house was rented for $10 or $15 a month. I earned a reputation for being a good furniture salesman and I stayed there until I was an old man.

"I said a prayer for my wife and little
daughter."
—Reverendo Donato Ruíz
(1881–1978)*

*Protestant ministers working in Mexico during the 1910s
faced many difficulties, especially if they had links with foreigners. Reverendo Donato Ruíz, a native of Zacatecas who
later moved to El Paso, remembers how playing host to two
Anglo American missionaries got him into trouble with the
federales.*

In 1913 when I was the pastor of the First Baptist Church in Torreón,
the federalist troops entered the city after Villa's revolutionaries had
left. The federalists came demolishing everything they could, and I was
aware of everything that was going on. A Catholic priest wrote an anon-
ymous note to the mayor of Torreón and another one to the chief of
police, telling them that I was a revolutionary spy and that I was har-
boring revolutionary spies in my house. Two North American missionaries were in my house and one of them had become sick and was in
bed. Then the chief of police sent word that two women detained at
the jail had said they knew me and if I would go and state who these
women were and what they did, they would be released. I went to the
jail, but there weren't any women there. The chief of police ordered

*Interviewed in El Paso in 1975 by Oscar J. Martínez. On file at the Institute of Oral
History, University of Texas at El Paso.

that I be put in a cell that was very small. For seventy-two hours they didn't give me anything to eat or drink.

On the third day they took me out of jail at midnight. I thought they were going to kill me and I said a prayer for my wife and little daughter. Later they threw me in a train car full of prisoners that was going toward Saltillo. After five days of traveling almost without food we arrived at the Coahuila State Penitentiary, where I was for one week. From there they took me to San Luis Potosí to an infantry regiment. By chance, the head of the regiment was an acquaintance of mine who had heard me preach in Torreón. When he saw me enter his barracks, he sent for me. He put his pistol on the desk and asked me what I was doing there. "If you don't tell me the truth, I'll kill you right here. Tell me why you're here. Are you a revolutionary or aren't you?" I answered him, "I am the pastor of the First Baptist Church of Torreón, and I am nothing else." Then he gave an order that I be sent to the hospital as being gravely ill, but I wasn't ill. I was in the hospital one week and I received help from the doctors. One told me to keep my head in my hands and not to say anything and another advised me not to take any medicine: "Don't take any pills. Put them under the mattress. Drink milk in the morning and beans or broth at noon. Don't eat or drink anything else." When I left the hospital I went with my brother who lived in San Luis Potosí.

> "Have mercy on us."
> —Mother Elías de Sta Sacto
> (1879–   )*

The deep antagonism against the Catholic Church long present in Mexico resurfaced with great force during the Revolution. Priests and nuns became the object of persecution by the government as well as troops in the field. Mother Elías de Sta Sacto, a member of the Carmelite order, recalls abuses inflicted on the Church and on individuals by Carrancistas.

As soon as the Carranza soldiers entered a city they seized the keys of the churches, and they said the government was the owner of the churches, and the holy communion would belong to the people. The soldiers took the ciboria and emptied the contents, the sacred Hosts, into the oats for the horses. Many times the Catholic ladies used to come to me and say, "Mother, they have emptied the ciboria to give to the horses." I did not believe it. I could not believe such a thing. But I went with them, and we tried to find out. The soldiers would take the vestments and put on the horses' necks, and different profanations like that. They also shot the tabernacles in almost every church. There was no place, no town, where there was not that kind of profanation. I saw many times how they burned up the confessional. Once I was going down to Mexico City and I saw in a church where hundreds of men had

*Interviewed in Washington, D.C. in 1920. *Investigation of Mexican Affairs,* Senate Document 285, 66th Congress, 2nd Session (Washington, D.C., 1920), pp. 2649–56.

241

shot the ostensoria, and then disappeared. The soldiers used to drink from the chalices and the ciboria, and then threw them down in the street. Several times widow women used to come to our door, because they knew we were nuns, and used to bring the chalices there to sell them. I bought them sometimes for 10 cents each.

Once I met with six or more women who said they were sisters, and they said, "Have mercy on us." They said they spent two years up in the hills with the soldiers, and they did not know where to go; they could not find any convent or place to stay. They said they were about to become mothers. Of course, I did not know whether to believe it or not. I said to them, "Well, you had better go some place, some maternity house, and pray to God and have more faith, because it is not your fault." I did not see them any more. Afterward I saw a big crowd in Colonia Roma in Mexico City. I saw imitation nuns, sisters, and priests, some of them wearing the sacred vestments. I never could believe they were real priests; one of the ladies who was there said to me, "Don't you believe them when they say they are priests. They are just trying to make fun. That is the way they slander the priests, because they say the priests do nothing but drink and dance with the nuns."

[Shortly after these events Mother Elías de Sta Sacto left Mexico and took refuge in Habana, Cuba, where in November 1914, she wrote a letter to the archbishop of New Orleans relating further outrages. Excerpts of that letter follow.]

All the communities of nuns have been expelled from the entire Republic, being given but a half-hour to leave and not allowed to take with them a change of clothes, and in many cases not even a breviary to pray. Many sisters have been taken to the barracks and police stations where their vows of chastity were in great danger. The furnishings of the Catholic schools and colleges have been stolen and in them have been planted the mixed lay schools with boys and girls together, from which there may be expected nothing but corruption and evil. Immorality has increased to such a degree that they have profaned not only virgins but have violated nuns, carrying them away by force where they now suffer horribly. To the great suffering of my soul I have seen in Mexico the sad and lamentable fate of many sisters who have been victims of the unbridled passions of the soldiers. I found many bewailing their misfortune that they were about to become mothers, some in their own homes, others in maternity hospitals. Others unable to flee from despair have surrendered to a life of evil and, filled with desperation and shame, have complained against God, declaring that He has abandoned them.

I have seen many sisters of different orders, dressed in the latest style, showing themselves on the balconies, losing the little spirituality remaining to them, and singing and playing the piano all day, saying that it is dissimulation to hide the fact that they are nuns for fear that they be carried away by Carrancistas, or Zapatistas, or Villistas, etc. Some priests, deserving of confidence, have told me that in one hospital there are fifty sisters that had been seized by the soldiers, of whom forty-five are about to become mothers, although they have religious vocations and are bound by vows. The Carrancistas deny this, saying that the nuns went with them voluntarily because they were held in the convents by force. In Celaya and in Mexico City I have seen others whom they have compelled by force to enlist in the Red Cross, and under this pretext holding them as slaves to serve them as though they were their own women, and if many look after the sick there are also others who have lost their chastity. In general, many young girls, after having been forced to live with them, have been thrown out, and many have been killed in the streets as though they were animals.

I wrote that when I was in Cuba. When I went back to Mexico they took me prisoner. They took me off of the train, and they said, "Are you the superior of the Carmelite Order?" Of course, I didn't deny it. I didn't say, "I am not," but I said, "I don't know what you mean." They said, "Are you a sister? How many sisters have you?" "I have no sister." Of course, I meant to say my own sister. I was dressed like a widow. I was taken in a dark room with a novice, and we promised to each other we would not separate from one another. At two in the morning they called us and said, "Now, ladies, it is your last chance. Where is the money?" "What money?" I said. They said, "The dowers of the sisters." I said, "I haven't any." "Well, how many sisters have you in your house?" "I haven't any." "Are you the superior of the convent?" "I am not." I had resigned my office; I was not the superior at that time. They said, "Well, would you like something to save your life?" I said, "I will not do anything. You would make me happy if you killed me, because my

243

husband died long ago." I meant our Lord Jesus Christ. "And I want to meet Him." Well, they didn't know what to do with me, because they could not scare me.

We were left alone without eating anything, and the next day at midnight they called again, and said, "Now, ladies, this is your last chance." I said, "I hope it will be for good. Will you please finish now?" They asked me the same questions about the money and the sisters, and I repeated over what I said before. Then they called the soldiers around me with their guns and told us to kneel down, and we knelt down. The novice was so scared, and I said, "Make up your mind to die. What is the use to get scared? It is better to die now than to be like the other sisters." The same questions were asked, and I gave the same answers. So the men shot like they would kill me. I was scared, but I didn't die.

The next day an Indian came to me and said, "Little sister, do you want to be free?" I said, "Why do you call me sister?" He said, "You have on your forehead like every sister has, and you can't deny that you are a sister." Well, I didn't say anything more. He said, "Do you want to be free today?" I said, "I don't believe you. I don't trust anybody." He said, "I will open the door for you if you will give me some money." I said, "I have no money to give you." I had in my clothing about $1,400 to pay the expense of the sisters to take them to the United States. So he opened the door for me, and we left. Another Indian offered me a horse in order to run away. Well, I never had ridden a horse, but I had to learn that day. And then it started to rain so hard we could not see the way any more, but at last we reached the railroad, and we went into Mexico City about 3 o'clock in the morning. That was the last thing that happened to me.

"Are you a *gringo?*" . . . "No, señor."
—Margarita Candelaria (1904–   )*

Refugees sometimes went through a process of step migration within Mexico before fleeing to the United States. Margarita Candelaria, of Mexican-Anglo parentage, remembers her family's move from Aguascalientes to Madera and finally to El Paso.

In 1914, my sister and I were attending a Catholic school in Aguascalientes and living with my grandmother and aunts. Our parents were in Chihuahua at the time. My father was working for the Northwestern Madera Lumber Company as a carpenter. One day during the examinations the revolutionaries came to the school, and there was concern because of their opposition to the Church. The nuns quietly shut the doors and windows, and classes were suspended. They got into the school but there wasn't any shooting. They left peacefully.

The communications to the north were interrupted and people in Aguascalientes went through a few experiences. Of course, being children, it was a lark for us. We didn't care or didn't know the hardships that the grownups had to go through. All we wanted was something to eat, to play, and so on. My grandmother and aunts had a big house with a patio and a large backyard with chickens and rabbits. The only thing we lacked at times was milk.

*Interviewed in El Paso in 1976 by Oscar J. Martínez. On file at the Institute of Oral History, University of Texas at El Paso.

245

Just as the communications started again from the north, my uncles, one of whom was in Chihuahua and the other in Mexico City, came to Aguascalientes to evacuate us on the train. On the way to Chihuahua, three locomotives broke down. One turned over along with some train cars, the boiler busted on the other one, and so on. One of the turned-over cars was a banana convoy, so we had fresh bananas. The people got off the cars and traded or bought eggs and other things from vendors on the way, and we built fires and cooked our food. When we got to Chihuahua City, mother picked us up and took us to Madera.

Our stay in Madera coincided with Villa's downfall and the arousal of his anger toward Americans for the help the United States had given his enemies. Although my father was partial to Villa, he knew that Villa was after the scalp of the Americans, so he decided to join others who were leaving Madera for the border. A train was formed and several Americans left at about seven that night. At 11 P.M., the Villistas started drifting in. It was snowing heavily and the poor revolutionaries, who were mostly from the south and not accustomed to the snow of the north, were cold and hungry. They would knock at any house where they saw a light, asking for food or shelter. Of course, we weren't in a position to give them food, and we were afraid.

One night my brother's godfather came and took us to his house because he was concerned about our safety since there was no male among us. A short time after we left some revolutionaries got into our house. They had orders to quarter themselves in any empty house, so they broke into our place. When mother got there it was a mess. They were cooking tortillas and a whole piece of bacon in the oven, and lard was dripping on the floor. The colonel in charge told my mother, "Señora, we are not dislodging people. I'll be very happy to leave your house, just give me time." So they did, but as soon as they left the Carrancistas moved in. It was the same story. Carranza's people also had orders to move into the empty houses of the Americans.

One day my brother and I were playing outside when a Carrancista came by. Generally we were not supposed to go out because our parents were afraid that being Americans we might be victimized. We were both redheaded and freckled. The Carrancista asked my brother, "Are you a gringo?" And my poor brother said, "No, señor."

There were shortages of one thing or another in Madera, but the people would share. The men would go up in the *sierra* and hunt,

246

bringing wild turkey and honey, or somebody would kill a pig and share it with the others. Then farmers would come by and we would exchange things. The only thing I lacked was good shoes. I was accustomed to wearing American-made shoes, and they didn't have them.

In 1916, there was a big scare when those sixteen Americans were killed in Santa Ysabel. My father was supposed to be on that train, but the hotel attendant did not awaken him on time, and he missed it. As he reached the station, the train pulled out. My mother knew that he was trying to reach us at that time, but there was no communication. At the end of the year, we decided to go north, since we hadn't heard from father. A train was assembled and seven families occupied a boxcar in a train bound for Juárez. Mother took a big trunk, a sewing machine, and some mattresses. It took several days, I forget how many, to make the trip from Madera to Juárez. At one point a tunnel had been destroyed and it took a long time to get the train through there. When we got to Juárez, my father was there to meet us.

In 1917 my father returned to México as an employee of the American Smelter and Refining Company. We went with him to Chihuahua City, but he was moved from place to place: Mexico City, Monclova, Rosita, and so on. We stayed in Chihuahua City since we had missed so much schooling and mother thought it important that we catch up. During the flu epidemic of 1919–1920 my mother died from pneumonia. My father was in Monterrey at that time. He came over and we were un-decided whether to go with him or return to the United States to live with an aunt. The family saw the advantage of having the children attend American schools, since we were Americans, and decided to move to El Paso.

"We dragged that sack home."
—Amparo F. de Valencia
(1905–)*

Hunger, disease, and other sufferings plagued people throughout Mexico. Amparo F. de Valencia, who was born in Baja California, recalls privations endured by her family.

During the Revolution I saw hunger. Sometimes one ate and sometimes one didn't. What good was money? Everyone suffered because one couldn't buy anything. Everything was scarce. If someone was discovered with food supplies a squad of soldiers would come and take them to the barracks. There was a Chinese man who made food available to us, but we younger ones couldn't go buy it because it came from the black market. He was rich and well-known, having businesses all over Mexico. When there was something available we were the first family to know about it. My mother and other adults would go get half a kilo of coffee, a kilo of beans, or a kilo of rice. Just small quantities, because that's all there was. There was no wheat because there was no harvest; corn was used to feed the horses. Thus there was tremendous hunger all over.

There was a man who had a big bakery, and he had a big stack of sacks full of old, hard bread that he would send to Sinaloa for feeding pigs. Even that was sold to people or given away sometimes. Once my brother and I went and bought a sack for about fifty centavos or a peso.

*Interviewed in National City, California in 1979 by Oscar J. Martínez. On file at the Institute of Oral History, University of Texas at El Paso.

248

We dragged that sack home. The bread was full of ants and other things, but we felt happy.

Disease was another problem. When someone got smallpox, they locked the house and would not let anyone in. A policeman kept watch to make sure the sick person was not taken out. The victim would die there, because there was no medical assistance. All the doctors were away taking care of the wounded who were involved in the fighting. We would be in school two or three months and then miss the next six, because the teachers had to serve as nurses. Students lost a lot of time.

When things were very difficult we fled to Almagres, an island near Guaymas. We joined a bunch of families and lived in a circus tent. The children loved that island because we didn't have any worries, unlike our parents. We were there two months until things began to quiet down.

When father passed away in 1918 [he was a naval officer who died while serving on active duty] we left for Nogales, Sonora, intending to enter the United States. We could not cross because mother was a widow and the children were all small. She needed a provider, but she was a proud woman and never remarried. She was thirty-five when father died; he was fifty-six. After three months we went back to Guaymas. General Plutarco Elías Calles was then governor. He summoned all war widows to give them their husbands' salaries, but mother was fed up with the Revolution, and she didn't want to go. The government owed her 30,000 pesos, but we never collected that money. Mother preferred losing it to having to deal with people who had caused us so much harm, according to her.

Mother started working at home. She was a very able woman, knowing how to do everything. Even the maid we had learned from mother— how to make *menudo, tortillas,* and how to sew. That's how mother was able to support us, by sewing. As the oldest I was in charge of picking up orders and delivering the finished product. We would make at least twenty pesos for an order, and with that I worked miracles. I would buy a little of this and a little of that to make that money stretch, just like ants do.

In 1919 we returned to Nogales, Sonora, hoping to be able to cross the border. However, mother got a well-paying job in a clothing factory, and we stayed there longer than we expected. During that time I took over the household, playing "mother" to my three younger sisters. We lived in Nogales until 1923.

"You never see your *gringo* daddy anymore."

—Lucy Read (1906–)*

Pancho Villa's characterization as both a cruel and a kind man is supported by testimonies of border people who came in contact with him. The following memoir by Lucy Read, who was born in San Buena Aventura, Chihuahua, of a Mexican mother and English father, and whose family settled in El Paso, falls in the first category. Aside from her comments on the Villistas, Read adds interesting details about her family's acquaintance with Gen. John J. Pershing.

One of the most terrifying experiences of my childhood was when the notorious Mexican bandit, Francisco (Pancho) Villa, entered our lives. Early in the morning of February 1916, during the absence of Father, the Villistas raided our home. We awoke to the sound of shattering window glass, the pounding of doors, and the angry voices of Villa and his men demanding to know where our father was. Villa began questioning Mother and started pushing and mistreating her. Mother answered that Father was in Sonora, but he did not believe her and went about searching our home.

When he couldn't find Father, Villa gave orders to post guards in all the doorways and windows, so none of us could escape. He said that

---

*Written memoir. Second place winner in the 1976 Historical Memories Contest of the El Paso County Historical Society. *Password* 22:1 (Spring 1977): 26–30. Reprinted by permission of *Password*.

he would punish us. My older brother, George, who was fifteen years old, disguised himself as an old lady and dressed into some of Mother's clothing. He escaped through the back garden exit where no guards had been posted. There he ran to Sierra Madre to seek help.

I was crying for fear of what he would do to us and kept hanging onto Mother's skirt. Just then, Villa reached out to me and pulled my hair. I still recall his very words; "Now *guerita* (fair one), you never see your gringo daddy anymore." He grabbed Mother and threw her to the floor where she fainted. I ran to one of the guards asking for a glass of water for Mother, but his reply was, "I'm sorry. Don't get too close to me, and don't let my general see you talking to me because he will kill us both."

One guard came over and told another, "General wants you to pour the oil on the family so we can burn them alive." The other fellow said, "Oh no, I just can't do that. What about the poor children?" The reply was, "General said, the whole family." Within minutes some of Villa's soldiers arrived with two wagonloads of coal oil to carry out instructions.

Earlier that day, one of my uncles who lived a few blocks away, took note of the suspicious activities and sent a telegram to Casas Grandes asking for help for our family. He was informed that a party of Carrancistas, who were in pursuit of Villa, were due to arrive in our town.

All this time, Villa's men were stealing everything in sight such as clothes, shoes, blankets, and jewelry. What they couldn't take they went about destroying. Soon Villa's soldiers were running back and forth opening cans of coal oil and pouring it over our home and furniture.

Just as they were ready to pour the oil on us, we heard the roar of cannon fire. At this interruption, Villa's soldiers made a run for their horses which were tied to the trees surrounding our house. They left our belongings scattered all over the place as they didn't have time to take what they had planned on stealing.

One of Villa's men walked toward us with a gun in his hand, and with a threatening tone said, "You'll escape from being killed this time, but remember, next time, you will all be killed." He rode away on his horse and left us trembling.

Shortly, the Carrancistas arrived to render aid. The party had orders to accompany us to Casas Grandes where a special military train would be waiting to take us to Juárez.

On our arrival, Mother got in touch with Father by wire at his residence in Sonora, asking him to come immediately to Juárez. Next day, when Father arrived, he was quite upset when he was told about our ordeal with the Villistas. So we stayed in Juárez a few days until Father made arrangements to go to El Paso. In El Paso we stayed at the Hotel Orndorff which is now the Hotel Cortez.

When things were back to normal in Mexico, we decided to go back. Our home was still in bad shape and in need of repair due to the destruction that had taken place, so we made the necessary repairs and were pretty well organized again. We heard rumors that Villa would again try to kill us if we returned home.

In the year 1916, we heard that the United States, with the permission of President Carranza of Mexico, was sending an expedition into Mexico to pursue Villa because of a raid that occurred on Columbus, New Mexico, where he killed seventeen men. These forces consisting of ten thousand men were led by the American brigadier general, John J. Pershing.

My father used to keep the British and Mexican flags flying over our home. Most of the revolutionaries that passed by seemed to have great respect for him as they would always stop and salute the flags. When General Pershing arrived in our town, he set camp about five miles from the city limits. The first trip Pershing made into town, he saw our flags and came over and introduced himself to Father. Since Father was the only foreigner in town, they became fast friends and Father extended an invitation to General Pershing and the Red Cross officers to stay in our home. Soon, they began to stay over weeks at a time, and we began to feel as if they were part of our family.

General Pershing took a liking to me since I was about the same age as one of his daughers. He would sit me on his lap and tell me that I looked a lot like one of his little girls, who at that time was living in San Francisco, California, with the rest of his family. It was always a special treat for my sisters, brothers, and me when he would bring us candy from the U.S.A. I can still taste the delicious striped peppermint candies. Father valued General Pershing's friendship and, to show his appreciation, would hold dances in our patio for the American soldiers so that they could have a good time and get acquainted with the people of our town.

Pershing was unsuccessful in his attempt to catch Villa and in the year 1917 received orders from the United States to withdraw his troops and

252

leave Mexico for an overseas assignment. He advised Father to leave Mexico for awhile as our lives were still in danger. Father agreed and we made plans to leave in the company of Pershing and his soldiers.

Our trip to Columbus, New Mexico, was very enjoyable, but we parted company and settled in Old Mesilla on a large farm. During that time, we found out that Villa had burned down our home and destroyed our cattle; so there was nothing to go back to. Father was very sad during this period and became ill and depressed. Eventually he lost the silver mine in Sonora.

"They took our source of living away from us."
—Aurora Mendoza (1901–   )*

Chihuahua native Aurora Mendoza briefly relates abuses suffered by her family and initial problems of adjustment to life in the United States.

We came to El Paso, Texas, in 1917, two years after the Revolution began to affect us on our ranch in the outskirts of Chihuahua. There were eight in our family and I was the youngest of three girls. We left Mexico because they took our source of living away from us. The soldiers took our horses and our cows. What were we going to do on a little ranch without those animals? We couldn't support ourselves without them. The federalists and the revolutionaries came and took with them whatever they wanted from our ranch and from neighboring ranches. Many times they came and we didn't know what side they were on. They told us not to go out after such and such an hour and if we *did* go out they would shoot us. Because of that nobody went out and then they could rob whatever they wanted. More important than the animals which they stole were the men and boys who were forced to join the army against their wills. My brother was one of the ones that they took. He stayed in the army until the Revolution ended.

We left Chihuahua in November of 1916 and didn't arrive in El Paso

*Interviewed in El Paso in 1976 by Jose A. Balli, Jr. On file at the Institute of Oral History, University of Texas at El Paso.

254

until January of 1917. We were on the road a month and a half because we stayed for a while with some relatives on a ranch before getting to Juárez. We didn't have time to bring anything with us, just the clothes on our back. No furniture or household items. My parents and five children came. The only one who didn't come was my brother who was still in the army. When they let him go, he came right away to live with us in El Paso.

We were afraid while we were coming because we had heard that on occasions the soldiers attacked the trains, and because of that we were anxious to get to the border. We were lucky that nothing happened. When we arrived, we crossed the international bridge without needing any papers. In those days no one had to report that they were going to cross over to El Paso. We went from Juárez to El Paso on the streetcar. Since the streetcar didn't go all the way to my aunt's house, we had to go on foot from the station. She lived near the center of town on a street that wasn't paved and in a neighborhood which was fairly uninhabited. My father got work without much trouble. My brothers found jobs right away, too. We lived in my aunt's house almost six months. From there we moved to some apartments near the river. Later we lived in several rented houses in that same neighborhood until we finally bought a house in 1941.

I had been in a Mexican school until the third grade. When we got to El Paso we didn't know anything about the laws, and we didn't realize that it was mandatory that we go to school here. Since we were newcomers, they didn't tell us anything about that, and we never found out for ourselves. Also, since I was already fifteen years old, we thought that I didn't need to continue going to school. That's why I didn't continue studying.

"He would send word for us to leave immediately."

—Ora Watson (1905–   )*

Affluent families who had association with the government in power were especially unpopular with the insurgents. Ora Watson, a native of Coahuila, recalls Villista harassment because of her father's service to Carranza.

When the Villistas were trying to assassinate Don Venustiano Carranza and attempting to hurt all those who favored him, my father was working for the government in Torreón, Coahuila. Whenever it seemed like Villa would attack Cuatrocienegas, Coahuila, where our family lived, Carranza would let my father know, and he would send word for us to leave immediately. The Villistas would hurt those families that had money; they would try to rob them, to take jewelry, money, arms, everything of value. We would then leave on the first available train, whether it was a freight or a passenger train, it didn't matter. We would stay wherever we could, in places where there would be no danger to our family.

On one occasion, we encountered a burned bridge on the way, and the train tried to return on another track but encountered another burned bridge behind us. Thus we couldn't move until they repaired those bridges. We waited three days on the train, with little to eat. The

*Interviewed in South Texas in 1974 by her granddaughter (name unavailable). Used by permission of the Texas Southmost College Oral History Program, Brownsville, Texas.

men killed some cattle and cooked the meat over the fire. We ate it without salt or anything. That was all we had to eat when something like that happened. At other times, we arrived in small towns and stayed there until things calmed down sufficiently to continue traveling toward Salinas Hidalgo, Nuevo León, where my grandparents lived. We would stay at Salinas Hidalgo for some time and then return to Cuatrocienegas when peace returned there, but soon the alarm would be given again, "Here comes Villa," and we would have to leave and endure many difficulties once again.

During one period when we were at Salinas Hidalgo, the only thing we ate was *atole* because there was nothing else available. After a while we didn't want to cook it any longer; we hated it, but the choice was to drink it or starve. At that same time, a very prominent man from Salinas Hidalgo was hiding at my grandparents' farm. They had him locked up in a very small house. We found out that they were after him, they wanted to kill him. He felt safer there. He would eat *atole* just like us.

Every time we fled our house, we would place our valuables on the floor and cover them with the wood we had for the stove so the Villistas would not take them. We always carried our jewels with us whenever we left, but on one occasion my mother forgot and left them on top of the piano, and the Villistas got them. The greatest fear we had was that Villa would abuse the women. He cut off an ear of every woman he abused; that was his mark.

When Carranza had to flee Mexico, Father rode on the same train. He had gone to Mexico City to pick up one of my sisters who was visiting an aunt there. Things got pretty bad, and Father and my sister left with Carranza. On the way they encountered a burnt bridge and could not continue, nor could they return to Mexico City. They had to stay in a little town, and that's where Carranza was murdered. Carranza had told everyone to leave on foot if they wanted to save themselves, that he would stay there. Father and my sister, accompanied by many others, walked until they got to a farm, where later another train picked them up and brought them to the border. Father knew that he would be hurt by Carranza's enemies if he didn't leave, because he was Carranza's *compadre* and both had been born in the same town. So he came first and then little by little he brought the rest of the family. We crossed through Eagle Pass and lived several years in San Antonio.

257

We stayed for some time with a *compadre* of Father's. We suffered quite a bit because Father had not brought enough money with him. We were a burden because it was difficult to support all of us. Later when Father was able to bring more money from Mexico we bought a house and our situation improved. However, it was not the same as what we were used to. There were always problems and sufferings because it was very difficult to live outside one's country.

"Why me?"
—María Cristina Flores Carlos
(1906–   )*

Jalisco native María Cristina Flores Carlos recalls a frightful incident as a teenager at the hands of some revolutionaries.

I was very young and didn't really pay much attention, but I saw the fear of people who complained about the Revolution. Bunches of revolutionaries would arrive in our town, but I didn't know who they were. I would hear people call them *"gauchos"* and *"Villistas,"* but they were all the same to me. The only thing I feared were the bullets. When I would hear bullets I would run and hide behind a trunk. I felt secure there, and when it was over then I didn't care much about it.

When I was about fourteen the revolutionaries scared me. One day I was returning home from the store in plain daylight when I saw one of the revolutionaries come toward me from the streetcorner. He was drunk, and I have always been very fearful of drunkards. He grabbed my hand and pulled me hard. He threatened me with a gun, saying, "I'm going to take you with me, you. . . ." I answered, "Why me? I haven't done anything to you." Then one of his fellow revolutionaries told him, "Come back, *compadre.* Why do you want her, she is very young. Leave her alone, *compadre.*" I was trembling, but I didn't want to let him know of my fear.

*Interviewed in National City, California, in 1979 by Oscar J. Martínez. On file at the Institute of Oral History, University of Texas at El Paso.

259

We kept on walking, and he continued saying he wanted to take me with him while the others told him to leave me alone. Then as he turned his head I quickly ran into the home of someone I knew and left him holding my *rebozo*. He said, "She got away, that. . . ." I hid there and didn't leave until the afternoon. I went home with a fever and dropped into bed.

It was horrible! I got scared and became ill. I was in bed for about a month. After that I was very afraid. When the revolutionaries would arrive I didn't leave the house.

American doctor attends to injured Mexican woman. (Courtesy, U.T. El Paso Library, Aultman Collection)

Clearing the grounds of the dead after the capture of Juárez, 1911.
(Courtesy, U.T. El Paso Library, Aultman Collection)

Huertistas and refugees en route to Presidio, Texas, 1914. (Courtesy, U.T. El Paso Library, Aultman Collection)

Refugees cross the Rio Grande. (Courtesy, U.T. El Paso Library, Ault-man Collection)

Refugees carrying all they can cross the Rio Grande. (Courtesy, U.T. El Paso Library, Aultman Collection)

American refugees trek across the desert near Columbus, New Mexico, 1916. (Courtesy, U.T. El Paso Library, Aultman Collection)

Mormon refugees, El Paso, 1912. (Courtesy, U.T. El Paso Library, Ault-man Collection)

Refugee camp, Ft. Bliss, Texas, 1914. (Courtesy, El Paso Public Library, Photograph Collection)

Foreigners in Mexico

"We are going to kill you and cut off
your fingers and toes."
—Anita Whatley*

*Many U.S. citizens who lived in Mexico were engaged in
farming and ranching. The isolation of rural life left them
totally on their own when fighting broke out or when lawless
elements invaded the area. Anita Whatley, a native of Tex-
arkana, Texas, remembers the night her family was terrorized
and robbed.*

We had a ranch forty miles from Parral. My father had spent from
1910 til 1911 on the ranch on account of his health, and he was better
off there than he was in town. That left my mother practically with the
responsibility of running the dairy business. We had a good deal of fine
stock cattle, in the neighborhood of 200 registered Jersey cows.

On the night of July 4, 1911, my mother was awakened by someone
having hold of her throat. We had left the door open since nothing was
going on then. She thought it was a dispute between two milkmen; one
had been trying to drive the other off. As soon as she awoke she found
the room full of armed men. They asked for our arms. We had a little
.22 rifle. So, thinking it was in our room upstairs where my sister and
I slept, she came up there and knocked on the door and told me to get
up. I asked her why, and she told me there was robbers and they asked
her for the rifle. I took it downstairs and gave it to them. Then they
asked me for keys, and I gave them the keys. They took the money that
was in the drawer, and said, "This is not enough. We have information

*Interviewed in 1920. *Investigation of Mexican Affairs,* Senate Document 285, 66th
Congress, 2nd Session (Washington, D.C., 1920), pp. 1084–85.

that you have about $5,000 in the house." Of course, it was the beginning of the month and the time when all the bills were to be paid, and they presumed there would be a good deal of money in the house. I said, "We haven't." One man acted as spokesman, and said, "We know you have it; we have the information you have money in the house." From the way they acted, they knew how things were run around there. And the leader said, "Take these three girls (my two sisters and myself) and shoot them." Nobody said anything for a moment or two; nobody made any moves. In a moment he took me by the arm and said, "You come with me." Well, of course, my mother grabbed me and said, "No." I made her turn me loose. So they took me out in the patio, a man on each side, and they stood me up against a wall. They stepped back and the leader raised his rifle and said, "Will you give me the money?" I said, "No, we have not got it." And he said then, "You *gringos* love money better than you do your life." I said, "No, if I had it I would give it to you." He said to one of the men, "Give me your knife." Then he came close and held it to my throat but didn't hurt me. Then he turned me loose. There was a little sidewalk there, and I stepped down on that. He said, "We are going to kill you and cut off your fingers and toes." He took off my bedroom slippers and did cut my foot but not very much. It hurt a little bit anyway. Then one of the men said, "Let's go, these people haven't any money," and they left.

The next morning this man that we were afterward sure had something to do with the robbery, came to my mother and said, "I know two of the men who were here last night. I saw them on the street this morning, and if you will protect me, I will go down to the *comandancia* and denounce them." Well, of course, we sent for my father, and this man gave him the information. They went down and had the men arrested. Shortly after that they took my mother and me down to the jail, and they lined up all the prisoners in the patio. They took us out one at a time and said, "Now, look at these people and see if there is anyone here who looks like any of the band that was at your house." Well, my mother did not identify any of them, but I picked out a man whom I was sure was the leader. And the judge said, "Well, he is convicted, just as good as convicted." About a month after that, they changed judges and they turned the man loose and that was the last I heard of it.

"We cannot permit Americans to have
arms in our territory."
—Junius Romney (1894–?)*

*It is ironic that persecution prompted the Mormons to settle
in Mexico and that similar circumstances drove them back
into the United States. In the first instance, this group suffered
infringement of their religious and civil rights; in the second,
they found themselves vulnerable bystanders in factional
crossfire and uncontrolled banditry. Junius Romney, a native
of Utah who served as the presiding officer of the Mormon
colonies in Chihuahua, relates the difficulties which led to the
exodus of 1912.*

Our relationships with the Mexican people had always been friendly
with all parties and factions of the people. We had taken no part in their
politics, and when the Revolution began it was our policy to be strictly
neutral. During the Madero revolution some efforts were made by local
officers to draw us into the federal ranks. They made some requests that
we help them, but we made known our position and maintained it, and
it was not long until they respected our position. In fact, developments
showed them that it was the wiser course for us to keep out of it, and
they seemed to appreciate that; and we also made known our attitude
to the revolutionary faction, and they approved of it.

*Interviewed in 1912. *Investigation of Mexican Affairs*, Senate Document 285, 66th
Congress, 2nd Session (Washington, D.C., 1920), pp. 2574–90.

263

When the Orozco revolution was hatched and developed in our immediate section we thought it wise to continue the same policy that we had pursued before, and so, when it was necessary, we announced our attitude to both parties and appealed to them in every instance to give us protection. We explained to them that all we asked was to be left alone in our business, that we would not render any assistance to either party, but would attend to our own business and not mix in it.

When we went into Mexico [in the 1880s] we had taken firearms with us. Almost every man took some sort of firearms with him for the defense of his family. The Apaches inhabited that country when we first went in there. We had no military organization, but we had arms in our homes for our protection, and we were in perfect harmony with the people there. We received kind treatment from both the revolutionary party and the federal government, with the exception of the stealing that was done by the revolutionary party and their followers and sympathizers.

Matters gradually grew worse because of the unstable conditions in the country, and some people took advantage of the situation and cut pasture fences and stole horses and cattle wherever they could get them. Then a habit grew up among the Orozco revolutionaries of exacting from us things that they claimed to need. It had also been more or less the custom in the Madero revolution to make exactions upon us, but they had always given us receipts. We could protest and use every peaceable means of avoiding giving anything to them; but when they would come and make demands and threats, our policy was to give them as little as possible and get them to give us a receipt. In a few instances we got those receipts applied on our taxes, but a good many of the people never realized anything on them.

Conditions finally grew a little more strained, and shortly after the Orozco revolution began they made up their minds to disarm us. Salazar had taken possession of Casas Grandes, and had demanded our arms and ammunition. They sent a force of thirty-five men to Colonia Juárez, under the leadership of Enríque Portillo. There were not a great number of them then, and we did not feel justified in giving up our arms. The American consul, Mr. Edwards, had approved of our refusing to give them up. We told them they could not have any of our guns, and that if it came to a matter of choice between using our guns or giving them up to them, we would use them. Before we gave them this ultimatum, they had already arrested one man, and had written out a receipt for another gun and pistol. Portillo then went back to Casas Grandes. The next morning I went to see Salazar to tell him the same thing. I took two or three men with me. They decided to leave us alone, and not to interfere with our guns. They said they did not want any trouble with us, and as long as we continued to be neutral they would respect our rights.

I went back to my home in Colonia Juárez, and in the latter days of July, Salazar sent for me to come over and see him. I went over with Mr. Bowman, one of our colonists at Colonia Dublán, and manager of the largest mercantile institution there. He had come over to Colonia Juárez during the night to bring the message that Salazar wanted to see me. When we called on Salazar he was very much wrought up and said he had sent for me to tell me that they had withdrawn all kinds of guaranties from our people, that they would not give us any kind of protection, either for our lives or our property. I called his attention to the fact that he had given me written guaranties and verbal guaranties and that I had always felt that they were good, that we had relied on him to make good on them, and he replied in Spanish, saying, "Those are words." He intimated that they could be changed at any time he wanted to.

He then told me that they had made up their minds in consultation with Orozco to take from us all our guns and ammunition. I told him that we did not feel justified in giving them up, but he insisted that we must do it. I asked him then for sufficient time to bring our women and children out. There were then approximately about 2,000 rebels right there in the neighborhood of Casas Grandes, and they had five cannons. They were in the outskirts of Dublán, at the stockyards. They had several rapid-fire guns. I asked him for time to remove our women and children before giving him a reply. He refused to grant that request. He said we would be a menace to them if we got our women and children out first, and that there was just one thing to do, that we must deliver those guns and ammunition immediately.

After arguing with him in every possible way that I could, we discussed the situation. When he seemed to be a little convinced in his own mind, he and Demetrio Ponce would go out and talk a little while about it in another room, and then he would come back and say, "Anyhow, it is just a superior order that I have from Orozco, and I have no authority except to comply with my orders." Then I asked him to give me time to see Orozco, and he said, "No, we have been acting the fool by giving guaranties to you people as long as we have. This thing has got to be done right now. Anyhow, we cannot permit Americans to have arms in our territory, because intervention is now an established fact."

When I could not get any permission to get away the women and children, I said, "Well, I will go and consult with the people and see what they say about giving up their guns." He said, "No, you cannot leave here until that order is complied with. You remain right here until that is complied with." I said, "Then that means that we are prisoners, does it?" He said, "Yes, you cannot leave here until that order is complied with." I said, "Then, I will be with you a long time, because I do not think it will be complied with. I could not give any order to the colonists to bring in their guns and deliver them. We have no military organization. What few guns there are belong to the individuals. They have brought them in and paid for them themselves. They are their own property. I have no authority to order them to bring them in."

Then they went out and discussed it a little longer, and Demetrio Ponce said, "Well, you can make a suggestion to them to do it, and if you do that, they will bring in the guns. That is what we want them to do." I said, "I will not make any such suggestion, and I will not issue any such order from Casas Grandes, because if I did my people would regard me as a traitor. They would think I had been in league with you, and I have told them all the time of these guaranties you have given. When you have demanded a list of the guns, I have told them that you have given your word of honor that you would not interfere with the guns. I cannot issue any such order and do not intend to. I will stay with you, and you can do as you please with me." I happened to tell him in that conversation that I was not afraid of him and was not afraid of what he could do to me, and it made him angry, and he said, "Well, you can go home to the colonists; neither am I afraid of you. I will come and get the guns, no matter where I have to go for them." I said, "Do you mean to say you would invade our homes and take our guns by force?" He said, "We will take the guns wherever we have to go to get them. If you want to deliver the guns as gentlemen, you can do it, but if you do not, we will proceed against you just as we do against the federals. We will consider you our enemies, and we will declare war on you immediately."

266

You could not just thoroughly understand our situation unless you were down there and saw our houses. They are very scattered, one or two on a city lot, and so on. We had no opportunity to do any fortifying. We had been pursuing a course to maintain peace with them and friendly relations, and to have made any preparations for war would have been equivalent to a declaration of war, and, of course, they would have immediately taken issue with us. So we were in a very delicate position. We could not make a hostile demonstration of any kind. We could not even throw up a wall of dirt to get behind or anything.

So I went down to Dublán and discussed the matter. They sent fifty armed men along with us; they never left us at all without armed men in reach. When we got down to Dublán, there were three or four hundred of them just across the river at San José, and there were about a hundred of them just helping themselves to the merchandise in the Union Mercantile right in the town. These fifty came right along and surrounded the house where we were. I called in a number of colonists to discuss the situation. We asked them to wait just a few minutes while we discussed it. They did, and we decided that the only thing that we could do was to deliver our guns.

We sent out word to the colonists of what we had decided, and we got permission to bring our guns and deliver them at a certain place in the town which they designated so that they would not go into our homes. Of course, men used their own judgment somewhat. We just told them the situation, that we could not see anything else to do. Of course, under those conditions, knowing that we could not get our families out, they reluctantly gave up their guns. Some brought them and some did not. Some who had more than one gun brought one. They brought the poorer class of guns.

They collected quite a number of guns and quite a considerable amount of ammunition, but only a small part of what we had at Dublán. Then they sent these same fifty men over to Colonia Juárez. We had consulted over the matter there, and had decided that we could not do anything else, so we delivered to them some guns. They did not get all there were at Colonia Juárez, not as large a percentage as they had gotten at Dublán. We had a little more time to consider it, individuals did, and they did not give them up as freely at Juárez as they had done at Dublán. Then they went on in a few days to Colonia Pacheco.

We began immediately to ship our women and children out. We felt as though we were in imminent danger. The women and children thought it was no place for them. We got transportation the best we could and sent them with enough men to take care of them and organize them, so that they would not come without any kind of direction. We sent out the older men and a few able-bodied men to look after them, but kept most of the men there to look after the property.

From then on the rebels began making things a little tighter and a little tighter. They went down to Dublán en masse and looted some dozen homes with men present and pleading for them to spare their property and to respect their rights. During the looting of the homes they would poke the owners around with the points of their cocked guns. They would also hold pistols in the faces of the men, and made threats that if they did not cease their pleadings for their property, they would shoot them. I think it was on the evening of August 1, after having previously taken different amounts from the stores at Dublán, for which they had given receipts, that they took between $30,000 and $40,000 from the Union Mercantile, and for this they refused to give a receipt. We took into consideration the different developments in Dublán, the looting, the threats that had been made against our lives, the continued less favorable attitude of the rebels, the fact that they had required all kinds of guaranties and had taken our arms, showing how absolutely prejudiced they were against us, Salazar's oft-repeated threat that he would bring intervention at any cost, and we concluded that it would be impossible for our people to remain in the colonies and witness the wholesale destruction of their property, which was the accumulation of years.

We fully expected an attack to be made upon us, and reprisals to be made for the execution of a man who had been carrying on a regular campaign of loot. On the 1st day of August the band to which this soldier belonged came into Colonia Juárez, about seventy-five in all, and asked if the Mormons had executed any more of their soldiers, or if the guard had executed any more of their soldiers, and the guard replied that they had not. The rebels said it was a good thing they had not, that they were not satisfied with the execution of that man. They said that whenever the Mormons wanted to get a man executed, they just worked up a charge against him and brought about his execution, and they were going to get even with them. They were going to get revenge on the

Mormon people for the execution of this rebel. He was executed by the rebel soldiers without our having had anything to do with it, other than to bring evidence before them of the criminality of the man. That was one of the things that led up to our exodus. So on the morning of the 2nd of August we evacuated the colonies.

"We went from caviar to beans."
—Sybil Jonsoni Ludlow (1904–   )*

Among the foreigners who migrated to Mexico right before the outbreak of the Revolution was the Albert Fredrick Jonsoni family, whose roots were truly international. Mr. Jonsoni was a native of Italy, his wife Rose hailed from Australia, and four of their children were born in South Africa. They lived an affluent life-style until their fortune changed in 1910 with the unexpected death of Mr. Jonsoni. Sybil Jonsoni (Mrs. Fred Ludlow) relates what happened to the family in the next few years.

We were a happy, well-to-do family consisting of Mother, Dad, brother Albert, and sisters Violet, Ruby, and myself. On December 5, 1906, tragedy struck. It was Violet's birthday, and Mother and Dad had gone downtown to pick up the birthday cake. Meanwhile Violet told the cook she could leave because Violet wanted to make the tea and coffee. She struck a match to light the stove, and somehow her long hair caught fire. She panicked and grabbed the kitchen curtains, which only intensified the fire. When our parents returned, she was in terrible pain. She died in Dad's arms with a smile on her face.

Mother became very depressed and our doctor suggested to Dad that we travel for awhile. In March of 1907 we left our home [in Cape Town,

*Written memoir. Second place winner in the 1981 Historical Memories Contest of the El Paso County Historical Society. *Password* 26:2 (Summer 1981): 86–90. Reprinted by permission of *Password*.

South Africa], going to Ireland, England, Belgium, Germany, France, Switzerland, and Italy. Dad had a brother in Venice and we stayed there a month. Then back to South Hampton, where we set sail for America, docking in New York. After a month there, we took a train to Tacoma, Washington. My parents liked this part of America very much so Dad bought a home in Gig Harbor (near Tacoma). Here my brother Gordon was born. We stayed in Gig Harbor nearly three years. Then a friend talked Dad into going to Mexico, where there were oil and mining activities. We sold our home and moved to Guadalajara in 1910. All went well for a few months, then Dad received a cablegram urging him back to Cape Town to settle some business affairs. He left intending to come back on the return ship. We never saw him again. He died of a heart attack in Rhodesia.

We had always had plenty of money so Mother, thinking all she had to do was write for more, didn't economize. She found out on writing that because Dad died without a will, the estate was tied up until my brother Albert became twenty-one.

Albert quit school in his senior year to look for work. He found a job in the state of Chihuahua, where they were building a new dam called Boquilla. Once more we moved, this time to Santa Rosalía, the nearest town to Boquilla.

Needless to say our life-style changed drastically. We went from caviar to beans. Mother had to learn to cook, wash, iron, and keep house. She sold some of her treasures, and we adjusted to a new way of living.

Then came the Revolution. Pancho Villa had gathered a band of men together to fight the *federales,* who were in power at that time (1910). Villa soon took many of the small towns, and each day we heard rumors that he was coming our way. We were afraid to leave our homes. The federales built trenches in the form of crosses down the center of the streets to protect themselves. Finally one day at 2 P.M., they attacked Santa Rosalía. Bullets whizzed by in all directions. The Villistas won. Most of the federales were killed. The Villistas robbed the stores, and then marched on.

Albert came as soon as they left and took us to Boquilla to live in one of the company houses, which had just been built above the dam.

We had barely got settled, when the Villistas moved into Boquilla. This time not a shot was fired; they marched in and took possession. This happened in December. The train from America with our Christmas supplies was on the track. The first thing the Villistas did was loot the train. You would see them open cans of plum pudding, taste them, and then spit the food on the ground.

Albert always wore a Stetson hat, and one day he came home from work wearing a large, dirty sombrero full of holes. He told us that one of the soldiers asked him how much he wanted for his hat. Brother answered, "It's not for sale." The soldier pulled out his gun, took the hat, put his old dirty one on my brother's head, and gave him an I.O.U.

Another time, the Villistas took our donkey, tied him to a post by the neck and by his tail to another post; then, they lined up with their guns and tried to shoot off his tail. They also stole Albert's race horse.

A rumor circulated that the Villistas planned a dance at the company's club house, and the general said that all American women were to attend. Mr. McKenzie, the company superintendent, called the men together and told them something had to be done at once. As a result all the women and children and one man were loaded in a motor boat (the only one in Boquilla) with a week's supply of food and were taken to the island. Guns were given to all the women and to Mr. Roland, and they were told to use them on themselves if the Villistas came after us. The week passed and food was running out by the eighth day. Mr. Roland and the women had only coffee, while the children had tortillas to eat. On the ninth day around 11 A.M., we heard the putt-putt of the motor boat. We all fell to our knees and prayed that it would be our men. It was. Everyone was crying and laughing at the same time. The Villistas had moved on and we returned to Boqilla.

My brother was worried and thought we would be safer in Durango. He went with us to get us settled. We found a home for rent at 212 Calle Principal. Our neighbor on one side was a priest, and on the other, a famous artist, Lupe García.

We loved Durango, because so many nice things happened to us there. My sister Ruby was sixteen, and the fellows would give her a *"gallo"* almost every week. . . . One of the young men who was eager to take my sister Ruby out had a coach with two white horses and a driver sent to our home every afternoon to take us where we wanted to go. If we went to a show or the confectionary for a soda, we were always told it had been paid for.

Then one night about 11 o'clock the Villistas, under the command of Tomás Urbina, surprised the *federales* by attacking Durango. The battle raged for three days and nights. The *federales*, with the exception of about ten, were all killed.

On taking the city, the first thing the Villistas did was to loot the grocery, jewelry, and department stores, then set fire to the buildings. They gave orders that all homes should be left open day and night. The Villistas would enter your home at any time looking for guns, horses, or even a pretty girl. Lupe García, who had moved in with us, took some brown shoe polish and painted sister Ruby's face. Each time the soldiers came into our home, Ruby got on her knees by a tub of clothes and pretended to be the maid doing the laundry.

I saw Villa twice. The first time he was dressed in khaki and wore a cap. The second time he was resplendent in a black uniform with silver buttons and a large black hat also trimmed in silver. He always rode into a town on a beautiful horse. Behind him were the soldiers and behind them a bunch of bedraggled women carrying pots and pans.

Our troubles increased after this. Villa burned all the railroad bridges and tore down the telephone wires. We couldn't communicate with my brother. Our money ran out and Mother started selling her jewelry and finally, the furniture a piece at a time, until four of us were sleeping in one bed. Month after month went by and still no word from my brother. We gave him up for dead. At last there was nothing more to sell and we were hungry. Mother swallowed her pride and went to the consul for help. He scolded her and said that he was in Durango to help British subjects and that he would give us enough to live on until we heard from brother.

Finally one day a messenger came to our home with a telegram. When Mother took it, she fainted as she thought it was a death message. One of the neighbors read it to us. It was from Albert, saying that he would arrive in Durango the minute the bridges were mended. Two weeks later he came, and our friends in Durango turned out en masse to greet him. The band played, people clapped and yelled, and Albert was carried on the shoulders of our friends down one street and up the other for about an hour. It was a joyous time for all. After our evening meal, Albert told us what he had experienced during the months we were separated.

The company had sent him to Columbus, New Mexico, as an escort for the women and children of the American workers who wanted to leave. On the way back he was captured by Villa, who accused him of

273

being a spy. No amount of talking could convince Villa to the contrary. Albert was thrown in jail and told he would face the firing squad in three days. The sentence was to be carried out when Villa returned from a raid on some big ranch to get food for his men. Brother said, "I was wearing a white suit and there were so many fleas, lice, and bedbugs that I couldn't brush them off fast enough, and so I just watched them crawl over me in a steady stream." On the third day he was taken out of his cell and stood up against the wall before a firing squad of six men. He was asked if he had anything to say. He replied, "Only that I am not guilty." When he spoke, one of the members of the firing squad broke away, ran and put his arms around brother, and shouted, "He is not a spy; he is Don Alberto and I worked for him on the Boquilla Dam." So, due to one of God's miracles, he lived to come back to us.

Albert paid all the outstanding bills. We packed our few belongings and went back to Boquilla with him where we again moved into one of the company houses. We went through two more battles while there.

Then in November 1916, the superintendent, Mr. McKenzie, told us that we must leave our homes and go to the United States, as Villa said that he would shoot every *gringo* he found. We boarded a train for El Paso that night with much fear, as we had heard about the 300 families who had left before us in March. The Villistas had halted their train inside the Cumbre tunnel (which is about 160 miles southwest of Juárez), and set fire to the tunnel exits. All burned to death, including Mr. and Mrs. Abel and their four-year-old son. They were related to the Visconti family, friends of ours in Santa Rosalía.

We hadn't traveled far when the men sighted Villistas coming. They told us to lie flat on the Pullman floors. The men got their rifles, and for a while it was quite lively with shots coming from all directions. However, the train outran the bandits, and we pulled into Juárez at 3 A.M.

When we got to El Paso, we took the first hotel we came to on San Francisco Street and found out the next day we had spent the night in a bawdy house.

And so a family born in four different continents—South Africa, Europe, Australia, and America—finally ended their wanderings in the Rio Grande Valley, El Paso County, in the state of Texas.

274

> "If we should live to be a thousand
> years old, we could never forget it."
> —Mary Trowbridge Ritter*

*The following letter, written by Mary Trowbridge Ritter,
tells of one American family's plight in north-central Mexico
in 1913. Ritter had lived in Torreón for ten years with her
son George, an engineer, and her sisters and their families.
She describes the hardships suffered during the siege on Torreón and the nightmares endured as they sought to flee Mexico.*

My sweet, dear, cousin Grace,

Your letter arrived last night and brought gladness to us all. Yes,
indeed, we have had a terrible time, and if we should live to be a
thousand years old, could never forget it nor fully become reconciled
to the losses and sorrows we have all had to suffer. We were all a happy
family in our lovely home in Torreón until the Revolution began in 1910.
Then, six times we had to collect our belongings and flee to the United
States for safety. And of course the expense was great because we were
ten people.

Then early last year another insurrection broke out. This time we all
decided to face it and run the risk with George. He could not leave
because his boss was sick in New York. Things looked so dangerous that
I could not make up my mind to leave him, and all my sisters said they

*Letter written on March 5, 1914 at Berkeley, California. *American History Illustrated*
13:7 (1978): 20–24. Reprinted by permission of AHI and Marian Fullenwider of Pontiac,
Michigan.

would stay too—none of them would leave me. As a result we found ourselves bottled up in a besieged city. On February 6, 1913, the rebels surrounded and cut off our city completely. Of course, we were all sure the siege would be lifted soon. But day followed day, week followed week, month followed month, and the siege continued. Food became more and more scarce and expensive. Lard was four dollars a pound, eggs were fifty cents apiece, and sugar was two dollars and fifty cents a pound. A quart of milk so thin that it was blue, brought five dollars. Coffee and salt were almost unheard of at any price. Early in the siege George had told us to lay in a large supply of food, so our household was much better off than most families. We even had salt to season our food.

The importance of little things slipped out of all proportion. I had a collection of rare birds and there was no birdseed in Torreón. Then for my birthday an American friend gave me two pounds of the precious stuff. Somehow he had arranged to have some smuggled through the lines of the besiegers. I felt as if I had drawn a lottery. My beautiful birds. I wonder where they are now.

George had asked us to stay inside our house, but even through the windows we saw pitiful sights. Horses, burros, dogs, and kittens fell and died of hunger on the streets. And the pitiful tales and heartbreaking scenes of hungry and sick children were too horrible to ever forget.

All of these things seemed minor, though, when the rebels actually attacked our city in late July. For four weeks we were under fire. Soldiers fought and died in the streets, so many of them that the authorities could not bury them all. They piled them up and tried to burn them.

George now insisted that all of us women and children stay inside, but often, when there was a lull in the fighting—and George was out of the house—we would open the door to peer out—until we saw the starving dogs and pigs eating the remains of the partially burned corpses. Then we were glad to stay inside—and give up using lard to cook with.

All of us worried about George because he had to go out to tend to his business. He did have several narrow escapes, but he seemed to be lucky.

Our darling sister Ada became ill; the constant fear and tension were more than she could bear. Soon she was unable to leave her bed, and every day she seemed a little weaker.

276

During a revolt within the city the Madero rebels massacred 335 Chinese in one day and over one thousand dead were dumped into wagons, taken outside the city, partially burned, then left. Terrible epidemics broke out—typhoid fever. Maudie's youngest son was also taken sick with typhoid.

In September, the already serious situation became even more frightening. The rebels brought up cannon, and for twelve days and twelve nights, Torreón was bombarded. During this period we discovered the real tragedy of life. On the last day of the bombardment Robert, our precious seven-year-old, Bobbie, Mattie's only child, became ill. When the doctor came, his verdict was terrifying; Bobbie had scarlet fever and the doctor could do nothing to help him for there was no medicine in the city. In spite of our loving care, he died at 8 A.M. on the fourth day. We had to bury him on the same day. As there was a lull in the fighting we thought we could get him out to the cemetery; so George got a carriage and hearse and the minister. At four o'clock we went with his heartbroken mother to try to bury our precious dead. We hurried to do so, but even that last rite was denied us for we were fired on so much that we had to hurry back to the city. We left some Mexicans to bury him. It broke our hearts to have to leave him with them, our precious baby, but we were forced to. The rebels kept firing at us all the time till we reached the city again. George went out the next day and everything had been done all right.

The cannonading was not resumed, but the fighting went on as fiercely as ever. But we hardly noticed what went on around us. We were overwhelmed by our troubles and our sorrow.

In September a messenger on horseback came from the American embassy in Mexico City. He told all the Americans who were living in the city that we must leave at once.

How hard it was to leave behind the personal possessions we had collected over the past ten years. To think that we will never see any of them again. But the decisions had to be made. Necessities were packed—in small bundles in case we had to walk; in suitcases in case we had to form a caravan; in trunks in hopes a train could get through. We wept as we packed. But all that was nothing to what was before us. We little dreamed we were to pass through such horrors and such dangers.

On September 25, 1913, our rickety train pulled out of Torreón with

277

four hundred Americans aboard. The engine was one that had been discarded as worthless, then pulled out of the junkyard and carefully repaired by our American men. It pulled eleven cars: one Pullman car for old or ill women and for mothers with new babies; a boxcar which had been converted into a hospital car with four cots and carried Meriden our fifteen-year-old who was confined to bed with a diseased hip, his younger brother Perry who had typhoid fever, and a man with scarlet fever; two baggage cars; one boxcar filled with supplies, and seven day coaches into which the rest of us four hundred were crammed like cattle.

The trip to the Texas border in times of peace took twenty-four hours. This time we all expected to meet difficulties because we would be passing through areas where rebels and federals might be fighting. Also we had been told that a trainload of federal troops would be escorting us and they might provoke trouble. So we packed provisions and clothes for four days, thinking that would be plenty. Well—we were one month. One, solid, horrible, long month, without a bed to sleep on or a table to eat at or even a change of linens, and not knowing what moment would be our last, for we were in constant danger.

I won't dwell on our many hardships but in a disconnected way will mention some of the events.

We traveled only in the daytime for fear of treachery. Bridges had been blown up and rails torn out of the roadbeds and taken away. The men—bankers, doctors, lawyers, engineers—took up rails after we had passed over them and laid them in front of the train. We carried materials to build a bridge and at each river the men built the bridge, then took it down again after the train had passed over it. At one point they built three bridges only one hundred yards apart. This made progress agonizingly slow. Moreover, at intervals, fighting broke out and we had to go back over the same territory over and over again. At one point we discoverd we had ridden over a mine containing twenty-six pounds of dynamite three times, but the percussion caps were faulty and did not explode.

Another time we stopped only thirty feet from another big mine of dynamite. This time the soldiers in the military train with us captured the man that tried to blow us up. They cut out his tongue, gouged out his eyes, then hung him up on a telegraph pole just outside the windows of our coach and filled him with bullets.

And there he remained. And there we remained—for three days and three nights—for ahead of us the rebels had blown up the bridges and behind us the railroad tracks were all torn apart. We had to stay on the train—live, sleep, eat on the train with that horrible object hanging outside the windows. They odor was terrible and the flies crawled everywhere—on the dead body, on the telegraph pole; even the ground crawled with flies. Finally the men finished building track and bridges and the train was able to move again.

Poor George worked day and night to keep our old discarded locomotive alive; he even built a pump to carry along so as to replenish the boilers when we came down to some river or puddle, for the way, the only way, of getting water on the road as by dipping it up in buckets, forming a bucket brigade. Every man had to get in and work. They all worked with a will, I tell you; not only were they working for their lives, but all knew what every mile meant, and we were driven back and forth over the same places so many times, and things looked so hopeless, I almost lost heart and hid away to have my cry out, but nobody saw me cry. There is good American stuff in me yet, in spite of my many long years in Mexico, but nobody can ever know how near I came to being a downright coward!

The Methodist minister's wife had a sweet little baby girl born while we were stalled between two burning bridges in the midst of a battle. One day we left the train just long enough to bury a little boy who had died during the night.

Sickness broke out on the train—three new cases of typhoid and other fevers. Our Maudie began to run a high fever and was taken to the Pullman car where dear Ada was slowly fading away. However, a few days' rest took care of her fever and she was able to return to the day coach.

I had one problem that I didn't talk about at the time. Before leaving Torreón, I had sewn pockets around the hips of my corset to conceal the family's money. When George mentioned this ruse to some of his friends, they came to ask me to look after their money too. So I was almost a walking bank. In order to keep the money safe, I wore my corset, in that terrible heat, for the entire trip. I perspired so much that I lost thirty-two pounds, and when I finally was able to take the corset off, the money was all stuck together, and it took a lot of drying out and careful handling to separate the greenbacks.

The train went through the rebel lines so often that I grew used to it and never once thought of my corset. But that was only part of the trouble. The federal troops were just as bad. We had eleven long trains of soldiers along with us most of the way. We felt almost as if we would have been safer alone. We could not pass; they would not let us pass; in fact, they used our train as a shield against the rebels. Half of the time we were between the rebels and the federals who were supposed to be protecting us.

After three long weeks of this sort of traveling, we had worked our way to within thirty-two miles of the border at Laredo, Texas. At this point, when we were almost certain we would succeed in reaching our goal, we were turned back and had to go back south to Monterrey. The failure almost overwhelmed us. In desperation we went east, across to Tampico, a port. There we were able to get a boat, the Swedish freighter *Texas*. It had accommodations for only twenty-four people, so the ill and old people were given the cabins, and we poor well ones had to take the best we could get. They put the men on the main deck and all the women and children on the hurricane deck. On this hurricane deck we ate, slept, and watched for the longed-for land. The hot sun burned us, the rain soaked us, the cold night winds chilled us, but we didn't mind. All hands were thankful even for that kind of transportation. And we could breathe freely and speak freely for there were no rebels and we were off of Mexican soil. Finally thirty days after we had left Torreón, we landed in Galveston, in God's country, safe, but far from well.

We hurried on to our family's home here in Berkeley to recuperate. Two weeks later our dear sister Ada died of exhaustion. She was one of five who did not survive the ordeal. Hattie also spent some weeks in the hospital to recover from the terrible experiences she had suffered. Slowly, we began to regain some semblance of composure, but none of us will ever be the same; we have suffered so much, all joy and laughter seem hollow.

We are, however, consoled by thoughts of the many friends we were surrounded by during our ordeal. Many brave and noble characters came to the front that were never suspected of any force of character before and very few proved to be cowards.

Every time I recall the trip, I am more and more proud of the fact that I am an American.

Some time I will write again. I wish you would send this on to the Dean, for it is so hard to write it all. It's all too terrible and nearly makes me sick to think of all the horrors and sorrows. It hurts too much yet, so if you don't mind, please share this letter with the family.

Your cousin who loves you and often thinks of you.

Mary Ritter

> "Any person who should be heard
> to complain . . . should be sus-
> pended by a rope . . . until . . . he
> sincerely repented. . . ."
> —Will B. Davis, M.D.*

*Americans used whatever means were available to flee Mex-
ico in times of crisis. In the spring of 1914, a large group of
refugees traveled on the German freighter S.S. Marie from
the west coast port of Manzanillo to San Diego, California.
Will B. Davis, a consular officer at the American consulate in
Guadalajara, accompanied the group. When he wrote his
memoirs, he included a vivid description of that trip. Especially interesting is how the refugees organized their life aboard
ship to make the best of their difficult situation.*

After having waited for so long a time without avail to have their
baggage inspected by customs officials before leaving at a little before
4 o'clock, the Americans agreed to pay the *jefe político* at the port eleven
hundred pesos (equal to $550 American money) to have the matter
attended to, for they had all become convinced—and had been told by
other than Mexicans—that they might be held there indefinitely unless
this was done—unless they paid graft money to the officers of the port.
This arrangement having been consummated, the women and children,

*Will B. Davis, M.D. *Experiences and Observations of an American Consular Officer
During the Recent Mexican Revolutions* (Los Angeles: Wayside Press, 1920), pp. 25,
28–32.

the small baggage, and a part of the men were permitted to go aboard the Marie at a little after 4 P.M.; but sixteen of the men were held, and later carried by army officials to the American consulate, where they were forced to witness violation of the American flag and a portrait of President Wilson, which said officers sacked from the Manzanillo consulate and delivered to the mob, who, in fiendish glee tore them, spat upon them, trampled them under foot and ended by burning them and then throwing the ashes in the faces of the American spectators, accompanying these savageries with exclamations of the most insulting kind.

The Marie left Manzanillo at 7 P.M., April 25th, and it was not until after she had nosed well out to sea, that the Americans felt that they could breathe in safety. They would have felt happy at that time, even had they been on a coal barge—or anything that promised to carry them from those shores, and out of the reach of those menacing Mexican mobs.

At that time of the year, it was quite warm in those southern latitudes, and consequently—(although but few of our people were provided with blankets, and none could be procured aboard ship)—sleeping upon the bare upper deck during our first two nights out, was not uncomfortable; but with our progress north, the nights were cooler, and before we reached San Diego, they became uncomfortably cold; but all our people were courageous and they endured every inconvenience or discomfort of the voyage uncomplainingly. The days, however, were pleasant throughout the entire trip, and those who had suffered from cold during the night could thaw out the morning after. The only cabins on the boat were officers' quarters, affording ordinarily sleeping room for sixteen persons only. The officers were very kind, and doubled up among themselves, to afford accommodations for our aged and infirm. The dining room was arranged to accommodate sixteen at a table, with fixed chairs for that number. The only service people on the boat were the cook with helper, and a couple of roustabouts. The captain had taken on all additional provisions that he could procure in the Manzanillo market— which was not much—to feed us until we could reach San Diego.

On our first night at sea, the Americans laid down anywhere upon the upper deck—each as best he could—and went to sleep early, for all of them were experiencing a sense of relaxation following a long state of tension, and an added great fatigue from travel under very uncomfortable conditions. Breakfast consisting of coffee, bread and butter, was served in the dining room the following morning—and every other morning during the trip—each passenger taking his turn, sitting or standing—mostly standing—while holding his food and coffee cup in either hand.

Early on the morning after sailing, a general meeting was held by our refugees, and an organization formed, by electing Mr. Michiel Slattery as a sort of *generalissimo,* with powers to appoint service committees, to see that each properly performed the duties assigned to him, and to supervise the enforcement of all rules and regulations that were adopted for our government during the voyage. One of the first resolutions that was proposed, and adopted by unanimous vote, was, "That any person who should be heard to complain of the service on 'this here boat,' should be suspended by a rope over the hatchway until he, such culprit should, by word of mouth—or some sign that could be well understood—express, indicate, or make known, to the entire satisfaction of his executioners, that he sincerely repented of what he, the culprit, had been guilty by word or deed; and that as to spoken words which should not have been uttered, the culprit, retracted the same, took them back, masticated and swallowed them, and would endeavor to never again be guilty of such misdemeanors, or their like; and that in so far as any deeds of kind would, in penance for same, do and perform double menial service throughout the remainder of the trip." Needless to say, no one was heard to complain, in any manner whatever, of the service, or the ship's accommodations, during the voyage.

One of the most important committees appointed was that of the meal-serving gang. At all meals—excepting breakfast—the Americans would form in two parallel lines on the outer gangway of the deck, and the members of the meal-serving committee would pass along the human lane so formed, those of the advanced guard handing out on either side, plates, knives or spoons—according to what food was to follow—sometimes soup, rice, or oatmeal porridge. Next the bread and butter gang would pass along; and another, perhaps, handing out potatoes or eggs, and—(on one or two occasions during the trip)—meat, of some sort. When soup, rice, or oatmeal porridge, or anything of a liquid or semi-liquid nature was being served, two of the "waiters" would carry the caldron between them, while a third would ladle out rations to whomsoever, on either side, would hold out his plate to receive it. Our menus were not very extensive at any of the meals, but such food as was served was well cooked, and was quite palatable. However, the eggs—which were served in abundance—had come all the way from China, and when they were not boiled real hard, it was difficult to distinguish the good from the bad ones—before breaking the shell. About every third egg had not yet spoiled. On this trip I learned that however hard one tried to boil a spoiled egg, it could hardly be done.

As stated, the Marie was a tramp freighter; therefore no provision had been made in her construction—though a splendidly built vessel— for the personal comfort of others than her limited number of officers; and consequently, she had been provided with only two toilet rooms, on the upper deck. This inconvenience to a passenger list of 300 souls was overcome by assigning the most convenient and commodious of the two to the women and children, and maintaining toilet room committees posted at the doors of each.

On a bulletin board, the names of the officers of our organization, the names of the members of the various committees, and all the rules and regulations were kept posted; and when an article had been lost or mislaid, or a meeting was to be held, the same was also announced on the bulletin board, as well as such "news" as may have leaked through the atmosphere. (The Marie was not provided with a wireless apparatus.)

On our third day out, there appeared on the bulletin board the following announcement: "A baby girl was born last night to Mr. and Mrs. (I cannot recall the name now), and christened 'Julia Marie,' in honor of our courteous captain, Julius Davidson, and the good ship Marie. Mother, babe and father doing well." There was general rejoicing over this announcement, which seemed to gratify the officers of the boat as much as it did the passengers.

A few hours before reaching the port of San Diego, a meeting was held, including the boat's officers, when expressions of appreciation were indulged in for the courteous treatment extended by the officers to the passengers. A gold watch which had been purchased from the stock of a jeweler aboard, by general subscription, was presented to Captain Davidson, by Mr. Slattery, who was also charged with having the watch appropriately engraved after we should arrive at San Diego.

On landing at San Diego, we were met by members of the Red Cross Society, who took charge of, and furnished the financially embarrassed members of our party—which included nearly all of them—with hotel and other accommodations for the time, and afterward, transportation to their respective destinations in the States. But with all this kindness, it made one's heart ache to see so many destitute Americans—men, women, and children—gathered in and about the San Diego Red Cross headquarters—(there were may others besides those who came over on the Marie)—during those times. Many of these people had been prosperous before the recent revolutions had begun in Mexico; and some of them had accumulated competencies sufficient to have enabled them to live in comfort the remainder of their lives; but all, except a few, had lost everything, and the "few" who had not had been compelled to abandon what "all" they may have had left and flee the country. The greater number of those with whom I have been able to keep in touch since have fared poorly. Some seemed incapable of readjusting themselves to their changed conditions, and to begin life anew again in real earnest; others were already too old for any kind of undertakings.

"I never reaped one dollar from my investment."

—William C. Garrett*

The big battles of the Revolution had ended by the late 1910s, but clashes continued between rebellious factions and the Carranza government. William C. Garrett, a naturalized U.S. citizen of British extraction, relates various difficulties he and other foreigners encountered during a period of such instability in the northeastern state of Tamaulipas.

It was at the time of the rebellion that Luis Caballero raised against Carranza in the early spring of 1918. The soldiers came out from Victoria and marched past by plantation to the north, where they were met by the government troops, and a fight occurred in which a great number of them were killed. In fact, I understood it was such a mix-up that they did not know which were which, and every man was shooting at the first one he could see.

During this time I went and hid in the brush. One or two men who had come out from Victoria and had felt that they did not want to join the rebels came to the plantation and told some of the men that worked for me that they would like to hide there. One of them took his saddle off and put it on the porch of my house and turned his horse loose, leaving his cartridges in a bag on his saddle. I was not aware that the man was there or that his saddle had been placed where it was.

*Interviewed in Washington, D.C., in 1920. *Investigation of Mexican Affairs*, Senate Document 285, 66th Congress, 2nd Session (Washington, D.C., 1920), pp. 1961–75.

About sundown my men came to me and said that the fight was over and that it was perfectly safe for me to come back, that everyone had gone. So I returned to the house, and was sitting on the front porch. In a few moments I heard some shooting at the gate and trampling of horses, and I turned to make for the brush. Then I heard a rifle shot, and I looked around and found one of the men was riding toward me. I stopped and asked him what he wanted, and he told me that the captain wanted to see me. I went up to the captain and asked him what he wanted. He was on his horse, flourishing his revolver, shooting it at the same time. He said, "Give me $5,000." I said that I did not have money there; that it would be foolish for me to keep so much money on the plantation. He said, "Give me $5,000," at the same time striking me on the side of the face with his revolver and shooting it off. He knocked me down insensible, and when I came to I found that they were ransacking the house, taking everything they wanted, breaking open my trunks. They had tied my Chinaman to the house, and he was begging and imploring them to leave him alone, and he gave them all the money that he had. Then they let him loose and told him to cook them something to eat.

After they had finished they came to me, drew their sabers, and pounded me all over, telling me to get up. They put their revolvers at my head and said, "Now, I am going to kill you, you damned *gringo*." I staggered to my feet, and they said, "Now, give me what money you have." I told them that I had a little money that I kept for the payroll next Saturday, and that I would let them have that.

I had about 120 pesos, partly in American and partly in Mexican money. At that time American silver was current in Mexico just the same as Mexican money. I also had about $40 in paper money. I had given this to one of my men in the morning to take care of, thinking that if trouble occurred it would be safer with him than with me. So I told them that I had some money that I would give them. They jumped on their horses, all of them, saying, "It is mine! It is mine! It is mine!" With their horses and swords they pushed forward to this house where the man had the money. I went to him, and he brought it out. I handed them the sack of silver and dropped the pocketbook with the paper money on the ground and kicked it in the grass. Then the captain said, "Give me $1,500 more." I said, "No; that is all the money you will get.

That is all the money I have." He said, "Well, we will find out." So they drove me back to the house, where there was a large tree, and they put a rope around my neck and pulled me off the ground twice.

Then they asked me about the saddle. They seemed to be under the impression that this man had come and sold me the saddle, and so they made a great fuss about it. I told them that I had not seen it before, that I knew nothing about it. So they went and took all my books, my accounts, and brought them all out and put them under the saddle, took some kerosene and soaked the whole thing, and gave me matches and said: "Now set it on fire." I had no compunctions whatever about burning up their own saddle, but I did regret burning up all my accounts.

My men who had seen me knocked down had run away to the brush and gone down to Victoria, where they told my friend, Mr. Robert S. Tice, who was the superintendent of the Quaker school at Victoria at the time, that they had seen me killed. He sent a telegram to my wife to that effect, but very fortunately the telegraph wires were all cut, and the telegram did not go through. After that, I left on the first train that left Victoria for Laredo, and came out, reporting the matter to the authorities at Matamoros.

On another occasion conditions got so bad that it was advisable to leave. I had thought that it was just a temporary affair and that matters would settle down. I got options on some land and went to London and arranged for the purchase of this land, the money to be placed in the bank in New York against the deeds. I returned to find that conditions, instead of improving, had gotten considerably worse. After great difficulties I succeeded in getting to Tampico by boat, and went up country to find that the men who had given me the options had been obliged to leave the country. After waiting there for two or three days the town was attacked by Carranza's men under General González, and I was in the town when it was taken by this general.

General González treated me with the greatest amount of courtesy. When I went to see him and asked him for a permit to leave the country, he referred me to his secretary, who, I noticed, was a Mason. Catching sight of my Masonic badge, he put out his hand, saying: "What can I do for you, *señor?*" and offered to do anything in his power to help us. We obtained passes that were very firm in their expression that we should be protected, and nine of us rode from Victoria to Matamoros.

While on the way we received the greatest amount of courtesy, with the exception of one experience that we had with one drunken Mexican, who came upon us accidentally in the brush at night and was going to shoot us all.

They looted Victoria, especially the businesses of those men who were loyal to the old government, and especially the Spaniards. There were two or three Spaniards. They broke open the large stores and the banks; they took all the property out and distributed it among the people. They broke open the safes in the banks, and burned the jail and the courthouse. All the records were burned at the time. I think it was a matter almost beyond the control of Pablo González. I think that the men took the matter into their own hands.

I went to see Luis Caballero, who was the governor of the state of Tamaulipas, and I could get no assistance whatever from him. He would utterly ignore it. On one occasion I went to the governor's palace and waited two days before I could get any audience with him. I sent in my card, and told him that I would like to have an interview with him to complain about the way in which I was treated and in which these roving bands of soldiers would come out to my place and would come in and demand anything, and would come and live upon the people who were working for me and demand food from them. But he absolutely ignored and refused to do anything for anyone who was a foreigner. He was very, very bitter against foreigners.

I invested all the money that I had. When I came out I had my suitcase, and that was all. I was fortunate to be able to bring that out. I never reaped one dollar from my investment in Mexico in any way. The cultivation of henequen is a very lucrative enterprise. A well-cared-for plantation, one that is producing, will bring from $75 to $100 an acre each year. I had hundreds of acres of it at the time I left.

My experience with the workmen who lived on my plantation was very agreeable. My opinion about them was that they were very tractable, that they were very easily handled as long as they were treated right. I noticed also that they would rather work for a foreigner than they would for a Mexican. They seemed to think that they were better treated. They never had to wait a day for their money. I always had their money ready for them on Saturday afternoon, and I never owed one of them a single peso. They were good workmen. They would come and work for the money that I paid them, and I paid them at the same rate as was customary in that vicinity. I thought that they were excellent workmen.

It is my impression that Mexico was greatly benefited by the investments that were made by foreigners. Otherwise, the country would have remained in virtually a dormant state. It was foreign capital that had come in there at the request of the Mexican government that has developed Mexico to the conditions that it is today—or that it was before the present troubles occurred. It appeared to me that the Mexicans had become alive to the improvements that the foreigners had made and had sent their sons to the U.S. and abroad to be educated, and when they came back they were naturally as bright, as intelligent, as the majority of men who can be found. One would say: "I have a son who is an engineer. He can conduct this business." Another one would say: "I have a son that understands railroading. He can run these railroads." And so they said: "You people get out. We will run this business. We will run it ourselves. Mexico for the Mexicans!" The property of the foreigners would be turned over and be used entirely by them. Now, the Mexicans were glad to have foreigners come and invest their money and improve the country. But just as soon as this was productive and the returns came in, then the story was different: "Now we will take it; and we will handle it ourselves."

I know several men who were in Chimal and several who were in Columbus. They were farmers—a fine class of people. A good many of them came from the western part of Oklahoma. They had gone there and invested all that they had and were doing well, had built nice homes, had fine cultivated land, had imported stock, and had put up stores and improved the land, had schools, and were getting along splendidly until this revolution came. They were advised by the United States government to leave. Great numbers of them got up at a minute's notice, and left everything that they had there and came back to the United States, and when they came back again there was not a thing left. Everything was gone. A great number of their houses were pulled down; the stock were taken, the horses were taken, and the cattle, a great number of them killed and eaten.

A man named Mark Johnson and his mother lived on a farm about a mile and a half north of Victoria. They had a dairy farm there, and kept a quantity of cows. On one occasion my wife and I were staying with them overnight when some Mexican soldiers came and demanded some

291

fodder. They were told that the fodder was needed for the cattle, and the soldiers said they needed it for their horses, and they were going to have it. Mr. Johnson told them that if they could get an order from the general, he would let them have it. This man immediately drew his revolver and pointed it at his head, and said: "That is all the order you will get." I went up to the man and told him to put his revolver up, that we were not armed, and there was no occasion to speak in that way. Another man who was with him talked to him and calmed him down, and they went off. The next day, I rode into Victoria and saw Gov. Luis Caballero and made a complaint to him about this matter, and we were told that if this man could be located he would be punished. We found the man and went back and told the general where he was, but no notice was ever taken of it.

No foreigners in Mexico were permitted to have any rifles or revolvers. When you went in the country they would search your suitcases and trunks particularly for revolvers, and if they found them they would take them away. On one occasion I was going across the border to Mexico, and, if I remember right, there were eight Americans on the train. We had all passed the customs. It was the time when we had to travel in baggage cars with planks across for seats. A few minutes after the train had started a man came up and said he would like to see the suitcases. So one American said, "Why, my suitcase has been examined by the customs." The man said, "I would like to see it again." He had a badge showing that he was a customs officer. He opened the suitcase and went through it very carefully and found a revolver. He said: "You are not permitted to bring revolvers into this country; it is against the Mexican law. I will take this." He put it in his belt, and went up to the next man and searched his suitcase and could not find any, so he said: "Have you got a revolver?" The man said: "No." He put his hands around his waist, and found one in his belt, and he said, "Yes, you have. I will take that." Then he came to me and said, "Have you got a revolver?" I said, "Yes." He said, "I will take it," and he took a revolver away from each one of us. Then he went back in the car, and said, "This is against the law, your bringing revolvers into this country. You may consider yourselves under arrest, and you will all get off the train at the next depot and go back to Matamoros with me." So we talked it over, and a few moments later he came back again, and he said: "I have been considering the case of you fellows, and if you would like to sign a paper donating these revolvers to the Mexican army, I will let you all off." So we decided that as he had the revolvers already we might just as well give them to him, and so we did so, all of us, and he disappeared off the train at the next station. No doubt he sold them for his own advantage, but that is something I know nothing about, what he did with them.

"Smiles spread across the features of
most of the Chinamen."

—Harry Morgan*

*As had been the case in previous attacks on Juárez, Villa's
last attempt to capture this city in June 1919 precipitated a
large migration to El Paso. Local reporter Harry Morgan
wrote on the meaning of the Revolution for the juarenses who
were forced to flee to safety.*

Two minutes after the firing began the rush across the river from
Mexico started. The first to cross was a body of about 350 Chinamen.
Fearing an attack these people, the entire Chinese population of Juárez,
had gathered their few worldly belongings to flee to safety on American
soil when the first shot of the battle was fired.

There was no attempt on their part to conceal the joy of being safely
housed in a building which flies the stars and stripes. Once inside the
immigration building smiles spread across the features of most of the
Chinamen, and groups chuckled and talked excitedly in their native
tongue. A bundle containing a few clothes and small articles of value
was all most of the Chinamen brought with them. Some brought blankets
and as soon as they had been permanently assigned to the basement of
the building many laid down on the floor and fell asleep, perhaps feeling
secure for the first night in many.

The rush of Mexicans for this side of the river was not as heavy as

*El Paso Times, June 16, 1919, pp. 1, 2.

294

had been expected. All night following the cannon firing a steady stream of Juárez inhabitants filed across the bridge. None except those who had passports was allowed to enter this country before the battle started. Then came a rush of a hundred or more, most of whom did not have credentials to cross the border. According to previously made arrangements, these people were herded into the immigration house and later were housed in an adjoining building. If the exodus had been so great that the immigration house would not have held all the Mexicans, preparations had been made by the military authorities to corral them east of Santa Fe Street.

Genuine pathos marked the flight of the Mexicans. Half-clad women, their hair loose, fear written on their faces, ambled across the bridge, holding scantily dressed, crying babies to their breasts. Shawls and blankets trailed in the dirt. To them the night of terror was just another page in Mexico's lengthy chronicle of revolution. To flee from their homes, leaving behind everything they possessed of worldly goods which, meager as it might be, was their all, was only a repetition of former experiences. To leave their humble homes in the wake of war and at the mercy of their fellow countrymen was not a novel thing, but its repetition made it no less terrible.

Little children old enough to walk but incapable of understanding, tagged along at their mothers' skirts, their eyes tearful, yet full of innocent wonderment. They had been born in the throes of revolution, and life to them had been little more than a recurring series of bloodshed.

One of the most pathetic sights was that of a ragged old man, who hobbled across to the American side, carrying a few clothes gathered up in his rapid exit from home on one arm. In the other arm he carried his provisions for an indefinite stay—two loaves of bread. His wife had hurried ahead of him and the two were placed together in the immigration building.

The international bridge was the scene of a steady flow of Mexicans between 8 o'clock and midnight. All who came over at that time were required to show passports and practically all of those who did come across brought the bulk of their personal property with them.

The situation at the international crossing, intense as it was all night, with bullets hitting near, immigration officials working overtime, and the American troops massed in force, was not without its humorous moments. Soon after the firing ceased yesterday morning, the Mexican inhabitants along the river began to emerge slowly from their adobe homes. One lad, not more than sixteen years old, walked down to the edge of the stream, stepped into the water, and pulled up a rifle that evidently had been discarded by one of the fighters. Happily, the boy ran back to his home, shouted something to those inside, and ran toward the center of Juárez. Fortune had made him a soldier in an instant, although it is doubtful whether he knew who was in possession of the city.

An hour later people started to cross into Mexico from this side. After the situation in Juárez was understood, the Chinamen and Mexicans without passports who had crossed during the night were sent back.

It was a sad Sunday morning across the river. Men, women, and little children were curiously walking about the town, viewing the remains of dead Mexicans lying in the streets. Barefooted children unknowingly stepped about the bloody bodies of the soldiers, looking at their ghastly wounds and walked away to view the next tragedy of the fight, the blood on their little feet making imprints on the pavement.

"I done this just through an act of humanity."
—Joseph Allen Richards (1884–?)*

Distrust and antagonism toward Americans continued in Mexico for some time after the peak years of revolutionary troubles. This is illustrated by the following incident which occurred in Baja California in 1919. U.S. Army employee Joseph Allen Richards found the bodies of two murdered American aviators who had been lost during a rainstorm, and his method of reporting got him into difficulty with Mexican authorities. Richards's attempt to pass for a German reveals U.S. perceptions of Mexican anti-Americanism in contrast to high esteem for Germans, presumably because the latter had befriended Mexico in its conflicts with the United States.

I was a passenger on board the Mexican steamer called Navari, of Santa Rosalía. I had come from the mouth of the Colorado River on the same boat, and we had no drinking water, so we pulled into the Bay of Angel to replenish the stock of drinking water—eleven kegs. I took a keg and went up to the spring and filled it. I was the first man back to the boat, so I began walking around the beach looking for sea shells. I smelled an awful strong odor, and about ten feet from where my keg was I seen a mound of dirt sticking up. I went over there and I seen a

*Interviewed in 1919. *Investigation of Mexican Affairs*, Senate Document 285, 66th Congress, 2nd Session (Washington, D.C., 1920), pp. 967–77.

297

human skull in the sand. I dug the skull up and looked at it; it was such a small skull. Then I took part of a turtle shell and dug in the sand and hit against a boot. I reached down with my hand, got hold of the boot, and pulled on it. I pulled him clean out of the sand. About 6 inches of sand was over him. I pulled him out and made an examination of him, and I seen he had on the army uniform. This man had on high-laced boots, with knee-cord Army pants. I searched him, and in his right-hand pocket he had a pair of gold cuff buttons, with the fancy letter "C" on them, and a pair of bird wings, with a propeller in the center of them. It stood straight up and down. There was also one little short silver bar. That is all this man had on him. I went and got a shovel then from the boat, and we dug this other man up. I took their clothes off down to the knee and examined them and found black hair on one and sandy hair on the other. The other man had in his watch pocket just one of those propeller wings and a lieutenant's bar. He had on a pair of ox-blood shoes, leather leggins, marked: "Hanan Brothers, New York." One man's head was crushed, and the other man's back was all bloody. There was no meat on the skulls. I judge they had been there about ten or fifteen days. I then dug a grave four feet deep, put both of them in it side by side, and buried them and went on to Santa Rosalía.

I went aboard an American steamer called the Providencia of San Francisco, made a sworn statement, and showed the captain the things I had taken. The captain was just about ready to leave. He said: "As quick as I get out of the three-mile zone, I will wire." I don't know what he meant by that. When I went ashore nobody bothered me for an hour, but when the Providencia pulled out I was arrested. They took me up to the office and asked my business aboard the Providencia. I told him [the police officer] I went up there to see if I knew any of the crew; he called me a "Goddamn liar!" He says, "You went up there to report the finding of the two murdered men." I says, "I don't necessarily know they were murdered." He says, "That is what you told the captain of the boat you went to. You Goddamned *gringos* come down here and start trouble when we don't bother you." I says, "I have not started any trouble at all." He says, "You will wish you hadn't before we get through with you." He wanted me to sign a document there. I did not know what was on it. I refused to sign it. He went outside, then two policemen came and took me to jail. I was in prison from Saturday, about 11 o'clock, until Sunday evening. They stripped me naked and put me in a little cement hole that was all dirty and filthy; there was no toilet in there. I asked the guard for a drink of water and he said, *"Besame el culo"* meaning kiss my ———. I did not say nothing. So when the new guard came on I asked him could I have a drink of water. He said, "Sure." He then asked me if I had any money. I said, "They taken $10.50 away from me." He said, "I will get it for you."

I stayed there without any clothes until they let me go. About four in the evening they gave me my clothes and took me up on the hill to the *juzgado menor,* that is, the lower court. The secretary of the town, a man who was half Mexican and half Frenchman, told me I was charged with robbery. I asked him who in hell I had robbed, and he said, "You robbed dead bodies." I says, "All right." Then he put up the argument to me, "Why didn't you come to the Mexican authorities when you landed here with this story and these articles instead of going to an American captain on the boat?" He says, "You are in Mexico now, not in America." I told him I did not know any different; I was ignorant of the law. He says, "Well, we have got a charge of robbery against you and the charge of molesting corpses before an inquest was held." I told him I was ignorant of both laws; I had not robbed anything. I got kind of bewildered in talking Spanish. I got all mixed up; I did not know anything about them big words. So I went and got the *juez de primera instancia,* who was also the mayor of the town. He was a Mexican but he talked English good as I do. He says, "I cannot act officially, but I will give you a little help. You ask whatever you want to and I will interpret it for you." So then I just put the case up to the district attorney. I says, "Suppose I was to come along and find your brother and father murdered in the sand, and I was to dig them up and try to find out who they were and bury them a little deeper, so the coyotes would not eat them up. Would you call that an inhuman act or a human act? I done this just through an act of humanity." They got to studying it over a little bit, and the captain of the port came up again while I was arguing my case. He says, "Throw the *gringo* bastard in jail; don't let him go. He done reported to the United States now, so you might as well hold him."

So they got to figuring how many days the Providencia had been out of Santa Rosalía. She had been gone a day and a half. I says, "All right, you call me a *gringo* if you want to; I never said I am a *gringo.* I am a German, born in Berlin; I am not a *gringo.*" The captain of the port asked me, "Can you talk German?" I says, "Just as good as I talk English."

299

He says, "I will damn soon find out whether you can or not." But he never got anybody up there to talk German to me. If he had, well, I don't know. . . . They asked me two of three times where I was going. I told them South America. Then they went and got this Italian [who was a fellow passenger on the Navari] and asked him if I was going with him to South America. He says, "Yes, I am paying his way." So he told them I was going to South America, and they let me go.

I was born in Chicago, Illinois, but I absolutely know that they are anti-*gringo* in that country. They have no use for an American in the port of Santa Rosalía. There were 12 German boats interned there, and the Germans are pretty strong in Mexico. A German is treated like a prince. They have got the freedom of the city, and have had it for five years.

[Richards left Mexico via Nogales, where he reported the incident to American officials. He subsequently traveled in a U.S. destroyer that had Mexico's permission to retrieve the aviators' bodies. From information gathered, the flyers had been picked up by a fishing boat seventeen days after their emergency landing, were subsequently murdered, and then taken to the port where their bodies were found. Apparently the motive was robbery.]

"My gosh, it's raining."

—Fred Bailey*

Banditry continued to plague Chihuahua even after Pancho Villa retired from revolutionary activity. Fred Bailey, a native of England and 1920 graduate of the Texas College of Mines (now the University of Texas at El Paso), remembers the uncertain climate that kept him and other Americans ever-mindful of possible danger.

Just before graduation, I was offered two jobs, one at the iron mines in Minnesota and the other in the silver-gold mines close to Parral, Chihuahua, Mexico. I did not have enough money to pay the transportation to Minnesota, where I really desired to go; so since transportation into Mexico was paid for me, I accepted the Mexico job. During summer vacations I had worked in New Mexico as a miner, assayer, and surveyor, but now I was entering the business world as a mining engineer. It was during the many periods of revolutionary activity in Mexico. The trains ran only during daylight hours, and sometimes not at all, if the revolutionaries had been active in destroying railroad tracks and bridges. We traveled only as far as Chihuahua the first day. The train we were on was the first to leave Juárez for several days, and it looked like about half the city of Chihuahua came to meet that train. We, a group of twelve

*Interviewed in El Paso in 1974 by Robert H. Novak. On file at the Institute of Oral History, University of Texas at El Paso.

Americans, were met by the American consul who entertained us that evening in the Chihuahua City Foreign Club. We left Chihuahua the following day en route to Parral in the same state of Chihuahua. The entire trip from Juárez to Parral took five days. (It can now be made by automobile in about ten to twelve hours.) Several bridges had been destroyed both to the south and to the west of Jiménez, a small railroad junction town. We were obliged to remain in Jiménez three days along with a large number of federal troops, who were also awaiting transportation from that place. We occupied ourselves playing poker and drinking tequila.

We eventually left Jiménez on the first train headed toward Parral in over a week, and this was a freight train. We were permitted to travel in one of the empty box cars, which like all the other cars on the train was loaded with soldiers and their families. They rode wherever they could, both on top of the cars and underneath on the rods, where boards had been fastened securely to make a sort of platform.

A rather embarrassing but somewhat amusing experience or episode happened to me on this trip. The train was traveling very slowly because there were so many small bridges that had been destroyed and replaced with cribs made of ties, and also because many of the rails were probably held in place with the minimum amount of spikes. At any rate, another person and I were sitting on the floor of our side door pullman with our legs dangling outside. Disregarding the inconvenience and hardships of travel, it was really a beautiful sunshiny day, with not a rain cloud in sight. Nevertheless, a few drops started to fall, and as I held out my hand to catch or feel them, I said, "My gosh, it's raining." The fellow sitting next to me scrambled back into the car and said, "Hell, that's not rain. A soldier on top of the car is satisfying the call of nature!" Well, imagine my embarrassment, chagrin, and mortification; I had just been unintentionally baptized by the Mexican army.

I had been hired to work for The Alvarado Mining and Milling Company located near Parral. This company no longer exists, but one of the operating mines was the famous old Palmilla mine, where Don Pedro Alvarado previously had made his fortune. Other mines were the Alfareña and Preseña, all shut down now, but in their heyday all very good producers of gold and silver ore. At one time they were operated by the American Smelting and Refining Company, along with their Veta Grande Mines near Minas Nuevas, a town about five miles from Parral.

302

It was during a Sunday evening concert that word was received of some bandit activity on a road from Parral leading to one of the mines. Our general manager, who also was at the band concert partaking of the festive spirit, started rounding up all the men from our camp so we could go home together. He sent word to our camp for some of our mounted and armed watchmen to start toward the city in order to escort us home. The distance to the camp was about four or five miles. In the meantime, the military headquarters had also been notified of the bandit activity, and a detachment of soldiers had been sent out on the road we were going to travel. The soldiers started ahead of us and did not know that our mounted watchmen were coming toward them, and of course our watchmen did not know that the soldiers were also en route traveling toward them. It was too late to notify either group, so it was up to us to get moving, overtake the soldiers and notify them about our watchmen, then keep going and notify our watchmen about the soldiers before the two groups met head on. It was very urgent that we do this, because our mounted guards did not look any different than the mounted bandits would look like, and a clash between soldiers and watchmen could easily have occurred. We were traveling in automobiles, so we caught up to and passed the soldiers, but on a rather sharp curve, and about this same time our guards came around the other end of the curve. Before either group could be notified, they all started reaching for their rifles, with us in the middle. Fortunately, notification and recognition was made before any shots were fired, and the story had a nice ending. It sounds nice now, but at the moment of the meeting it was somewhat of a hair-raiser and thriller.

There was a lot of bandit activity in the Parral district during 1920 and 1921. It was the home ground or headquarters for Pancho Villa, and while a lot of crimes were probably not committed by Villa and his men, he received credit for all of them.

Practically all of the mines were silver and gold producers. It was not uncommon for bandits to appear and take the bullion, because it could be easily disposed of or sold.

Two of my classmates had hair-raising experiences that I think are worth mentioning. They were Rolene Tipton and Walton H. Sarrels. Tipton and I were working as mill shift bosses for the San Patricio Mining Company. The mine and mill complex was in a rather isolated place about thirty to forty minutes walk over the mountain from the headquarters camp where we lived. On this certain day, I was on second shift and Tipton on grave yard. He relieved me about midnight, and sometime after I had left, he was approached and surrounded by a group of bandits who demanded the key to the bullion melting room. We had just melted the previous day and the bullion was to be shipped out after sunup. He figured that discretion was the best part of valor and so delivered the keys. He was marched up the hill to the melting room. He was able to witness the loading of the bullion on the pack animals, and when the bandits left, he was locked in the room. The mill crew had been placed under guard during the robbery, and afterward they sent word to the headquarters camp about the hold-up. Tipton was eventually released from his temporary prison.

The experience of Sarrels had an amusing ending. He was in charge of a small mine near Jiménez. Most of the mines in those days had lots of horses, mules, and so on, as the main means of transportation. One day a large group of armed horsemen arrived at the camp and demanded to see the *jefe*. When the *jefe* (Sarrels) arrived, he was amazed and somewhat dumbfounded, as was the head bandit or revolutionist, to find that they had been schoolmates at the Texas School of Mines. This man, who had become one of the leaders in the Villista movement told Sarrels that he meant no harm to anybody. He just wanted food and horses, which he could take if not freely given. He completed his mission in a friendly atmosphere, and so there was no unpleasant aftermath or consequence.

After Pancho Villa terminated his revolutionary activity, he was given, and lived on, a good-sized ranch not far from Parral. The government, so it was said, paid him a fee for as long as he kept the peace. I am not sure of the amount, but I think it was one million pesos per year, which at that time was five hundred thousand U.S. dollars. I am also not sure of the year, but I think it was in 1923 that my wife and I, along with other foreigners, were invited to attend a very large party or dance at the Parral Foreign Club, given in honor of Pancho Villa and General Martínez of the Mexican Army, who had come to Parral to make the first payment. I mention this incident just to show the possible mental strain under which Pancho Villa lived, even under peaceful law-abiding conditions, especially when in large crowds.

Pancho carried two guns on his belt, one on either side, with the belt full of bullets, and there were several of his heavily armed escorts around the dance hall. As I recall, he only danced one dance, and while dancing remained on the edges of the dance floor with his back to the wall, facing always to the people or dancers and the inside or center of the room. He never rotated or turned while dancing, and never ventured into the middle of the dance floor. If anybody had any ideas of taking a shot at him, he was at least going to face them and not be shot in the back. Also, his dance partner was in front of him.

I was still living in the Parral district when Pancho Villa was killed, while riding in an automobile on the Parral city streets.

Epilog

Ten years after the outbreak of Revolution, large-scale fighting had ended in Mexico, but an unsettled political climate and persisting attempts at social change led to continued instability. Open power struggles were not over, as President Venustiano Carranza discovered when rebellion broke out in April 1920. Sonora Governor Adolfo de la Huerta and others who opposed the president's attempt to install a hand-picked successor proclaimed the Plan of Agua Prieta, which called for Carranza's ouster and the return of sovereignty to the states. As the insurrection gained support, Carranza evacuated Mexico City, but within weeks he was dead from an assassin's bullet. Carranza's demise paved the way for Sonorense Alvaro Obregón to become president. Yet once in office Obregón, too, faced opposition from followers of Adolfo de la Huerta, regional *caudillos* (chieftains), and die-hard supporters of the slain Carranza. In 1922, two border uprisings, one at the Tamaulipas frontier and the other in Ciudad Juárez, broke out against Obregón. The Juárez incident resulted in thirteen deaths and eighty-six arrests.[1] Obregón served out his term, passed the presidency on to Plutarco Elías Calles in 1924, then managed to get re-elected in 1928, only to fall victim to a religious fanatic's fatal bullet shortly after the election. The final major political revolt that affected the border occurred in 1929, when followers of General José Gonzalo Escobar seized Juárez from the federal forces, some of whom retreated across the border to Fort Bliss, Texas.[2]

Apart from political disturbances, violence also resulted from religious conflict, land distribution, and personal feuds. Defenders of the Catholic Church, known as *Cristeros*, put up strong resistance to government enforcement and antireligious laws enacted in the 1910s. The conflict

307

at times had tragic consequences, as federal troops sought to crush the *Cristeros*. In 1927, for example, the army burned to the ground San José de Gracia, a small town in Michoacán, forcing much of the local population to flee. Bloodshed also occurred where the government attempted to distribute land to the peasants. The landowners' recourse to violence to protect their property led to many deaths among people of all ages. Given the climate of lawlessness prevailing much of the time and the thousands of weapons that remained in private hands after the Revolution, it was inevitable that personal disputes regularly ended in shootings and deaths.[3] Thus, the 1920s brought only limited relief to people anxious for peace and normalcy.

This chronic instability aggravated the country's long-standing economic problems, which meant low productivity, food shortages, inflation, and unending poverty. Such conditions drove hundreds of thousands of Mexicans northward to the border in search of peace and economic opportunity. During the 1920s, about half a million Mexicans entered the United States legally, more than twice the number of immigrants recorded in the previous decade.[4] These newcomers swelled the Mexican-American population in the border region, making the group more visible to the dominant Anglo-American majority. Many of the immigrants of the 1910s and 1920s believed that eventually peace and prosperity would favor Mexico, permitting them to return to their homeland. For many of them, however, it was not improved conditions south of the border that induced them to move. Hard times in the United States during the 1930s created such strong pressures that hundreds of thousands of migrants had no choice but to "repatriate" themselves to a Mexico that was by then peaceful but still terribly poor. For most of these involuntary repatriates, the stay south of the Rio Grande would be brief. Scores of them made their way back to the United States by the 1940s as part of a substantial and prolonged human movement northward that continues to the present day.[5]

As students of the borderlands well know, in recent decades the problem of migration has dominated U.S.-Mexico relations. Yet we should not lose sight of the many other problems complicating those relations: trade, smuggling, distribution and quality of water pollution, urbanization, industrialization, population growth, health, and transportation.[6] In contrast to the 1910s, the two nations have consistently sought diplomatic solutions to these problems. In consequence, although the border region remains a trouble-ridden zone, the days of mass violence are over. This has been a welcome change for the area's residents, who might eagerly relate reminiscences of bygone border troubles, but who would rather not live through such times again.

NOTES

1. Armando B. Chávez M., *Historia de Ciudad Juárez, Chih.* (México, 1970), pp. 432–36.

2. Ibid., pp. 441–43.

3. Lawrence A. Cardoso, *Mexican Emigration to the United States, 1897–1931* (Tucson: University of Arizona Press, 1980), pp. 71–73.

4. Mark Reisler, *By the Sweat of Their Brow: Mexican Immigrant Labor to the United States* (Westport, Conn.: Greenwood Press, 1976), p. 268.

5. There is a large and growing body of literature on Mexican immigration to the United States. Recent works include Cardoso, *Mexican Emigration to the United States;* Arthur F. Corwin, ed., *Immigrants and Immigrants: Perspectives on Mexican Labor Migration to the United States* (Westport, Conn.: Greenwood Press, 1978); Juan Ramón García, *Operation Wetback: The Mass Deportation of Mexican Undocumented Workers in 1954* (Westport, Conn.: Greenwood Press, 1980); Mario T. García, *Desert Immigrants: The Mexicans of El Paso, 1880–1920* (New Haven, Conn.: Yale University Press, 1981); and Reisler, *By the Sweat of Their Brow.*

6. A guide to the literature on contemporary border issues is Ellwyn R. Stoddard, ed., *Borderlands Sourcebook: A Guide to the Literature on Northern Mexico and the American Southwest* (Norman: University of Oklahoma Press, 1983).

Bibliography

Listed below are sources cited in the footnotes plus works that address topics mentioned or discussed briefly in the text.

Primary Sources

Archival Collections:

Oral History Interviews, Institute of Oral History, University of Texas at El Paso.

Oral History Interviews, Archivo de la Palabra, Instituto Nacional de Antropología e Historia, Mexico City.

Records of the Department of State Relating to the Internal Affairs of Mexico, 1910–1929. (Microfilm copy)

Government Reports:

Investigation of Mexican Affairs. Senate Document 285, 66th Congress, 2nd Session. Washington, D.C., 1920.

Proceedings of the Joint Committee of the Senate and the House in the Investigation of the Texas State Ranger Force. Austin, 1919. Texas State Archives.

Secondary Sources

Unpublished Sources:

Estrada, Richard. "Border Revolution: The Mexican Revolution in the Ciudad Juárez–El Paso Area, 1906–1915." Master's thesis, University of Texas at El Paso, 1975.

Rocha, Rodolfo, "The Influence of the Mexican Revolution on the Mexico-Texas Border, 1910–1916." Ph.D. dissertation, Texas Tech University, 1981.

Books and Articles:

Acuña, Rodolfo. *Occupied America: A History of Chicanos*, 2nd ed. New York: Harper and Row, 1981.

Aguilar Camín, Hector. *La frontera nomada: Sonora y la Revolución Mexicana.* Mexico: Siglo Veintiuno, 1977.

Almada, Francisco R. *La Revolución en el estado de Chihuahua*, 2 vols. Mexico: Biblioteca del Instituto Nacional de Estudios Históricos de la Revolución Mexicana, 1964.

Azuela, Mariano. *The Underdogs*, translated by E. Munguia. New York: New American Library, 1963.

Bailey, David C. "Revisionism and the Recent Historiography of the Mexican Revolution." *Hispanic American Historical Review* 58:1 (February 1978): 62–79.

Beezley, William. *Insurgent Governor: Abraham González and the Mexican Revolution in Chihuahua*. Lincoln: University of Nebraska Press, 1973.

Blaisdell, Lowell. *The Desert Revolution: Baja California, 1911*. Madison: University of Wisconsin Press, 1962.

————. "Was It Revolution or Filibustering? The Mystery of the Flores Magón Revolt in Baja California." *Pacific Historical Review* 23:2 (May 1954): 147–64.

Braddy, Haldeen. *Pancho Villa at Columbus: The Raid of 1916*. El Paso: Texas Western Press, Southwestern Studies, No. 3 (Spring 1965).

————. *Pershing's Mission in Mexico*. El Paso: Texas Western Press, 1966.

Cardoso, Lawrence A. *Mexican Emigration to the United States, 1897–1931*. Tucson: University of Arizona Press, 1980.

Carr, Barry. "Recent Regional Studies of the Mexican Revolution." *Latin American Research Review* 15:1 (1980): 3–14.

Chávez M., Armando B. *Historia de Ciudad Juárez, Chihuahua*. México, 1970.

Clendenen, Clarence C. *Blood on the Border*. London: Macmillan, 1969.

————. "The Punitive Expedition of 1916: A Re-Evaluation." *Arizona and the West* 3 (1961): 311–20.

————. *The United States and Pancho Villa: A Study in Unconventional Diplomacy*. Ithaca: Cornell University Press, 1961.

Cline, Howard. *The United States and Mexico*, 2nd ed. New York: Atheneum, 1963.

Cockcroft, James D. *Intellectual Precursors of the Mexican Revolution*. Austin: University of Texas Press, 1968.

Corwin, Arthur F., ed. *Immigrants and Immigrants: Perspectives on Mexican Labor Migration to the United States*. Westport, Conn.: Greenwood Press, 1978.

Cué Cánovas, Agustin. *Ricardo Flores Magón, la Baja California y los Estados Unidos*. Mexico, D.F.: 1957.

Cumblerland, Charles C. "Border Raids in the Lower Rio Grande Valley, 1915." *Southwestern Historical Quarterly* 57:3 (1953–1954): 285–311.

————. *Mexican Revolution: Genesis Under Madero*. Austin: University of Texas Press, 1952.

──────. *Mexican Revolution: The Constitutionalist Years.* Austin: University of Texas Press, 1972.

──────. "Mexican Revolutionary Movements from Texas, 1906–1912." *Southwestern Historical Quarterly* 52:3 (1948–1949): 301–24.

──────. *Mexico: The Struggle for Modernity.* New York: Oxford University Press, 1968.

──────. "Precursors of the Mexican Revolution of 1910." *Hispanic American Historical Review* 22:2 (May 1942): 344–56.

──────. "The Sonora Chinese and the Mexican Revolution." *Hispanic American Historical Review* 40:2 (May 1960): 191–211.

Davis, Will B. *Experiences and Observations of an American Consular Officer During the Recent Mexican Revolutions.* Los Angeles: Wayside Press, 1920.

de Wetter, Mardee Belding. "Revolutionary El Paso: 1910–1917." *Password* 3:2 (April 1958): 46–59; 3:3 (July 1958): 107–19; 3:4 (October 1958): 145–58.

Fabela, Isidro. *Historia Diplomática de la Revolución Mexicana,* 2 vols. México: Fondo de Cultura Económica, 1958–59.

Fyfe, Hehn Hamilton. *The Real Mexico: A Study on the Spot.* London: William Heineman, 1914.

Gamio, Manuel. *The Mexican Immigrant: His Life Story.* Chicago: University of Chicago Press, 1931.

García, Mario T. *Desert Immigrants: The Mexicans of El Paso, 1880–1920.* New Haven: Yale University Press, 1981.

Gerhard, Peter. "The Socialist Invasion of Baja California, 1911." *Pacific Historical Review* 15:3 (September 1946): 295–304.

Gerlach, Allan. "Conditions Along the Border—1915: The Plan de San Diego." *New Mexico Historical Review* 43:3 (July 1968): 195–212.

Gómez-Q., Juan. "Plan de San Diego Reviewed." *Aztlán* 1:1 (September 1970): 124–32.

──────. *Sembradores: Ricardo Flores Magón y El Partido Liberal Mexicano: A Eulogy and Critique.* Los Angeles: UCLA Chicano Studies Center, Monograph No. 5, 1973.

Guzmán, Martín Luis. *Memorias de Pancho Villa,* 2nd ed. México, D.F.: Compañia General de Ediciones, 1951.

Hager, William. "The Plan of San Diego: Unrest on the Texas Border in 1915." *Arizona and the West* 5:4 (Winter 1963): 327–36.

Hall, Linda B. "The Mexican Revolution and the Crisis in Naco, 1914–1915." *Journal of the West* 16 (October 1977): 27–35.

Harris, Charles H. and Louis R. Sadler. "Pancho Villa and the Columbus Raid: The Missing Documents." *New Mexico Historical Review* 50:4 (October 1975): 335–46.

———. "The Plan of San Diego and the Mexican–United States Crisis of 1916: A Reexamination." *Hispanic Mexican Historical Review* 58:3 (1978): 381–408.

Harper, James W. "The El Paso–Juárez Conference of 1916." *Arizona and the West* 20:3 (Autumn 1978): 231–44.

Henderson, Peter V. N. *Mexican Exiles in the Borderlands, 1910–1913.* El Paso: Texas Western Press, Southwestern Studies, Monograph No. 58, 1979.

Johnson, William Weber. *Heroic Mexico: The Violent Emergence of a Modern Nation.* New York: Doubleday, 1968.

Katz, Friedrich. "Pancho Villa and the Attack on Columbus, New Mexico." *American Historical Review* 83:1 (February 1978): 101–30.

———. *The Secret War in Mexico: Europe, the United States and the Mexican Revolution* (Chicago: University of Chicago Press, 1981).

Lister, Florence C. and Robert H. Lister. *Chihuahua: Storehouse of Storms.* Albuquerque: University of New Mexico Press, 1966.

Machado, Manuel A., Jr. and James T. Judge. "Tempest in a Teapot? The Mexican–United States Intervention Crisis of 1919." *Southwestern Historical Quarterly* 74:1 (July 1970): 1–23.

Martínez, Oscar J. *Border Boom Town: Ciudad Juárez since 1848.* Austin: University of Texas Press, 1978.

Martínez, Pablo L. *El Magonismo en Baja California.* México, D.F.: Editorial "Baja California," 1958.

Meyer, Michael C. "The Mexican-German Conspiracy of 1915." *The Americas* 23:1 (July 1966): 76–89.

———. *Mexican Rebel: Pascual Orozco and the Mexican Revolution, 1910–1915.* Lincoln: University of Nebraska Press, 1967.

Mumme, Stephen P. "The Battle of Naco: Factionalism and Conflict in Sonora, 1914–15." *Arizona and the West* 21:2 (1979): 157–86.

Munch, Francis J. "Villa's Columbus Raid: Practical Politics or German Design?" *New Mexico Historical Review* 44:3 (July 1969): 188–214.

Niemeyer, Vic. "Frustrated Invasion: The Revolutionary Attempt of General Bernardo Reyes from San Antonio in 1911." *Southwestern Historical Quarterly* 67:2 (October 1963): 213–25.

Pace, Ann. "Mexican Refugees in Arizona, 1910–1911." *Arizona and the West* 16:1 (Spring 1974): 5–18.

Peterson, Jessie and Thelma Cox Knowles, eds. *Pancho Villa: Intimate Recollections by People Who Knew Him.* New York: Hastings House, 1978.

Raat, William D. "Diplomacy of Suppression: Los Revoltosos, Mexico and the United States, 1906–1911." *Hispanic American Historical Review* 56 (November 1976): 529–50.

314

————. *Revoltosos: Mexico's Rebels in the United States, 1903–1923* (College Station: Texas A & M University Press, 1981).

Rausch, George J. "The Exile and Death of Victoriano Huerta." *Hispanic American Historical Review* 42:2 (May 1962): 133–51.

Reed, John. *Insurgent Mexico*. New York: D. Appleton, 1914.

Reisler, Mark. *By the Sweat of Their Brow: Mexican Immigrant Labor to the United States*. Westport, Conn.: Greenwood Press, 1976.

Ritter, Mary Trowbridge. "Flight from Mexico." *American History Illustrated* 13:7 (1978): 20–24.

Rocha, Rodolfo. "Banditry in the Lower Rio Grande Valley of Texas, 1915." *Studies in History* (Texas Tech University) 6 (1976): 55–73.

Ross, Stanley R. *Francisco I. Madero: Apostle of Mexican Democracy*. New York: Columbia University Press, 1955.

Samora, Julian, Joe Bernal, and Albert Peña. *Gunpowder Justice: A Reassessment of the Texas Rangers*. Notre Dame: University of Notre Dame Press, 1979.

Sandos, James A. "German Involvement in Northern Mexico, 1915–1916: A New Look at the Columbus Raid." *Hispanic American Historical Review* 50:1 (February 1970): 70–88.

————. "The Plan of San Diego: War and Diplomacy on the Texas Border, 1915–1916." *Arizona and the West* 14:1 (Spring 1972): 5–24.

Smith, Margaret Holbrook. "The Capture of Tía Juana." *Overland Monthly* 58 (July 1911): 1–7.

Stoddard, Ellwyn R., ed. *Borderlands Sourcebook: A Guide to the Literature on Northern Mexico and the American Southwest*. (Norman: University of Oklahoma Press, 1983).

Teitelbaum, Louis M. *Woodrow Wilson and the Mexican Revolution, 1913–1916: A History of United States–Mexican Relations from the Murder of Madero until Villa's Provocation across the Border*. New York: Exposition Press, 1967.

Thord-Gray, I. *Gringo-Rebel (Mexico, 1913–1914)*. Coral Gables: University of Miami Press, 1960.

Turner, Frederick C. "Anti-Americanism in Mexico, 1910–1913." *Hispanic American Historical Review* 47:4 (November 1967): 502–17.

Turner, Timothy G. *Bullets, Bottles, and Gardenias*. Dallas: South-West Press, 1935.

Vasquez, Richard. *Chicano*. New York: Avon, 1970.

Webb, Walter Prescott. *The Texas Rangers: A Century of Frontier Justice* (New York: Houghton Mifflin, 1935; Austin: University of Texas Press, 1965).

Wilkie, James W. *The Mexican Revolution: Federal Expenditure and Social*

Change since 1910, 2nd edition, revised. Berkeley: University of California Press, 1970.

Wilkie, James W. and Edna Monzón de Wilkie. *Mexico visto en el siglo XX: Entrevistas de historia oral*. México, D.F.: Instituto Mexicano de Investigaciones Económicas, 1969.

Newspapers and Periodicals:

El Paso Herald. 1914, 1915, 1916.
El Paso Times. 1919, 1922, 1939.
Password. 1972, 1975, 1977, 1980, 1981.